D1261361

A VILLAGE WITHOUT SOLIDARITY

A
VILLAGE
WITHOUT SOLIDARITY

Polish peasants in years of crisis

C. M. HANN

1985
YALE UNIVERSITY PRESS
NEW HAVEN & LONDON

Designed by Mary Carruthers.

Filmset in VIP Baskerville by Clavier Phototypesetting and printed in Great Britain by The Bath Press, Avon.

Library of Congress Catalog Card Number 81–052242
ISBN 0–300–03353–2

CONTENTS

Preface

The fieldwork on which this study is based was completed shortly before the declaration of a 'state of war' in Poland at the end of 1981. Further short visits to the village of Wisłok during and after martial law showed that conditions there did not change significantly, despite the upheavals at societal level, and despite all the promises, in the context of general economic reform, to improve fundamentally the position of agriculture. At the local level, each succeeding visit reinforced an impression of continuity, of immunity to the vagaries of national politics. Indeed, the themes of continuity and stagnation were prominent in the self-descriptions of these villagers; and this is one of my justifications for describing them as peasants in this book.

But though the societal crisis might appear to pass the village by, in fact one of the most important causes of Poland's difficulties lies in the failure to satisfy the aspirations of the village, to permit agriculture to modernise effectively, without creating a new elite of prosperous 'capitalist' farmers. Thus, the main themes of this monograph are highly relevant to the recurring crises of the system. The rural population in the socialist period has been remarkably stable at around fifteen to sixteen million, most of them sustained by inefficient, privately owned small farms. There has been a steady exodus from the countryside accompanying the development of socialist industry, but many workers have retained their plots and either commute to the factory or reside only temporarily in the town. Moreover, the proportion of the workforce employed solely in agriculture exceeds that in other socialist countries, virtually all of which have enjoyed greater success in modernising agriculture and redeploying labour in the industrial sector. There may remain a considerable gulf between town and countryside throughout the socialist world, particularly noticeable in the quality of the local infrastructure, and explicable in part by the speed of industrialisation. But of all the Soviet bloc countries, only in Poland does this gulf correspond to that between a predominantly socialised sector (industry) and a predominantly private one (agriculture). Ideological implications have compounded the disadvantages of the rural milieu in Poland; yet because of much lower birthrates in the towns this is where a majority of Poles grows to adulthood.

In seeking the reasons why socialism in Poland should function so very poorly in comparison with other socialist systems, I am not inclined to look primarily (as some Western specialists do) to unique configurations of Polish history and the pre-socialist political culture. Nor do I see any reason to suppose that Soviet influence has been more malign here than elsewhere in Eastern Europe. Important though these factors are, I am inclined to agree with orthodox Soviet commentators who have suggested that it is the persistence of the private sector in agriculture that has played a major part in bringing the country to its present predicament. Low productivity in this sector has had far reaching effects upon the economy, whilst the survival of the peasantry has been vital in maintaining the strength of the church and has also, more arguably, preserved certain class differences, or at least a potential for class differentiation, of a kind not to be found in the collectivised states. From these facts, to be elaborated in this study, I would not draw the conclusions that Soviet ideologues may draw: if there is a contradiction between the persistence of an independent peasantry and adherence to the familiar 'extensive' industrialisation strategy pursued by most socialist countries, it does not follow that the only way to improve matters is to liquidate the former. Here, I am merely emphasising the need to recognise this fundamental contradiction. Consequently I am convinced that, however passive the peasantry has been compared to the industrial proletariat, an appreciation of economic and social relations within the rural sphere in the socialist period is indispensable for a full understanding of the collapse of the system.

A brief note on place names will bring out a subsidiary theme. The village studied lies in mountain marchlands which did not become truly Polish until very recently. Nevertheless, except where an English form seems permissible (Cracow, Lemberg), I have used the Polish names for places which fall within the current boundaries of the People's Republic (Wisłok, Sanok, Przemyśl etc.). This is merely because these are the names used by the majority of the present inhabitants. I do not wish to imply that they have greater historical legitimacy than other names used by non-Polish groups. Lacking any personal emotional involvement in the ethnic conflicts which have riven this region, I have endeavoured to describe them with

viii

impartiality. My own 'pluralist' sympathies may equally be construed as bias by some readers. But I find it difficult to sympathise with policies which aim at the forcible assimilation of minority groups, even if the results are dignified with the label of 'socialist integration'. The Polish achievement in this field is doubtless less striking than that of other socialist states; comparisons cannot be pursued in this study, for in Poland the minorities no longer pose major problems, but I hope to take up this theme on another occasion.

The project was begun in 1978, when I held a postgraduate research studentship awarded by the Social Science Research Council of Great Britain. It was completed after I had been elected a Research Fellow at Corpus Christi College, Cambridge. I have also accumulated debts to many individuals over this period. In particular, I should like to thank the following: Romuald Biskupski, Józef Burszta, Adam Fastnacht, Bogusław Gałęski, Teodor Gocz, John-Paul Himka, Henryk Jadam, Jan Jerschina, Jacek Kolman, Yarko Koshiw, Andor Korik, Iwan Krasovsky, Andrzej Kwilecki, Paul G. Lewis, Paul Robert Magocsi, Bronisław Misztal, Jerzy Motylewicz, Andrzej K. Paluch, Witold Potępa, Andrzej Potocki, Roman Reinfuss, Stanisław Stępień, Dennis Vnenchak, Jerzy Wasilewski and Zbigniew Tadeusz Wierzbicki.

The manuscript was completed in 1982 and revised in 1984. During these two years I have been working in other fields, but have kept in close touch with the village. I have tried to take some account (far from comprehensive) of the recent spate of publications on Poland. Though particular approaches and diagnoses may differ, many of these works are explicitly sympathetic to *Solidarity*. I would hope that sympathisers in Western countries will not judge me lacking in solidarity. However, this study shows that *Solidarity* did not everywhere enjoy the mass support that is sometimes assumed in retrospect. As a national movement it was not guaranteed to bring greater freedom to certain oppressed groups; in fact it was not necessarily conducive, at least in the short term, either to a more efficient economy or to a more pluralist society. The book reveals an unfamiliar part of the Polish scene, one as alien to some activists in the opposition as it is to the regime. I dedicate it to the officials and clergy in Komańcza who helped me in all my enquiries, and to their charges who are building the new community in Wisłok; and especially to the families of Krzysztof Ołtarzewski, Michał Opryszko and Michał Milasz, who welcomed me into their homes.

C.M.H. August, 1984

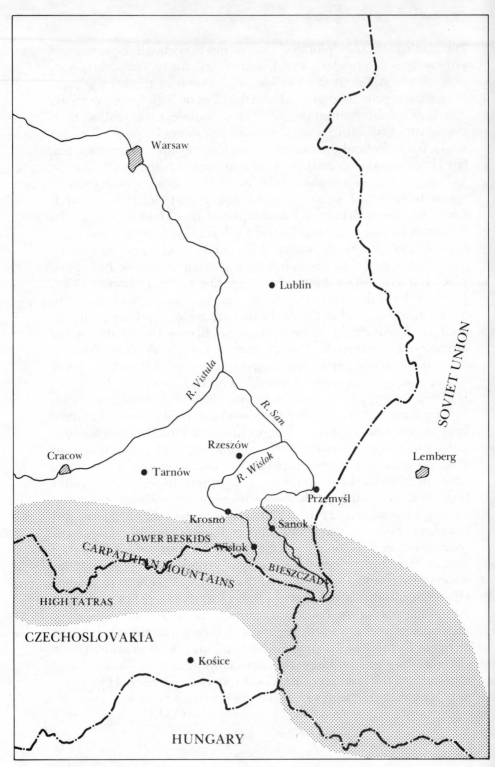

Map 1. Wisłok — general location.

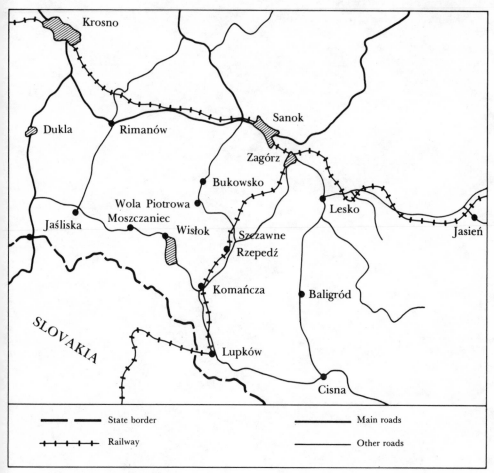

Map 2. Wisłok — regional communications.

CHAPTER ONE

Introduction

It is as well to begin with the problem of typicality, which always presents itself in a study of this kind and can create uncertainties in the minds of laymen and professional anthropologists alike. Poland is a large and diverse country with over thirty-five million inhabitants. Just over three hundred of them live in Wisłok, and the reader is therefore entitled to ask what general conclusions may be drawn from a detailed study of this one village.

Other anthropologists have had to confront a similar problem. Few of them have resolved it so explicitly as Paul Stirling in his study of a Turkish village in Anatolia, and to my mind he deals with it most satisfactorily.[1] The reader is informed that there can be no such thing as a 'typical' village, and Stirling's 'Turkish Village' in fact gives a composite picture of two very different settlements, situated quite close to each other geographically. However, the anthropologist does write in his introduction that he set out to select 'an orthodox Muslim, Turkish-speaking village of modest size, fairly far away from the direct influence of the cities, on the plateau which forms the largest part of Anatolia', and, whilst the 'typical' was nowhere to be found, 'it was at least possible to avoid choosing villages with obvious peculiarities'.[2] Hence, although the anthropologist is concerned 'to offer a model of social structure' and not to make general statements about all Turkish villages, nevertheless, it is important for Stirling that his villages resemble the other villages he has visited and that in key respects — geography, economy, religion and ethnic profile — they should conform to preponderant statistical norms for the country.[3]

In some contrast to Stirling's endeavour, let the distinctiveness of Wisłok be understood at the outset:

1. *Location.* Despite her forever changing frontiers most of Poland has always consisted of low-lying plain. Wisłok is located in the

1

Lower Beskid section of the Carpathian Mountains, adjacent to the most stable frontier Poland has had; before 1919 this was the Hungarian frontier, since then it has marked the boundary with Slovakia.

2. *Economy*. Whereas agriculture has long dominated in lowland regions, in this region it has often been subordinate to an upland pastoral economy and to forestry.

3. *Ethnicity*. Although never separated from Poland politically throughout the centuries that it has been inhabited, the local population was not Polish until very recently. Before 1947 Wisłok and most villages of this region were inhabited by Eastern Slavs who called themselves *Rusnaks* ('Ruthenes'). They spoke a language that is generally classified as a dialect of Ukrainian and is still alive in the region today.

4. *Religion*. Whereas the Roman Catholic Church dominated in Poland, the *Rusnaks* belonged to the Orthodox and Greek Catholic (Uniate) Churches, employing the Byzantine rather than the Latin rite.

Wisłok certainly bore close resemblance to hundreds of other villages in the *Rus* regions of the mountains (which included territory presently divided between the USSR, Czechoslovakia, Romania and Hungary), but it must be granted that this has always been a rather exceptional region in the Polish national context, whilst the present community in Wisłok is a distinct oddity. Yet it was not as a curiosity that I became interested both in its history and in its contemporary situation. My main interest was the general transformation of the rural scene in Eastern Europe in the socialist period, and my particular reason for going to Poland was that, alone among the states of the Soviet bloc, she avoided mass collectivisation. I wished to enquire just what this major difference entailed, both at the local level and for the development of the national society, with particular reference to the persistence of 'peasantry'. The project seemed all the more timely as the country plunged into political and economic crisis in 1980–1. The bulk of this book presents information I gleaned about a single community; let me now try to show why, given my main interests, a village unlike most other villages proved to be a singularly instructive setting for fieldwork.

Introduction to Wisłok

The village occupies a narrow valley in the Lower Beskid Mountains, close to the source of the river which also bears the name Wisłok

General view of the lower hamlet, including the school (centre) and the church.

(pronounced *Vees-wock*). This river joins the San north of the town of Rzeszów and eventually flows into the Vistula (see Map 1). The town of Sanok is located on the San, at a point where the foothills of the mountains begin to merge with the plain. With brief exceptions, Wisłok village has always belonged to the district of Sanok, the town being 38 km distant by the most direct route through the mountains. This district was historically part of the voivodeship (county) of Lemberg (*L'viv* to Ukrainians, *Lwów* to Poles), but, when this city was incorporated into territories of the Soviet Union after the Second World War, Rzeszów became the new provincial capital. Finally, since 1974 this south-eastern corner of Poland has been administered as part of a new, much smaller voivodeship with its centre at Krosno (see Chapter Five for details of the present system of administration).

The village also belonged to a *Rus* zone which preserved its separate identity until 1947. In common with the *Rus* population of most other villages of this zone, the inhabitants of Wisłok were then forcibly evacuated from the mountains and dispersed at the other end of the country on territories 'regained' from Germany. The

3

background to this tragedy is supplied in Chapter Two, which outlines the pre-socialist history of the village and the slow development of national consciousness amongst its inhabitants — a process which culminated only after the dissolution of their communities.

Many villages of the *Rus* zone disappeared permanently in the 1940s. In some areas, notably the more remote parts of the Bieszczady Mountains, resettlement did not begin until the 1960s. But in Wisłok, and other villages where economic conditions were similarly favourable, resettlement by ethnic Poles began almost immediately after the deportation of the indigenous population. Immigrants to Wisłok have therefore experienced the whole gamut of socialist policies over more than three decades. Their experience has differed, however, from that of the inhabitants of Polish villages in other regions, in that the formation and maintenance of this community have been more directly influenced by the socialist political environment, both by the general uncertainties this has created and by particular fluctuations in central government policy.

The population figure has been quite stable since the early 1960s, at about one-eighth of that of the pre-1947 community. However, continuing high turnover is an indication that the social integration of diverse groups of settlers has proved more difficult to achieve. Most were poor families who came to Wisłok from the overcrowded lowland regions of southern Poland, mainly from the voivodeships of Rzeszów and Cracow. Later these were joined by more heterogeneous elements, and occupation became a more significant marker than diversity of origin. Forestry workers formed one major group, and State Farm employees another. Some immigrants who began by working in the socialised sector were later stimulated to commence independent farming operations, in which case they would be more likely to build permanent homes in the village. A number of industrial workers, attracted to the region in the course of an extensive public works programme in the 1960s and 1970s, also settled as private farmers. Finally, some members of the indigenous population have been allowed to return since the late 1950s.

Obviously a rural community starting, as it were, from scratch in the socialist period is an exceptional case. In the Polish case it is not in fact so unusual, and recent developments in Wisłok may usefully be compared with the evolution of hundreds of other villages which obtained a new, Polish identity as a result of the frontiers established after the war. It seems that social integration proceeded more rapidly in the western and northern territories obtained from Germany, partly because both agrarian and industrial conditions were more favourable here, and partly because the resettlement processes were better coordinated and speedily concluded. In contrast, in the former *Rus* zone resettlement was delayed, due to difficulties presented by the terrain and also to the legacy of the violent conflict which had precipitated its evacuation. Reconstruction was particularly slow in the Bieszczady Mountains, a part of the former *Rus* zone which became popularly known as a 'Polish Texas', as a frontier zone and melting pot of classes, religions and nationalities. No sharp natural boundary separates the Bieszczady section of the Carpathians from the rather gentler, rolling hills of the Lower Beskids; geographers may assign Wisłok to the latter, but in the minds of most of her present inhabitants she falls within the section of Bieszczady.

This regional identification is interesting evidence of the self-perceptions of the new settlers, but it is nonetheless misleading. A village in Bieszczady proper, where the Forestry Commission and the State Farms dominate and the traditions of independent peasant farming have weakened substantially, would indeed throw little light on the fate that has overtaken the Polish peasantry as a whole. But in Wisłok, formation of the new community began almost at once in 1948, and the salient feature of the local economy remains what it has been for many generations past — independent family farming. This is no longer the case in many Polish mountain villages with a long and continuous history of upland farming. All too frequently, proximity to new sources of employment in towns, the expanding tourist trade, and other factors, such as the influx of dollars from relatives abroad, have undermined the farm economy. Wisłok is not immune to any of these factors. However, the special circumstances in which the community took shape, its relative isolation and the character of the relationship locally between the public (socialist) and private (peasant) sectors make this an excellent laboratory in which to study the effects of socialist policies upon the peasantry. At this point, the question 'Why Wisłok?' must revert back to the question 'Why Poland?'.

Introduction to Poland

Why Poland? Because no other state in the Soviet bloc has almost four-fifths of its agricultural surface in the ownership of more than three million private farmers. The Polish agrarian structure is quite remarkable in contemporary Europe; the parallels sometimes sug-

5

gested in Yugoslavia, or in some underdeveloped parts of 'capitalist' southern Europe, turn out to be less than satisfactory. More than 60 per cent of Poland's individual farms are smaller than 5 hectares in size (all holdings greater than half a hectare are counted as farms), and few of these provide the sole source of income for their owners. The problems presented by the peasant workers and by the category of 'dependents' in private agriculture require that statistics be handled with caution; but there is no doubt that, with more than one-quarter of her active labour force employed in agriculture, Poland has not advanced as far along the roads of industrialisation and agricultural modernisation as her socialist neighbours.

If the countryside has indeed changed considerably in the socialist period, this has been largely a side effect of imposed industrialisation rather than the planned consequence of policies to modify the agricultural sector. The Polish strategy, like that of other socialist countries, was founded upon systematic discrimination against agriculture, and especially against individual farmers. In the early phase of the construction of socialism this antagonism was rendered explicit, and policies corresponded to the general pattern in Eastern Europe. After 1956, when, in the wake of a political crisis, forced collectivisation was definitively rejected, the instruments to implement these policies had to be refined. Economic pressure could still be applied, because the supplies of essential factors of production were controlled by the authorities, who also had a virtual monopoly over channels of 'marketing'. The ability and the willingness of individual farmers to produce for such a market gradually declined. When this decline was particularly sharp and shortfalls intolerable, pragmatic adjustments were made to purchasing prices. Such policies could succeed in the short term, at least so long as the state of the consumer goods markets gave enough farmers the incentive to want to earn more money. The majority of peasants did not adjust production significantly, and the policies had uneven effects in different regions of the country. This market stimulus was always weak in isolated areas, where the disequilibrium on the consumer goods market was most serious. Such policies offered no long term guarantees to the private sector anywhere, and inevitably they had deleterious effects upon farm investment as well as production. Young persons were stimulated to seek regular cash income through urban employment, and many farmers found themselves without a prospective heir. The inadequacy of housing conditions (the waiting time for a flat in the capital is in the order of twenty years) and poor food supplies in the towns meant that many workers did not abandon their rural homes and were anxious to retain at least a smallholding. This further impeded the consolidation and more rational utilisation of agricultural land.

In socialist terminology it might be argued that changes in the *relations* of production in the Polish countryside have been less complete than in other socialist states, and have not kept pace with the transformation of the *forces* of production (mechanisation etc.). Yet even the latter has proceeded much less smoothly in Poland, precisely because the continued dominance of the private sector removed the urgency of the need to divert industrial resources into agriculture. Only in the early 1970s (and perhaps again now in the later 1980s) have policies designed to increase the productive capacity of the private sector been more vigorously pursued. For ideological reasons these have been hedged with controls and restrictions, because of the risk of negative (from a socialist standpoint) consequences for the class structure of the rural population. Indeed, the English 'farmer' has been a bogey-figure to politicians in the populist tradition and to many peasants themselves, as well as to communists. This has not helped to promote rural development.

Poland's failure to collectivise, which given the performance of the socialised sector in certain other states may be no bad thing in itself, was not mitigated by the implementation of any alternative long-term development programme. Instead, the agricultural sector as a whole was more completely deprived of investment resources, whilst individual farmers were subjected to slightly more subtle forms of discrimination. It seems reasonable to maintain that the resulting structural deficiencies in agriculture have contributed to recent upheavals in Poland, though it would be foolish to claim that the antiquated agrarian structure was the sole root of the general economic breakdown.[4] Criticism needs to focus upon the fundamentally unbalanced way in which industrialisation was implemented, and not on the performance of the private sector out of context. The record of the socialised sector in agriculture (consisting primarily of State Farms but also including production cooperatives along the lines of the Soviet *kolkhoz* and other types of cooperative) certainly does not suggest that full collectivisation in Poland might have led to better results.

Comparisons between the private and the socialised sectors of agriculture in socialist states often seem to involve elements of paradox. Western observers are surprised to discover that plot farming, though responsible for only a tiny fraction of the land surface, contributes a very large proportion of final output. Those who gleefully quote such statistics usually fail to point out the many ways in which the private sector is supported by and integrated into the socialised sector: without the latter the former might well be incapable of producing anything at all. During the 1970s all of the collectivised states made greater efforts than before to stimulate small-scale production outside of the socialised sector, such policies being carried furthest in Hungary, but also having considerable effect on more centralised systems such as those of Bulgaria, and East Germany. Yugoslavia raises different problems, for like Poland it has not been fully collectivised; but here too it may be said that a more substantial measure of market-regulated integration has been achieved, a) of private and socialised sectors within agriculture and b) of agriculture and industry in an overall economic strategy. No such integration or coordination of policies has been achieved in Poland. The private sector performs better in terms of crop yields, and incurs lower costs in livestock production. Moreover, there is a sense in which each tiny holding in the private sector, even those which feed only a single family, is a godsend in the short term to a socialist regime which has fudged collectivisation. Its input demands are low, so there is no necessity either to divert investment resources away from other sectors of the economy or to worry unduly about satisfying food demands. At the same time, the state's monopoly position as a buyer gives it full power to manipulate the farmer's rate of return — in other words, to exploit him in any commodity production he undertakes. The problem, of course, with an unsatisfactory distribution of holdings and the suspension of market forces, is to provide farmers with any incentive to go on supplying the commodities which townspeople need. In the long run, the failure to allow the private sector either to modernise along 'western' lines or to be integrated into a modern socialised sector results in low levels of investment in agriculture overall, and in large areas of land falling out of production.

The persistence of the peasantry

The macroeconomic consequences of these policies (e.g. upon industrial growth rates and upon the quality of the industrial labour force) are for economists to analyse. Political scientists and historians can help to explain how such policies came to be implemented, and sociologists can reflect on some of their wider social implications. The anthropologist is expected to provide an accurate picture of continuity and change at the grass roots, to reveal 'how the system really works' by combining his own insights with the perceptions of his informants. His task is perhaps unusually difficult in the case of a socialist society, if only because many Westerners have trouble in approaching these countries without prejudice. Reliable information has not always been available and still remains difficult to gather. Furthermore, the ideologists of these regimes leave themselves open to easy attack by steadfastly adhering to theories and explanations which, it is evident to even the superficial observer, social and economic circumstances flatly contradict. However, it is not enough to reveal the inadequacy of a socialist dogma, such as that which declares the harmony of social groups in socialist society, and insists that progress is taking place towards 'communism'. It is essential, if we ourselves are not to fall back upon 'ideology', to put forward some more satisfactory alternative theory: the simplistic 'totalitarian' model seems to be not even remotely adequate.[5] To the best of my knowledge this has not yet been done concerning the fundamental problems of class stratification in socialist societies, and no such ambitious attempt is made in this study. However, if his descriptions and analyses are to be of any value, even the empirical anthropologist must exercise theoretical care. There are limits to what one may assume to be unproblematic. The concept selected as problematic and central to the arguments of this study is that of 'peasantry'.

Definitions of 'peasantry' are not easily agreed upon; if 'peasant' is to designate any small-scale cultivator, does it not become too hopelessly broad a category in time and space? Most anthropologists have placed their studies of peasantries in the context of particular social formations. Marxists in particular have sought precision in this way, and insisted that peasantry in itself cannot constitute a mode of production; contemporary peasants are typically described by them as petty commodity producers, within a mode of production that is dominated by capitalism. Marx's own views on peasants (and possible modifications that he introduced late in life) have been much discussed, largely because revolutions have tended to occur in societies which had large peasantries. The role of that class in the accomplishment and consolidation of the revolution has been played out in different ways, in theory and in practice, in the major socialist states; but it is usually thought that within a short period of time the peasantry will lose its former distinctiveness as a class, and indeed, there are studies confirming that this has happened in, e.g. the Soviet Union and Bulgaria.[6]

However, a few socialist countries appear to go further towards recognising the compatibility of elements of traditional peasant economy with socialism (just as peasantry was compatible with both feudal and capitalist social formations in the past). From another angle, a few anthropologists have made preliminary attempts to analyse the conditions of the peasantry under socialism. Aiming to build on these foundations, one is still confronted by the initial problems of definition: what are the criteria for establishing the presence or absence of 'peasantry' in any given society?

It is impossible to specify very precisely a point at which peasantry gives way to a modern occupational grouping of commercial farmers, as has happened gradually in most countries of Western Europe in recent generations. In most socialist countries collectivisation is merely the most dramatic episode in the transformation of peasantry: the full process of transformation may still have a long way to go, given the late date at which industrialisation commenced and continued exploitation of certain elements of the old peasant economy, particularly in certain labour-intensive branches of agriculture. But in order to distinguish peasants, a) from commercial farmers in a developed capitalist economy, and b) from rural dwellers who have been effectively incorporated into the national labour market of a socialist state, it is worthwhile attempting a 'working definition'. It seems to me that the various features identified by different authors can be reduced to three general classes.[7]

Firstly, there are the sociological and political characteristics of peasantry. In the widely accepted stereotype, which owes something to Marx as well as to more recent contributions by cultural anthropologists, peasantry constitutes a numerically dominant but politically passive and subordinate section of pre-industrial states. Although peasantry may, in appropriate circumstances, have revolutionary potential, it is too fragmented and its inherent traditionalism (conservatism) ensures that it is unlikely to become the permanent beneficiary of upheavals it may engender (the problematic character of peasant political movements will be touched upon later in Chapter Five). The peasant is thus cast as the eternal 'underdog', he belongs to a 'part society' which, if not entirely a 'closed system', permits little mobility towards the other sections of society.

Secondly, there are economic features centred upon the identity of the household unit and the enterprise (the 'family farm'). The peasant labour process makes little use of capital equipment, but relies upon full mobilisation of the members of the family. The family is the crucial unit, and it works more to satisfy wants (determined by the traditional cultural standards) than in pursuit of the economist's 'maximum profit'. This does not mean that the members of the peasant household are any less rational or calculating than the managers of the capitalist firm, as is sometimes implied by romanticisers of the peasant economy. It is merely that an utterly different economic environment renders them relatively insensitive to changes in market prices. When due account is taken of this context, then the peasant's preoccupation with subsistence (a full stomach) and aversion to risk become entirely comprehensible.

Thirdly, following the socio-political and the economic characteristics of peasantry, one can perhaps suggest that the more fundamental, *necessary* condition for peasantry, is psychological. Land husbandry is typically the sole, or at least the principal means by which subsistence is assured. Consequently, there arises a powerful commitment to the land, and very often to a specific plot of land that becomes the property of the family, or its *patrimony*. Full personal ownership was the norm for the East European peasantry in the century or so between final emancipation from feudal restrictions and the establishment of the Peoples' Republics. This personal involvement with the means of production is severed by collectivisation. Contrary to those who might interpret this as perhaps no more than a formal change to 'administrative' domain, I shall contend that collectivisation necessarily inaugurates the demise of the peasantry. Even when the cultural stereotypes retain their force and when some fraction of the family's labour power is still expended in the traditional manner on plot farming, the loosening of the tie to the land is sufficient to entail the displacement of the family as the key unit of production and the substitution of new, individual relationships comparable to those of the industrial sphere. In general it has been individuals, not whole families, who have become cooperative members; and within a relatively short time they have tended to become indistinguishable from workers or employees in other branches of the modern economy.

Thus, a failure to collectivise agriculture may enable the persistence in the socialist state of a 'peasant mentality', and even of a separate 'peasant class'. This study will suggest to what extent this has in fact occurred in Poland, or may yet occur as policies change.

11

Of course, one is not dealing with the miraculous survival of the traditional peasantry, as it was described by Thomas and Znaniecki (1918-20). Changes in living conditions, in the employment structure (including the extent of industrial commuting) and the ubiquitous presence of socialist institutions have exercised great influence over village life. But the extent of discrimination against agriculture has been such that the many factors working for the *incorporation* of the peasantry into the national economy and into the new socialist society have, contrary to the experience of other socialist states, been outweighed by loyalty to traditional ideals and resistance to outside interference. Arguably it is the persistence of private ownership which has made resistance practicable, as well as serving as its symbolic fulcrum. The peasant was left in control of his productive base and, however susceptible to the manipulations of the authorities, he maintained a degree of freedom that was lost elsewhere with collectivisation. Thus he could choose to meet his cash needs through working in the socialist sector rather than through the production of agricultural commodities. And if he succeeded in achieving certain targets, let us say the construction of a large new house on his smallholding, he could quite well choose more leisure thereafter, and withdraw to archetypal peasant autonomy for so long as commodity production seemed not worth pursuing.

The modernisation of agriculture in capitalist countries has been achieved through mechanisation, ever greater specialisation and the establishment of larger farm units. The division of labour in the household has altered. Production is determined by the criteria of profitability, similar to those applied in industry. Hence farm families in Western Europe, though frequently owners of their land and attached to it by powerful ties of sentiment, can be said to have moved beyond the peasant labour process. In Poland also a minority of farmers has been able to make this transition. I have stayed with prosperous greenhouse owners on the Baltic coast, producing flowers and tomatoes for the large city markets, who started off as poor immigrants in the 1940s on former German soil. Farmers in other parts of the country have had to struggle harder to accumulate smaller stocks of capital, but some did manage it. Others were aided in the process in the 1970s, when generous government assistance was made available to selected farmers (see Chapter Three). However, even within this minority of farmers who were not short of land or machines and fulfilled some of what one might call the 'objective' conditions for transcending peasant status, a certain peasant mentality lingered. These farmers too were deeply suspicious of the intentions of the authorities. During fieldwork at the turn of the 1980s they often seemed quite unconcerned with expanding production and maximising cash profits, and were evidently content merely to satisfy immediate family demands for food products, and perhaps sell enough to generate a minimum cash flow.

Such behaviour was of course entirely rational in an economic context in which the local currency was increasingly ineffective, goods required as inputs for agriculture were unavailable, and consumer products were either unavailable or subject to rationing. Although most farmers were theoretically capable of expanding their commodity production, in the crisis of the 1980s few saw any point in doing so, whilst the majority had considered the market environment hostile all along. Only in quite exceptional cases have whole communities been characterised by dynamic expansion and innovation (an example is described briefly on p.114-15, where religious zeal provides a motivation transcending any dispassionate economic assessment). In this way peasantry survives *in spite of* certain objective economic possibilities — concessions by the authorities, necessary to avoid shortfalls but taken up only by small numbers of well-placed individuals. The majority has *resisted*, not because of any inherent peasant opposition to progress and commercialisation (let alone any collective notion of 'limited good'[8]), but because this was a natural response to discriminatory policies against the private sector and agriculture as a whole. The food crisis of the 1980s enhanced the value of private access to land and strengthened the retrenchment of traditional peasant economy. It became clear that not even very large increases in purchasing prices would be enough to stimulate output when there were no goods available on the market for the farmer to spend his money on. This was the crux of the breakdown most apparent in 1981, when a wide range of goods had to be rationed (including meat, butter, some other fats, flour and cereal products, sugar, confectionery, cigarettes etc.). It requires little imagination to see how the authorities might seek to create friction between the peasants and the townspeople, since neither group was obtaining the goods it required; but to most Poles it was perfectly clear who was responsible for the policies leading to this impasse.

Thus, the hypothesis is that what is specific to non-collectivised Poland is the degree to which agricultural policies have reinforced the essential features of peasantry, even when the general tenden-

13

cies of extensive socialist industrialisation were, as elsewhere, eroding its distinctiveness. In Poland it has survived tenaciously: elsewhere in Europe modernisation of the agrarian structure has proceeded in a great variety of institutional frameworks, and peasantry
has all but disappeared. In an isolated area such as Wisłok, where
peasant farming lapsed but was then carefully re-established in the
socialist period, the responsibility of state policies can most clearly be
demonstrated. In addition it is possible to show how economic
policies have also hindered progress in cultural fields and delayed
the full assimilation of the peasantry into socialist society.

Although the problems presently facing Poland are specific, the
study is also intended to contribute to wider, comparative enquiries
into the transformation of peasant society, including Western
Europe. Some explicit comparisons with other socialist states are
briefly discussed in the conclusion of this study. I have shown elsewhere (Hann, 1980) that elements of traditional peasant economy
may survive in even the most successful of collectivised states and
may indeed be central to its success. Now, certain inequalities between town and countryside may be universal; they may be unavoidable in any society undergoing rapid industrialisation and it is only
because socialist societies do set themselves the highest egalitarian
standards that one devotes so much attention to systematic inequalities within them. Nevertheless, there is a basic difference
between a state which permits an adversary relationship to develop
across that gulf, as has happened in Poland, where continued private
ownership of the land has given the peasantry a firm base from which
to *resist* exploitation, and, on the other hand, a state which allows its
rural citizens considerable scope to redress certain built-in inequalities of the system, thanks to extra earnings in plot farming or in
other diverse areas of the so-called 'second' or 'informal' economy.
In Marxist terms the latter, which gives very considerable encouragement to market forces, may be exploiting rural dwellers much
more than the former, where they have some power to resist. But it
does not follow that, because on the whole they may work less (and
certainly much less efficiently) than their counterparts in other
socialist states, the class position of the Polish peasantry is therefore
somehow superior. So many other factors must be considered, and
we would find the concept of 'exploitation' fully as problematic as
that of 'peasantry'. It is significant that peasantries which have been
successfully incorporated into socialist national societies seem to
show remarkably little desire to restore the old system; and indi-

viduals who enjoy the opportunities presented by a genuine market for household plot production do not pine for the loss of their private ownership rights to a slightly larger holding. We shall return to this theme in the Conclusion.

*   *   *   *

In that earlier study, as in the present one, a village unrepresentative of other villages afforded an apt illustration of the main principles of national policy. Another theme of that book central to the present monograph has to do with the emergence of a new community in the socialist period. In my Hungarian village, as in Wisłok, but for different reasons, the solidarity of 'community' could not be taken for granted as a legacy of the pre-socialist past. In spite of greater economic prosperity in Hungary, or perhaps because of this, the goals of socialist integration within the new community there proved to be elusive. This was a promising theme to pursue in Wisłok because it has been taken up for the whole of the Bieszczady region by several Polish social scientists in recent years. They have tended to paint a reassuring, optimistic picture of the 'formation of a new community' by means of the integration of diverse groups of immigrants. The evidence in the following chapters will contribute to a critique of these theories, and I shall tackle this question too in the Conclusion. Extrapolation to the national level is always dangerous; but it is the unrepresentative village which did not inherit the organic solidarity of community that affords more insight into the present national community, which was born at the same moment in history and likewise had to create a new cohesion.

The ethnographic present is the spring and summer of 1981, a time when there was little semblance of cohesion at the national level. Fieldwork was conducted at irregular periods before and after this, adding up to about nine months residence altogether. My first longer spell was in 1979, before the collapse of Edward Gierek's government and the emergence of *Solidarity*. By 1981, activist farmers were themselves engaged in a long and bitter battle to establish a free trade union to represent rural interests, along the same lines as those created by industrial workers in the preceding year. Many of the farmers' complaints touched upon matters dealt with in this book, including the various forms of discrimination practised against the private sector and the bureaucratisation of local institutions. Rural militancy was exceptionally forceful in the Bieszczady region (strikes, occupation of government buildings etc.). This then was the background at national and regional levels during my main stint in the village. My concern was to grasp the deeper causes of this crisis, but inevitably the vagaries of the political situation have left their mark upon the evidence I found, and which I present in Chapters Three–Eight. Chapter Two will outline the history of the *Rus* community in the centuries which preceded the foundation of the People's Republic, and may be skipped by the reader who is interested solely in the socialist period.

CHAPTER TWO

From Brigandry to Guerilla Warfare

This chapter is concerned with the history of the *Rus* settlement in Wisłok. It is not an exhaustive local history, but a brief outline intended to point up major developments before the socialist period; since the *Rus* community did not survive long under socialism, the chapter may be omitted by readers interested exclusively in the formation of the present community.

The Eastern Slav, Orthodox community with basically pastoral economy resists incorporation into feudal Poland

In the later Middle Ages, after the schism of 1054 between Rome and Byzantium which definitively established the Orthodox Church, it was religion rather than language or any other criterion which served as the principal distinguishing feature within the Slavic populations to the north and east of the Carpathian Mountains. In the westerly parts a Polish state was consolidated in the tenth century, after Mieszko's conversion to Christianity by the Latin church. The Eastern Slavs were converted from Byzantium. Temporarily unified in the Kievan *Rus* Federation, they eventually evolved into three distinct cultural and political entities: Muscovy (Great Russia), the Ukraine (Little Russia), and White Russia. Political, economic and religious differences between the two fundamental ethnolinguistic communities of Eastern and Western Slavs deepened over several centuries, but demarcation of the precise border at different periods has presented modern historians with an awkward problem. According to earliest written records, Wisłok was part of an administrative unit centred on Sanok and known as the Sanok Lands (*Ziemia Sanocka*). Very sparsely populated until late in the Middle Ages, it could not be assigned unambiguously to either ethnolinguistic community at this period. Between 1030 and 1340 the Sanok Lands formed the south-western corner of the Eastern Slav principality of Halicz within the Kievan *Rus* federation, and later the independent kingdom of Halicz-Volhynia. Polish sources claim, however, that this region belonged to the Polish state at an even earlier date.[1]

The Sanok Lands were definitively incorporated into Poland by the last monarch of the Piast dynasty, King Casimir the Great, in 1341. Thanks to the survival of written records, from this time onwards it is possible to trace the process of colonisation, which in this area proceeded from the more fertile lowlands in a southwards direction up the river valleys to the less hospitable parts of the Carpathians. This process was encouraged by the Polish crown, and expansion also took place in more easterly regions where the East Slav (*Rus* or 'Ruthenian'[2]) population was already substantial. Some of the beneficiaries were powerful magnates, others were members of the lesser gentry, a class so numerous in Poland that many of its members were almost indistinguishable from the mass of the peasantry. Those who were granted title to land then did their best to recruit more settlers from wherever they could be found. Immigrants from Germany were very numerous in the early period, and so too from the fourteenth century were their co-religionists, the Western Slavs or Poles. To the Sanok Lands, however, the largest numbers came from the east, particularly in the later phases of colonisation when the richer lowlands were already quite densely settled. They were Eastern Slavs and their religion was Orthodox. To complicate matters further it is also necessary to take account of a fourth ethnic contingent, the Vlachs. The Vlachs were pastoral nomads who originated in the Balkans and migrated in several waves from Transylvania to the northern reaches of the Carpathians; they were eventually assimilated by other groups in this region, but left indelible marks upon its pastoral economy and its folk culture.[3]

Apart from this diversity (but to some extent corresponding to the differences between ethnic groups) there was also significant variation within the Sanok Lands in the social and legal conditions of colonisation and in the means by which the new settlers obtained their livelihood. Broadly speaking settlement in lowland areas suitable for agriculture took place according to the standard terms of 'Magdeburg Law'. Such a settlement charter stipulated feudal dues and services similar to those enforced in towns and villages throughout the country. The rules applied in the colonisation of upland areas were of necessity quite different and typically expressed in the form of a 'Vlach' charter (*ius Valachium*). The terms were adjusted to the contrasting mode of subsistence, and dues were expressed not in terms of field crops or money but in terms of animals, their skins and their cheeses. Moreover, there was recognition of the great difficulties encountered by those breaking new ground in isolated mountain territory. The size of the 'fiefs' granted was larger than elsewhere, the headman (*kniaź* or *sołtys*) had far-reaching power locally, and for a lengthy initial period no dues of any kind were extracted. The more generous terms were doubtless necessary to persuade peasants to settle in such remote parts. Thus, although the colonisation was initiated and guided by the feudal state, feudal norms in force elsewhere were not strictly applied in this region. The early population was made up of volunteer peasants enjoying considerable independence, rather than of captive serfs.

Wisłok is mentioned for the first time in 1361 when, as a *loca deserta*, it was allocated by Casimir the Great to two brothers, 'Peter and Paul from Hungary'. This does not necessarily mean that Peter and Paul were ethnic Hungarians, only that they probably came to Poland from the south, from territories belonging to the Kingdom of Hungary. Nor does the reference to an 'empty place' imply that no previous settlement had existed in Wisłok: on the contrary, the way in which Wisłok is named in this document suggests the possibility of some short-lived earlier settlement.[4] Peter's descendants remained the owners of the new village during the fifteenth century and though they themselves preferred to reside elsewhere, in more congenial surrounds, they did much to develop it. By the sixteenth century more detailed information is available. In 1552 the village contained altogether 48 farms, 2 mills and an Orthodox Priest, and it would seem that the area of land exploited more than doubled in the period 1526–89. The names of the inhabitants in these early centuries confirm their East Slav origins. There is no surviving indication of a Vlach charter before 1561. However, it seems likely that such dues as were exacted in these earlier centuries cut into the surplus of an extensive pastoral economy (the presence of the mills is an indication that already some fields were cultivated, but this was a subordinate element).

The sixteenth century, which probably saw substantial increases in the population as well as in the land area exploited, also witnessed a more general closing of the frontier in the Sanok Lands. With all attractive sites now occupied, colonisation ceased in the early seventeenth century. Even the continued expansion of existing settlements was now impeded, partly because of a decline in Poland's international position and a lack of political cohesion. The monarchy was no longer the strong and unifying force it had been under Casimir the Great. The sixteenth century had registered many outstanding scientific and cultural achievements, whilst economic prosperity was founded upon the export of grain to the west. It was the gentry and especially the larger magnates who benefited from this trade, and who now sought to increase the efficiency of their manorial economy by stepping up feudal appropriations. The full impact of this 'Second Serfdom'[5] was experienced when this trade began to decline and the peasantry had to be further squeezed so that profits could be maintained. At the political level, the magnates succeeded in establishing an elective monarchy, to mask the reality of an anarchical aristocratic republic in stark contrast with the absolutist states taking shape elsewhere in early modern Europe. These developments affected all regions of the country, including those regions in the mountains not previously subjected to the feudal yoke. The weakness of the state left the peasants less secure against foreign invaders, and Wisłok was one of many villages plundered by Tartar invasion in 1624. At the same time it was considerably easier to resist magnate oppression in the mountain environment, and in the southern parts of the Sanok Lands the Second Serfdom was scarcely more fully implemented that the First.

Legally, Wisłok was still privately held, but eventually it passed out of the hands of the original proprietors. Most neighbouring villages belonged directly to the crown and were administered by its agents. Here feudal controls were weakest of all and the peasantry largely independent. The inhabitants of some nearby villages to the east of Wisłok retained great pride in having once belonged to the Royal Demesne, even after the Monarchy collapsed and this ceased to have any practical meaning. The ethnographer Roman Reinfuss found this tradition alive in Wisłok itself as late as the 1930s, despite the fact that in pre-partition Poland this village had always been privately owned.[6] This would suggest that the legal details of ownership did not matter much at all in mountain conditions; and such an interpretation is strengthened when one examines the record of peasant resistance in Wisłok in the course of the seventeenth century.

Resistance could take many forms. A mass struggle against the forces of exploitation was one possibility, illustrated notably by the Polish highlanders of Podhale (Tatra Mountains region) in the second quarter of the seventeenth century, but not imitated on any large scale in the Sanok Lands. Very common, however, in the more easterly sections of the Carpathians, was individual or collective *flight* from the oppressors. This was easy and effective: the feudal system could not work, because an oppressive Lord found himself left without a labour force. The third and most colourful strategy of self-defence was organised brigandry, which became endemic in the Sanok Lands in the seventeenth century, and which invites comparison with patterns of rural protest and banditry in other countries. The prominence of Wisłok men in the criminal records of the period derives in part from the village's location on the state border; it was relatively easy to accomplish a daring exploit on one side and retreat to a temporary refuge on the other. But apart from a catalogue of common crimes (particularly cattle stealing) there are also records of coordinated, mass attacks upon the manor houses of the gentry of the region, which was ethnically Polish. That these violent protests were on occasion organised and led by the Orthodox priest suggests that feelings were running high, and that ethnic and class barriers were closely related. It has been argued that the Orthodox clergy in the East Slav villages seldom lived at a much higher level than their congregations, whilst in the Polish villages of the lowlands the Catholic presbytery was more likely to be perceived on occasion as yet another oppressive feudal institution.[7]

It is possible that the seeds of much later bitterness were sown during the troubled years of the seventeenth century. In spite of the weakness of the Polish state, in the Sanok Lands some continuity of settlement (if not in every village) and of population was maintained. Despite the class conflicts engendered by feudal exploitation there was as yet no hint of ethnic antagonism between Eastern Slavs (or *Rusnaks*, as they presumably already described themselves) and Polish villagers with whom their contacts began to increase. Polish peasants did not identify themselves with the Polish aristocratic republic, any more than the *Rusnaks* could have considered themselves to be members of any national community. Despite the intolerance induced by the Counter Reformation, at the local level there was little religious antagonism. Many of the Polish Commonwealth's Orthodox subjects were formally brought into communion with Rome at the synods of Brest-Litovsk in 1595–6, which called into being the Greek Catholic or Uniate Church.[8] Some Orthodox Bishops, including the Bishop of Przemyśl, to whose diocese Wisłok belonged, refused to ratify this Union. When a successor finally did so in 1692 it made no difference to the *Rus* masses in the mountains.

They continued to practise the Byzantine rite and to use the Julian calendar, and this was more than enough to distinguish them from the ethnically Polish communities which came to predominate in the lowland areas.

Thus, the two main ethnic groups in the Sanok lands under the Polish Commonwealth were the Poles and the *Rusnaks*. The differences between them were clearly defined, in language, in economy (because the *Rusnaks* were concentrated in the upland areas and much more dependent upon their animals), and in religion. In Wisłok the *Rus* community was again consolidating its position at the end of the seventeenth century. It had successfully resisted full implementation of feudal controls under Polish Lords, maintained a mixed pastoral-agricultural economy in which the former (influenced by Vlach shepherds) was probably still the more important, and clung tenaciously to the practical essence of the traditional religion, despite the diocese's departure from Orthodoxy and acceptance of papal authority in 1692. The influence of the Polish Commonwealth, though it lingered on until 1772, was always slight in these peripheral lands. Yet in a sense the very instability of Wisłok during the seventeenth century renders it a faithful microcosm of the state to which it belonged; although most lowland villages were more stable and more effectively exploited by the manors, the aggregate of these exploitative relations was a highly unstable, unmanageable Polish state.

The Rus, Greek Catholic community expands and Austrian policies in Galicia transform both its economy and its political aspirations

After the turbulence of the seventeenth century the period up to the First World War was more tranquil. In it great changes occurred in Wisłok, for under Austrian rule economic progress was more rapid and a new sense of group identity emerged, thanks largely to a combination of Austrian policy and the designs of the Greek Catholic Church. The gradual disintegration of the Polish Commonwealth, caused by the refusal of the nobility to permit the central authorities to wield effective power, reached its predictable climax in 1772. As a result of the 'first partition' agreed in that year between Russia, Austria and Prussia, most of Poland's southern territories passed to Austria. Henceforth they were known as the Province of Galicia, a name derived from Halicz, centre of the East Slav Prince-

dom which had controlled most of this territory before its annexa-
tion by Poland in the fourteenth century. After the 'third partition',
agreed by the same great powers in 1795, even the rump Polish state
disappeared. It was not to reappear on the map of Europe until 1919.
During this period the Sanok Lands formed part of Eastern Galicia.
The provincial capital at Lemberg was the north-eastern outpost of
what became known in the second half of the nineteenth century as
the Austro-Hungarian Empire, or simply 'the Monarchy'.

Despite high mortality figures (indicated in the church registers,
which date from 1784 and employ Latin and Polish languages) the
population of Wisłok seems to have grown steadily during the eighteenth century. This could not continue throughout the nineteenth
century, as the figures given in Table 1 confirm. The population
exceeded 2,000 by the 1860s, and this imposed severe pressure upon
limited land resources. Areas formerly used as pasture were increasingly brought under cultivation, and by the beginning of the twentieth century the traditional extensive pastoral base of the economy
had been almost completely destroyed.

Year:	1808	1828	1859	1880	1900	1921	1931	1946
Population:	1760	1921	2034	1974	2271	2268	2767	2450

Table 1: Population of Wislok in selected years 1808–1946

Austrian administration probably had little immediate impact at
village level, and therefore the first detailed agricultural census they
took, which dates from 1787, sheds interesting light upon the farming system as it was before the developments of the nineteenth
century. By now there were altogether 324 peasant farms in Wisłok
covering an area of nearly 6,000 acres, more than double the forest
area under 'manorial' control. The dues these farmers had to pay
were no longer expressed in animal products but in crops and
money, as elsewhere. It is interesting to observe that in Wisłok, in
contrast to most lowland villages, they were extracted not from
single families but from groups of families which sometimes contained as many as 8 separate households. Almost all arable fields and
gardens were jointly held by at least two households. It has been
suggested that in this mountain village, unlike most of Galicia,
production was still organised on a large, collective base and not
devolved to individual households; if this was also true of other *Rus*
villages it would imply significant differences between their social
structure and that of Polish villages on the plains.[9]

23

Austrian administrators sought to regulate access to land carefully and were more successful in constraining the freedom of the local population than their predecessors had been. Since the peasants of Wisłok had never been greatly burdened by feudal obligations they attained no great benefits when these were finally abolished in 1848. But they were affected by the process of land registration, which took place at about the same time; the meticulous cadastral survey conducted in 1851 shows that many plots were already highly fragmented, although evidence of the original division, in blocks of land on either side of the river, could still be seen. Peasants were prohibited from making free use of the forests by an Austrian regulation of 1782. Although this was quite impossible to implement, it gradually became more difficult to exploit the still vast areas of forest in casual fashion.

In the course of the nineteenth century, the absentee owners of forest estates parcelled large areas out to local buyers, and also to outsiders interested in commercial exploitation. There was a growing demand for timber from across the Hungarian border, which occasionally meant cash and short-term employment for local peasants. Cash could also be obtained through farming, mainly by selling animals at district markets, which were attended by buyers from as far afield as Vienna. The more important sources of money lay well outside the region. Seasonal migration at harvest time, to work on the rich estates of northern Hungary or in lowland Galicia, was one possibility which numerous peasants took up from the late eighteenth century onwards. This was considerably facilitated in 1872 when the Austrians opened a railway line through the mountains, passing very close to Wisłok. In the closing decades of the nineteenth century horizons widened further. In common with many Poles from the equally overcrowded villages of the plains, thousands of *Rusnaks* sought work in the United States. Many were young men who had no intention of settling permanently in North America. They would return to their village after a few years, marry, and invest all their savings in farming (i.e. in the purchase of land), conforming in all respects to the norms of their native community.[10]

Land was the crucial scarce resource and the influx of dollars drove its price to very high levels (a foretaste of things to come in the socialist period when the dollar again became the effective measure of value). This was the most conspicuous aspect of the penetration of a cash economy. Money was also needed to buy other goods, made available by the first immigrant group to challenge the ethnic homogeneity of the *Rus* community. The Jews had for centuries been more welcome in Poland than almost anywhere else in Europe, and their penetration of even the most remote villages in the mountains was in tune with the new economic order.[11] They opened shops or taverns, usually a simple combination of the two, which obtained most of their income by dispensing alcohol. Sometimes they invested their profits in farming; they became the major source of credit in the community; and they maintained their ethnic and religious identity absolutely, for although they never numbered more than a few dozen in Wisłok, they associated themselves with larger Jewish communities elsewhere (the nearest to Wisłok being the small market town of Bukowsko, 12 km through the mountains).

The character of the economic 'development' experienced by Wisłok and by Galicia as a whole (for Wisłok exemplifies the general tendencies of this period) must be studied in relation to the expansion of Western Europe and the role of the imperial hinterlands of Austria-Hungary in the new capitalist system. It is plausible to maintain that Eastern Europe was condemned to a subordinate role and to 'underdevelopment' from the sixteenth century onwards. Certainly the Monarchy which actually governed East-Central Europe during the era when capitalist relations of production reached even the most isolated rural communities lacked the ambition and the means to develop all its sprawling territories. It obtained a surplus in agricultural products (from Wisłok it extracted little more than timber and migrant labour), and it used it to maintain an elaborate bureaucratic machine. It built many railways, but it could do little to develop industry or to alleviate agrarian conditions, the distress brought about by population expansion in the face of a chronic shortage of land. Migration was the sole hope of many peasants, Poles and *Rusnaks* alike.[12]

In the latter part of the nineteenth century and the early part of the twentieth, for reasons intimately related to this pattern of underdevelopment, village populations in East-Central Europe came gradually to be drawn into new patterns of political involvement with the wider societies to which they belonged. Previously, the main factor in such wider identification had been religion; but now new criteria for unity were discovered. One notable illustration was the formation of new political parties to represent the interests of the peasant masses. The Polish Peasants' Party, founded in 1895 in the East Galician town of Rzeszów, was the very first of many similar 'populist' parties which went on to wage a fifty-year struggle on behalf of the East European peasantry, until silenced (at least temporarily) by socialist governments after the Second World War.[13]

But the type of movement which had the greatest impact upon the Austro-Hungarian Monarchy in its later years was the expression, not of class or interest-group solidarity, but of growing nationalist sentiment amongst the many subject peoples. In Galicia, perhaps because of the recent memory of a Polish state, this happened earlier in Polish areas than it did amongst the Eastern Slav population. Polish leaders in Galicia succeeded in gaining a large measure of autonomy for the Province in 1860. This enabled Poles to dominate political and cultural life, as they had done traditionally, even in those eastern parts where they formed only a small minority of the population. Whether simply as a response to this assertion of Polish influence (which far exceeded anything that Poles were allowed to achieve in the Prussian or Russian sectors of their divided country), whether perhaps encouraged by Austria in order to counter this Polish influence, or whether due ultimately to cultural and economic forces similar to those which stimulated the national 'awakening' amongst Poles, there developed in the Eastern Slav territories in the later nineteenth century a movement proclaiming a Ukrainian national identity. Because no Ukrainian state had existed previously, at least not in the same sense that a Polish political formation had survived until 1795, the tasks facing this movement were formidable. In the absence of an appropriate political culture and the symbols of 'nation', it was first of all necessary for an intelligentsia to come forward and create them. Then the new Ukrainian consciousness had to be transmitted to the masses, and this took time, especially in the more remote mountain regions. Amongst the most westerly *Rusnaks*, long associated with Poles, success was not finally achieved until after the Second World War; in Wisłok it came a little sooner.

In the Sanok Lands in the nineteenth century religion remained the principal factor differentiating the population, together with langauge and other cultural features, and these differences were still not perceived in terms of national communities. Most villages were *either* Greek Catholic parishes *or* Roman Catholic parishes, but they were not strictly endogamous. A Polish speaker from a Roman Catholic village who married into a *Rus* village would adopt the dialect and the religion of his new community (and vice versa for in-marrying *Rusnaks*). The boundary between the *Rus* zone in the mountains and the Polish villages which penetrated the foothills remained firm. There were only a few islands of Polish settlement within the *Rus* zone, and equally few isolated Greek Catholic parishes on the lowlands. This pattern changed slightly under Austrian rule, as a result of new economic developments. Thus, a number of Polish families moved at this time to Komańcza, 10 km from Wisłok, in order to work on the newly constructed railway, and sufficient of them remained for them to be able to preserve their separate identity in a village that had previously known only Greek Catholics and a few Jews. However, because economic development was so limited, few villages were affected by such immigration. Wisłok in this respect seems to be typical. At the end of the First World War (during which it suffered considerable damage and human losses as Russian and Austrian armies struggled to control the nearby mountain passes), the handful of Jewish families was still the only non-*Rus* element in a population of more than 2,000.

There are few accounts of how the ethnic consciousness of these *Rusnaks* was evolving in the last decades of Austrian rule. The two main orientations which emerged can only be understood in the context of prevailing political alliances. Firstly, there was a current termed the 'Old Ruthenian', the adherents of which looked generally to Great Russia (Moscow) as the only existing East Slav state which might serve to focus the pristine unity of all Eastern Slavs. This orientation was viewed with deep suspicion by Austria, inveterate opponent of Czarist Russia. It was viewed with more enthusiasm by some Poles, content to endorse a vague pan-slavic sentiment which did not threaten their own more pragmatic objectives of gaining full power in Eastern Galicia. But it was the Ukrainian orientation which gained popularity amongst the mountain *Rusnaks*. This *was* a serious threat to Polish aspirations, and suited the 'divide and rule' tactics of the Austrians rather well. Those who espoused the new Ukrainian identity also believed themselves to be descendants of the true, original Eastern Slavs. They looked not to Moscow, nor to the creation of an autonomous *Rus* political formation in the mountain region, as did some amongst the Old-Ruthenians, but instead they proclaimed a new Ukrainian nation as the successor to the old Kievan unity. They were given considerable freedom to propagate their views by the Austrian authorities, and in most areas of *Rus* settlement they eventually triumphed over the Old-Ruthenians. They owed their success most of all to the committed support of the Greek Catholic clergy, the only intellectual elite available to transmit the new ideology to the mountain peasantry. The Greek Catholic

Bishops of Przemyśl were particularly active in the Ukrainian cause, to the fury of Polish political leaders in Eastern Galicia.[14]

At the end of the First World War the Monarchy collapsed, and before the resulting power vacuum in Eastern Galicia was filled by the newly established Polish republic, many areas were shaken by revolutionary upheavals. The *Rus* mountain areas, the most westerly parts of ethnic territory claimed by Ukrainian insurgents, were no exception. The Old-Ruthenians, many of whom suffered severe persecution by Austria during the war, managed to establish an autonomous republic. Some of their leaders sought desperately to affiliate the areas they represented with the new Czechoslovak state, but this proposal was rejected at the Versailles Peace Conference in 1919. In Wisłok, the Ukrainian orientation asserted itself more strongly. In November 1918 the local priest, Panko Shpilka, was instrumental in establishing a National Council in sympathy with the independent Western Ukrainian Republic, which had its capital in Lemberg. Delegates came to Wisłok from a wide area, representing most *Rus* parts of the Sanok Lands, and the priest worked assid-uously to foster contacts with the centres of the revolution during the winter months 1918–19. He was eventually arrested and the national movement suppressed by the Polish army. The short-lived Ukrainian administration in Wisłok and the environs was followed by twenty years of Polish administration.[15]

The Greek Catholic, Ukrainian community survives the trials of capitalist Poland and fascist Germany before succumbing to socialism

Poland's treatment of the ethnic minority groups within her new borders in the inter-war period left much to be desired.[16] Altogether they made up about one-third of her population. The Ukrainians were the largest single minority group, and they formed a majority in most of the regions which had formerly comprised Eastern Galicia. The *Rus* zone in the mountains was the most isolated part of the territories claimed by Ukrainian nationalist groups; but here, as we have noted, the Ukrainian orientation was not universally adopted by the *Rusnaks* themselves. For this reason *Rusnaks* were singled out for a less antagonistic approach than that adopted towards the more self-conscious Ukrainians of other regions. It was considered that the *Rusnaks* of Wisłok and hundreds of other villages in the moun-tains could at least be won over to an 'Old-Ruthenian' consciousness, if not fully assimilated into the Polish nation and state. Efforts were made to achieve these goals through control of the education system, through suppression of the main sources of pro-Ukrainian propaganda, particularly the Greek Catholic Church, and finally by the fabrication of new regional identities for the *Rusnaks*, in which the regime was aided by historians and ethnographers.[17]

Virtually no detailed academic studies of *Rus* territory were carried out before the inter-war period, and the bulk of research was conducted in the 1930s. Much care was taken in defining the boundaries of *Rus* sub-groups — not where they met Polish villages, for this was obvious to all, but where one *Rus* 'ethnographic group' shaded into another. According to the linguistic and cultural criteria inconsistently applied by different writers, Wisłok fell into the most westerly of these groups, the 'Lemkians', who inhabited a territory roughly corresponding to the boundaries of the Lower Beskids. Some writers held that the Lemkians had more in common with Poles than with the Ukrainians, since, despite their mixed East Slav and Vlach ancestry, they had always been part of Poland politically and had benefited from their contacts with Polish culture over many centuries. It was even suggested that the Lemkians were really the product of interaction between Vlachs and Poles, with Eastern Slav elements absent altogether; according to this view, it was merely as a result of some later cultural diffusion from the east that their language and religion came to differ from those of the Poles. The Polish academic invention of 'Lemkovina' had considerable influence on the *Rus* masses, and, combined with the 'Old-Ruthenian' legacy, the amalgam of blatant propaganda and serious ethnographical studies of differentiation within the *Rus* zone did help to ensure that peasants moving beyond a purely local group identification for the first time would move no further than to the 'Lemkian' or 'Old-Ruthenian' orientation. Thus, some who had previously identified themselves only as *Rusnaks* and offered this as a statement of their religion and their culture, not about their 'national' allegiance, now proudly assumed a 'Lemkian' identity. However sceptical they were when told about their intimate cultural ties with Poles, there were many who came to accept the line of the Polish authorities, that their own regional identity might as well be developed within the Polish state as in an independent Ukraine.

Despite Polish pressure, the inhabitants of Wisłok were not disposed to accept this view, and the eastern section of Lemkovina, which had supported the Ukrainian insurgents in 1918–19,

2. *Rusnak* woman in traditional costume. (Photo by R. Reinfuss, 1935.)

3. Typical *Rus* dwelling (1981).

remained overwhelmingly loyal to the Ukrainian cause. The pressure was most evident in education and in religion. After 1930, Ukrainian language materials were prohibited in the schools and teaching thereafter took place in the Lemkian dialect (a more archaic form of essentially the same language, written in a slightly different script). The Polish authorities were also determined to prevent the Greek Catholic Church from emerging as the national church of the Ukrainians. One important instrument used to achieve this objective was support for the Orthodox Church, not only in the eastern territories taken from Russia but also within Lemkovina, where 'Old-Ruthenian' sympathisers were encouraged to abandon the Greek Catholic Church in favour of Orthodoxy, the original church of all the Eastern Slavs. Many parishes did so, whilst in other villages, where only a part of the population wished to make this move, there was considerable sectarian acrimony. The Greek Catholic Bishop of Przemyśl was unable to counter these trends after 1934, for the Polish government succeeded in persuading the Vatican to create a separate 'Apostolic Administration for Lemkovina' with an amenable, pro-Polish Bishop at its head.

These policies differed from the blunter instruments used to repress this minority in other parts of inter-war Poland. Not surpris-

30

ingly the Ukranian nationalists accused the government of attempting to 'Polonise' the so-called 'Lemkians', by detaching them from
their church and from their larger cultural group. The Poles enjoyed
a measure of success only in the westerly parts of *Rus* territory, where
the Ukrainian cause had not gained a strong hold in the days of the
Monarchy. In Wisłok and most other easterly districts the challenge
to the Ukrainian identification and to the Greek Catholic Church
was unsuccessful. In Komańcza inroads could be made with ease
because there was an immigrant Polish population. Thus, a Roman
Catholic Church and also a monastery were founded here in the
1920s, the first time a Latin rite parish had existed in this part of the
mountains. In Wisłok a Pole who had married into the village was
instrumental in mustering some support in the 1930s for a small
evangelical church. However, this was more a product of the dis-
tressed economic circumstances of the period than a sign of any
serious weakening of Ukrainian sympathies.

It can be seen from Table 1 that the population of Wisłok rose
sharply in the inter-war years. This was partly because there were
now fewer opportunities to emigrate. It was also more difficult to
supplement incomes by seasonal migration, since the new state
borders of Czechoslovakia had to be crossed twice to reach potential

31

employment on the plains of Hungary. With the forests already depleted there was little the *Rus* population could do except try to intensify agriculture and to make more land available for cultivation by terracing even the most unfavourable stretches of hillside. There was little inclination to innovate, the diet was deplorable and mortality figures remained high. Yet Reinfuss, the outstanding ethnographer who visited the village in the 1930s, found that material poverty did not preclude great cultural vitality.[18]

In spite of the changes which followed the restitution of the Polish state in 1919 and the worsening of ethnic relations within it, particularly after 1930, there was still little or no antagonism at the local level between *Rusnaks* and Poles in the Sanok Lands. The zone as a whole may be seen as one of the few successes of Marshal Piłsudski's early 'federalist' designs for his country (policies which underestimated the strength of national feeling amongst minority groups, or at any rate overestimated the capacity of the Poles to control them). For a time it even seemed that class solidarity might overcome ethnic differences, notably when Polish and *Rus* peasants combined in massive protests at the height of the Depression in 1931–2.[19] Wisłok remained an isolated village, bounded on all sides by smaller, equally homogeneous, *Rus* villages; yet marriages with Poles were still quite common (Poles were outnumbered only by Jews at the market centre of Bukowsko). The rules applied were the same as in Austrian times — both partners adhered to the language and religion of the community in which they resided, and their children were raised accordingly. The presence of a police station, manned by Poles who were strangers to the community, was the major sign that much had changed in the outside world; but not until the end of the Second World War was the gravity of these changes brought home to the peasants of Wisłok.

In 1939, Wisłok was occupied by German forces (the Soviet-German demarcation line followed the line of the River San a short distance to the east). A short time later many of her able-bodied men were transferred to Germany as slave labour. The Poles at the police station were replaced by a Ukrainian staff. Throughout the war the Germans were astute in exploiting the accumulated grievances and aspirations of the nationally conscious Ukrainians, though they never showed themselves to be genuinely interested in satisfying the desire for independence. In the course of the war the *Rusnaks* were more exposed to Ukrainian influence than ever before; even the priests sent to Wisłok were from lowland regions of the Ukraine proper, with no knowledge of the 'Lemkian' dialect. Fresh conflicts developed in the *Rus* zone after the Nazis were driven back in 1944. A Ukrainian nationalist guerilla organisation based in the mountains, possibly with some German connivance, was able to continue the struggle for an independent Ukraine until 1947. The Ukrainian Insurrectionary Army (UPA), as it was called, committed innumerable atrocities against the civil population (mainly against Poles, but also against some *Rusnaks* who were considered to be half-hearted in their Ukrainian commitment). Guerillas were also involved in many military skirmishes with forces of the Red Army and of the newly formed People's Army of Poland. Originally based in regions that were incorporated into the USSR in 1945, UPA was able to survive in the *Rus* zones that were left under Polish control because it could attract men and supplies from villages such as Wisłok. Most of the fighting in fact took place outside the Lemkian region, in the 'Boikian' section of the Bieszczady Mountains. These *Rusnaks* had not been subjected to the same Polonising policies in the inter-war period and were firmer in their support for guerilla fighters, most of whom were not *Rusnak* natives of the mountains. The movement was liquidated by the Polish Army in 1947 in the course of a massive military operation (Operation 'Vistula'), during which all *Rus* zones in Poland, including Lemkovina, were evacuated and devastated.[20]

It may seem strange that such a recent invention of one set of Polish authorities could be dismantled so easily by another set, but Soviet power had transformed the situation. The new Polish state, far from possessing some of the most numerous minority groups in Europe, was ethnically one of the most homogeneous. As with other *Rus* groups in the Carpathians, Soviet policy was to submerge regional identities in the cause of consolidating a Ukrainian national identity.[21] When the new Polish-Soviet borders were agreed in 1945, it was decided to repatriate not only some millions of Poles who would otherwise have been left in the Ukraine and White Russia, but also several hundreds of thousands of Ukrainians from Polish territory, including Lemkians who had previously been encouraged by Poles not to consider themselves Ukrainian at all. The bulk of these transfers were concluded by the end of 1945, several hundred inhabitants of Wisłok being amongst those who were moved to various locations in the Ukraine. According to those who remember these events, a few went voluntarily — communist sympathisers and some of those most fervently loyal to the Ukrainian cause; but most went reluctantly, under considerable pressure from the police and the military. Terrorist activity continued to affect the village in 1946, when both UPA and the Polish Army were active in Wisłok. The population was still high, because many *Rusnaks* abandoned smaller villages and sought refuge here in houses left empty after the migrations to the USSR. It is difficult to gauge how many gave voluntary support to UPA, but at least some younger men were willing recruits. The Polish Army acted on the assumption that the entire village was collaborating with terrorists. Polish soldiers were responsible for the deaths of several civilians in at least one operation, which was speedily avenged by UPA. Overall there was little military activity in the Lemkian region, partly because the Lower Beskids did not offer adequate protection to guerilla bands. The decision to evacuate this region in its entirety was taken early in 1947 and cannot be justified on purely military grounds. It was implemented crudely and quickly. By the early summer of 1947 the entire *Rus* zone was empty, apart from a few pockets of Polish settlement. Some UPA leaders succeeded in escaping through Czechoslovakia to the West. The *Rusnaks* themselves were deported to the northern and western territories which Poland had acquired from Germany. In this new setting, where the better farms had already been occupied, often by virulently anti-Ukrainian Poles repatriated from the east, all *Rusnaks* finally had to take cognisance of the status they have officially retained to the present day: that of being the major component of the Ukrainian minority group in the People's Republic of Poland. The designation 'Lemkian', if it survived at all, was superseded as the prime level of ethnic identification. Those who went back to their native lands (as some of them were allowed to from the late 1950s) returned as Ukrainians, whatever orientation they had supported before the war; and it is as a Ukrainian minority in the new community in Wisłok that we shall have occasion to refer to them in later chapters.

*   *   *   *

We have traced the history of the *Rus* community in Wisłok from its earliest records down to its dissolution in 1947. For most of this period it was politically part of the Kingdom and the Commonwealth of Poland. Later it came under Austrian rule, before in the twentieth century it reverted to Poland. The inhabitants were once Orthodox, but became Catholic in 1692 without abandoning the

Byzantine rite. The Greek Catholic Church maintained its position until 1946, when it was proscribed at national level by the new socialist authorities. The economy of Wisłok was initially that of mountain pastoralism, but this gradually yielded to one based on agriculture as the population expanded. Emigration was the major systemic regulator in the underdeveloped Galician economy, but this did not prevent the fragmentation of agricultural land being carried to extreme lengths. Economic conditions were probably most severe in the inter-war period, when there were fewer opportunities to emigrate. Relations between the *Rusnaks* and the Polish peasantry outside the mountain zone were good through many centuries, until they were influenced by the growth of nationalist sentiment and finally poisoned during and immediately following the Second World War. It was the misfortune of the *Rusnaks* that they attained full national awareness as Ukrainians only when their communities were destroyed and they themselves forcibly dispersed by the Polish Army.

CHAPTER THREE

Reconstruction of the Private Sector

In no country have we seen a richer soil, and more susceptible of agriculture, than in Poland. Every acre, from Warsaw, is capable of great improvement, and the country at large might become the granary of the north of Europe . . .
Robert Johnston, *Travels* (London, 1815, p. 445)

The formation of a new community began almost immediately after the dissolution of the old. Its new ethnic profile was overwhelmingly Polish. The economic base on which this village was reconstructed reveals it to be a direct product of the socialist period. Socialist principles were energetically applied, notably in the development of State Farms and the Forestry Commission. However, greater reliance was placed on the traditional peasant economy, which immigrants to Wisłok were permitted, within limits, to rebuild. This peasantry may not dominate statistically, as opportunities to work in the socialist sector have increased, but it has been decisive in the moulding of a new local society. In this chapter we concentrate on how peasant farming has managed to adapt to adverse economic circumstances, how it can withstand a crisis, and how it is likely to persist in the future.

The legacy of the Rus community is plundered by the Polish rural proletariat (1947–1959)

The *Rus*/Ukrainian villages were evacuated by early summer of 1947. The remaining inhabitants of the Wisłok area were put onto trains at Komańcza and despatched to various settlements in the north and north-west of the country, leaving their houses and many other assets behind. Further action was taken to ensure that they would not be able to return. Some villages had already been damaged by fighting and fell into a rapid process of decay, whilst others were now destroyed by the Army or looted by Polish civilians. Half a dozen villages bordering on Wisłok experienced this fate and disappeared from the map. Wisłok itself was raided by Polish peasants from Bukowsko (the former Polish-Jewish market centre, 12 km away across the mountains), who made off with whatever they

36

considered worth taking. Spontaneous pillage from outside was complemented by the establishment within Wisłok of a new, extensive mode of production based upon the rapid plunder and squandering of the *Rus*/Ukrainian legacy. This began in the agricultural season of 1948, when about fifteen families were induced to settle in the village and commence independent farming operations. After a lag in the early 1950s more families followed, so that by the end of that decade the population was close to its current level of about 300 persons and the process of resettlement was effectively complete.[1]

The immigrants were Polish, their origins were diverse but had certain common features. The initial group was recruited from two lowland Galician villages, less than 200 km from Wisłok, which in different ways illustrated the negative consequences for the agrarian structure of underdevelopment in the capitalist period. One was a densely populated village of smallholders in which a large proportion of the population had no access to a viable farm, nor to any alternative form of employment. The other was a village dominated by a manor (*dwór*), in which a large proportion of the population worked as agricultural labourers, if they were fortunate enough to obtain work at all. In both of these villages the post-war Land Reform had had considerable levelling impact, but it had been impossible to allocate to every applicant an adequate size of holding. Those who were unsuccessful, and who were too slow or reluctant for other reasons to seek farms in the territories 'regained' from Germany, were easily tempted in 1948 by the promise of abundant fertile land and free accommodation ready for immediate occupancy. The opportunities were advertised by the authorities at District (*powiat*) level; they also assisted these migrants with free rail passage, special bank credits and exemption from taxes during the first years of residence in the new community. (See the Appendix for an example of how the experiences of one early immigrant were described in glowing terms in propaganda brochures aimed at enticing others to the region.)

Thus, it was not difficult for the authorities to recruit settlers, but since they had no practical strategy of economic renewal for this isolated region and no money to invest in it, they left these early immigrants to fend for themselves, with only minimal aid and advice. Unfortunately, just as it was not easy for the deported Ukrainians to adapt to lowland farming in Pomerania, so it was well nigh impossible for these Polish colonists, familiar with conditions on the plain but for the most part without any experience of running an

4. The church of the upper hamlet, destroyed by State Farm tractors in the mid-1950's. (Photo by A. Fastnacht, 1936.)

independent farm, to adapt to the mountain environment. The season was shorter, the soils poorer, yields lower — and disenchantment was swift. The alternative was to resort to a more extensive mode of production, and with relatively few farmers working large areas (though their legal ownership rights extended only to quite small parcels) this soon became the general practice. The authorities were willing to purchase hay in Komańcza for transport to lowland areas where the demand was high. The Wisłok immigrants seized their chance and spent most of their summers simply cutting the grass. They retained a little for their own few animals and earned enough cash with the rest to see them through the year. Whilst the men cut and carted the hay other members of the family would collect the abundant mushrooms, which also found a market in Komańcza.

Today some older men look back with nostalgia on these years of plenty. They moved into houses more spacious than any they had known before (with the pick of such a large number they naturally chose the best), and they cultivated or ravaged as large an area as they could manage. There was no tax to be paid and no rigorous demarcation of farm boundaries. In the long winters they did not need to worry about fuel, for they had only to dismantle the empty dwellings in their neighbourhood. They therefore neglected the forests, just as they neglected to maintain paths in other areas they did not need and to curb the wild growth of natural vegetation. As numbers increased in the 1950s and the socialist sector was built up, gradually some of these new farmers realised that it would not always be possible to survive merely by appropriating the fruits of the past labours of others. The demand for hay slackened, the mushrooms disappeared (because, so it was said, there was no animal manure to stimulate their growth and anyway the land and forests were so overgrown they could not be seen). When the period of tax exemption came to an end the Wisłok farmers too were subjected to compulsory delivery requirements, and limited to small and precisely demarcated plots. Few amongst the rural proletariat from the lowlands were able to adjust to these new demands. A positive example was set by immigrants hailing from other parts of the mountains (mainly near the Tatras, where land shortage was also acute), who were familiar with the techniques necessary to grow crops and breed animals successfully in difficult upland conditions. But they were a minority, and eventually the authorities became convinced of the need to devise some long-term development strategy to assist the rest of the new population. The next phase in the construction of the socialist farming community in Wisłok can be conveniently dated from the approval in 1959 of a far-reaching Development Plan for the entire region of Bieszczady and adjacent parts of the Beskids.

The locally controlled Agricultural Circle is unable to save the private sector from stagnation and decline (1959–1975)

The 1959 Development Plan was an ambitious charter for the Bieszczcady region which placed the main emphasis upon large projects and the need to build up a strong socialist sector. Thus, the period which followed witnessed a transformation of the local infrastructure in Wisłok. Electricity was introduced in the early 1960s and a few houses close to one of the new State Farms even obtained piped water. A new asphalt road was constructed to open the village to the world in two directions: eastwards to Komańcza, the larger settlement 10 km away and on the railway line linking the mountain zone to the towns of the lowlands, and westwards to the small towns of Jaśliska and Dukla. Regular daily bus services now enabled residents of Wisłok to commute to work outside the village. The main such opportunity was in Rzepedź, where a large sawmill was built up in the 1960s.

The private sector of agriculture was not transformed, any more than it was in the rest of the country. After the phase of plunder, which arose out of the specific circumstances of resettlement, conditions now came to resemble much more closely those prevailing in other parts of the Polish countryside. By now the State Farms and Forestry Commission were fully operative and the restriction of the private sector to the central parts of the Wisłok valley meant that farm boundaries were more effectively enforced within this area. Out of a total land area of just over 6,000 hectares, in the early 1960s the private sector was farming a mere 234 (whilst the State Farms had 2,738 hectares and the Forestry Commission most of the remainder). There was little variation in the size of the private holdings, which was usually restricted to 6 hectares per family (for comparison, the norm applied when new farms were established in the late 1970s was still only 8 hectares). Generally, this land was allocated in compact units near to dwellings but, though desirable in itself, this also made for considerable inefficiency and inequality. Some farmers received only flat, fertile land, part of which they would use as pasture, whilst others found themselves obliged to sow grain on steep stretches of hillside. Most of the outlying areas had passed to the State Farms, but since these did not have the resources to utilise them, large tracts ceased to contribute to production altogether. The pattern to emerge conformed to the highly egalitarian (at least on paper) pattern created throughout the country by the post-war Land Reform and reinforced by attacks upon the richer peasants (*kulaks*) during the Stalinist period, particularly up to 1954. As a productive system such a pattern of landholding had great deficiencies everywhere. In the lowland regions of the Rzeszów voivodeship, anything over 9 hectares was enough to brand a peasant as a *kulak*. In a mountain region, where pasture was plentiful, it did not make economic sense to enforce an upper limit of 6 hectares, and to require farmers by law to sell grain rather than animal products to the state.[2]

The Polish peasantry as a whole was not, at this time, well endowed with capital goods. The former proletarians, elevated to the status of peasant in Wisłok, had fewer than most. Some managed to bring a horse and cart along with them; others acquired these and other basic tools (plough, harrow) only after their arrival, with the aid of state credits. Not until the 1970s did it become possible for a few farmers to own tractors and other modern equipment. It was recognised before this that the facilities and services needed by individual farmers could be made available on some collective basis. The Agricultural Circle[3] was the institution revived after the political crisis of 1956 and charged with helping the private sector to increase its production, whilst simultaneously bringing it into closer contact with (and dependence upon) the national economy that was by now firmly under socialist control.

Agricultural Cooperatives, of which the revived Circle may be regarded as a particular type, had a long history in many parts of Poland before the socialist period. However, attempts in many parts of the country to 'persuade' peasants to join Soviet-style collective farms in the early 1950s were so counter-productive that there was now widespread suspicion and accusations of 'backdoor collectivisation' when a Circle was initiated in Wisłok in 1959 by the outside authorities. It had to be emphasised to the new members that individual ownership rights would not be threatened, and that no collective work was expected. When this Circle was established it was able to draw credits from the State Bank and several tractors were acquired. At this point peasants began to take more interest in its affairs. A managing committee was popularly elected, and a few local young men with the appropriate qualifications were taken on as full-time employees. It became possible to carry out all major tasks on the land by machine (since even threshing could be accomplished with the aid of a machine hired by the Circle from Komańcza). Not all farmers took advantage of the new facilities to the same degree; but some were induced to expand the area of their farms (and actually received formal permission to do so later in the 1960s), whilst even the least innovative families were pleased to reduce drudgery in the fields, and to release the horses for more remunerative work in the forests.

In spite of these benefits, there were few regrets when local control over the Circle was lost, as it merged in the mid-1970s with the Circles of neighbouring settlements. Some informants preferred that control should be vested in strangers, since they said this was the only way to avoid favouritism within the village. They also hoped that the number and quality of machine services might improve more rapidly in a larger organisation. It is possible that these later developments reveal not so much the peasant's deep-rooted hostility to all institutions smacking of 'socialism', but simply the inability of these *parvenu* peasants of diverse origins to make any cooperative institutions work. It is also tempting to feel that, had the locally controlled Circle been given a better chance in the 1960s (in terms of material equipment and competent extension services) then commodity production might have responded more impressively than it did.

The only exceptional measure of assistance granted in this period to farmers in the Bieszczady region was the provision of more generous credits to new settlers. In fact, almost all purchases of land and equipment relied entirely upon credits, in contrast to most lowland villages, where market prices were paid with cash. The incidence of re-emigration from Bieszczady remained high in the 1960s, and the predicament of new settlers did not differ basically from that of earlier pioneers, or from that of peasants elsewhere. They received little aid or advice from the socialist sector, into which considerable investment resources were being chanelled. Many of the credits to which they were entitled (some were reluctant to take them up) were used for housing or consumption goods; some were wasted, e.g. because of the lack of veterinary services. In any case credits could not command investment goods that were decreed to be unavailable to the private sector. In theory the Agricultural Circle was supposed to overcome this problem, i.e. to enable peasants to produce more without adding the private ownership of capital and machines to their private ownership of land. But so little was actually done through the Agricultural Circle that one must conclude that the authorities were determined not to permit the peasantry to modernise, even on these terms. For political reasons, the legal rights of ownership could not be revoked; but peasants were not encouraged to expand their farms to an economically warranted size. Access to capital was even more severely constrained, partly because in the economy as a whole resources were concentrated in industry, and partly because, within agriculture, priority was always given to the socialist sector. In such circumstances, the reaction of the third crucial factor of production, family labour, was understandable. Peasant farming ceased to be regarded in many households as a secure source of cash income and was replaced by wage-labour in socialist enterprises, both agricultural and industrial. Families neglected to invest in their farms, but kept them on mainly for subsistence purposes. Levels of commodity production (which is easily monitored in Wisłok, since apart from the State Farms everyone must 'market' almost all his produce through the official state channels in Komańcza) were very low, possibly lower even than they had been in the pre-war period, when the Wisłok fields had fed not 300 but almost 3,000 local residents.

There is little doubt about the long-term consequences of the agricultural policies pursued in Poland between the political crisis of 1956 and the adoption of a new course by the Gierek team in the

1970s. The failure to invest centrally, coupled with the failure to assure private investment, constituted deliberate negligence of a sector which traditionally had been the major national asset, and was no less detrimental than earlier crude attempts to impose collectivisation. Once the latter had been definitively rejected, as a political consequence of 1956, it was essential to work out some alternative strategy for the longer term development of agriculture. Under Gomułka this raised an insoluble ideological dilemma. The problems which resulted were apparent in Wisłok just as they were elsewhere. The average age of farmers rose as the young abandoned their heritage, and when farms without an heir reverted to the state the total area of land under cultivation began to fall. The fragmentation of holdings again became a problem as the new class of worker-peasants hung on to small-scale plots to meet subsistence needs. These long-term trends might be disguised by shorter cycles, influenced by climatic variation and by the alteration of purchasing prices by the authorities. The early 1970s saw something of a boom when, in years of favourable weather, prices were raised and compulsory deliveries to the state finally abolished. When output increased dramatically it quickly became necessary to step up fodder imports, since domestic production had become insufficient to maintain the animal stock at its new high level. It was inevitable that structural changes would have to be attempted, but these did not ensue until the mid-1970s.

If the petrification of an antiquated agrarian structure lay at the root of the national problem in this period, how much more absurd it was to reproduce such a pattern in a mountain environment where the evacuation of a densely settled population had created a unique opportunity to commence a new and more rational system of upland farming. Unfortunately, only the socialist sector was considered eligible to be established on this footing. It is true that amongst the proletarians who became peasants in Wisłok there were few who were well qualified to farm independently on any scale, let alone meet the challenge of a large uplands farm; but some might have, and they were denied their opportunity by rules which gave families no positive material incentive to produce more than they required for subsistence. Economic development was thus stifled by the rigid insistence on creating and maintaining a new village of egalitarian small-holdings, unaided by trained advisers and with only minimal access to modern technology. The only justifications were ideological; but as the economic costs became more apparent in the 1970s the ideology and the policies were revised at the national level and the Polish peasantry entered the most recent phase of its development.

Gierek places a 'wager on the strong'

In the early 1970s, with Edward Gierek having replaced Gomułka at the head of the Party, all farmers obtained a better deal within the previous framework of institutions and controls, primarily through large increases in the purchasing prices for their products. Gierek continued by attempting to modernise the structure in such a way that some farmers would reap much greater benefits than others. The most significant step in this direction was a regulation of 1975 which singled out a group of dynamic, innovating producers in the private sector for a variety of credits and subsidies. They were called 'specialists', because they were supposed to abandon the ideal of the autarchic and diversified peasant farm in favour of specialised commodity production and integration into the national economy. An initiative of this kind might have had little impact at local level, had not simultaneous steps been taken to reform the administration (see Chapter Five) and to increase controls exercised by the local Party apparatus over the allocation of goods, services and credits. The authorities began to intervene in farming more decisively than they had in the days when detailed production targets were set. They were out to achieve a qualitative change in the performance of the private sector, but the fate of their experiment in Wisłok illustrates its fate across the nation; let us see what happened in this period to the basic factors of production, land and capital.

The land market in Wisłok, as in other resettled parts of the mountains, remained more tightly controlled by the authorities than was usual in lowland areas of continuous settlement. Consequently, one observes here in greater relief the underlying pattern prevailing elsewhere. Priority still went to the socialist sector. However, the State Farms were now encouraged, indeed obliged, to release lands which they were not fully able to exploit. Thus, some plots were transferred permanently to peasant farmers (payment, as usual, by credit). Lands formerly belonging to the Agricultural Circle were distributed in smaller parcels, the large number of claimants proving the demand for land to be strong in all sections of the peasantry. Moreover, as some individual holdings were abandoned (on the retirement or departure of the owner), these, too, could now be sold off to augment existing farms. A few new immigrants about this time were allowed to commence operations with an acreage two or three times greater than that which had been granted to earlier settlers, e.g. the case of Krzysztof Ołtarzewski, described in the Appendix. The catch was that anyone wishing to obtain large credits, in order to pay the notional price attached to a large acreage, would need to qualify as a 'specialist' and, through contracting with the state, commit himself to farming his larger resources in a particular, more commercial way. Control was now vested in the Chief Executive of the council in Komańcza, who issued stern warnings to farmers and worker-peasants whom he considered to be neglecting their farms (usually on the grounds that they were selling nothing to the state). Such warnings could be followed up by the confiscation of plots and their re-allocation, either to other individual farmers or to the socialist sector. Thus, while the authorities came in the 1970s to tolerate great inequalities in the size of individual holdings, they were simultaneously concerned to obtain a much greater measure of control over the utilisation of these lands. This control was aimed at the large holdings of the new specialists and at the non-productive 'dwarf-plots' of worker-peasant households alike.

Reform was clear cut in the case of the Agricultural Circle, whose job had been to supply capital goods and services to the private sector. It was just after a new depot had been constructed for the machines, in the centre of Wisłok, that it was decided in 1975 to abolish the local organisation and transfer the equipment to Komańcza. In practice there was no longer any pretence that the newly constituted Cooperative of Agricultural Circles (*Spółdzielnia Kółek Rolniczych* — hereafter SKR) retained the democratic and self-managing character of the earlier Circles. It became necessary to travel at least to Komańcza, sometimes further to the SKR centre at Szczawne (20 km), in order to request services. It became much more difficult to get jobs speedily completed, since the technician was now a non-local employee of the SKR, who could not easily be persuaded to work longer than his stipulated shift. Such factors, combined with increases in the rates charged and continuing deficiencies in the availability of many kinds of machine, made for a high level of dissatisfaction with this channel of aid to the private sector.

Some peasants, the new specialists, were now for the first time in a position to make alternative provision. While the Circles were bureaucratised and distanced themselves from the peasantry, during the later years of the 1970s much more equipment (especially tractors) was sold to the private sector. The allocation of new items was strictly controlled by the local administration, which received its quota from higher levels. Thus, a peasant's access to crucial items for production depended not upon the market and possession of an effective currency, but upon his productive potential as estimated by the authorities, or upon some still more 'subjective' assessment, involving factors such as political loyalty or social needs. The Chief Executive in Komańcza acknowledged that decisions were often difficult to reach, and that he sometimes had to gamble on whom to support.

His options were fewer than might be expected because amongst Wisłok farmers the demand for modern technology was not so strong as their readiness to apply for more land. This could be attributed to ingrained conservatism amongst older peasants; but the fear that they would not be able to maintain machinery, either through lack of skill or lack of spare parts, was also common amongst younger members of the community. Some preferred to draw credits for large new buildings, including some so foolishly conceived that they were never properly utilised. The fundamental problem for the authorities was how to persuade individual farmers, specialist and non-specialist alike, to deploy the resources available to genuinely *productive* purposes. There were still some who were congenitally opposed to accumulating debts of any kind. However, most farmers had grown accustomed to owing large amounts of money to the State Bank since their arrival in Wisłok, and the policies of the 1970s merely increased the temptations: there was no stigma or shame in taking advantage. Of course, as before, many credits went to consumption or house-building, rather than the construction of farm buildings or the purchase of farm equipment.

The principal effect of Gierek's agricultural policies upon the private sector was to increase wealth differentiation. As a result of the more flexible land policy, of more generous credits backed by a better, though still imperfect, flow of goods, and the encouragement of private accumulation of the means of production (subject to close administrative control), overall production increased, in some cases quite impressively. There were tentative and partially successful attempts to integrate the private sector into the socialist sector, with a few specialists negotiating contracts to raise animals bred by socialist enterprises. Such specialisation as there was in Wisłok took place mainly in dairy production. However, it became necessary to import fodder to the village when the new specialists could not produce

5. Modern house of 1970's, built by the new headman.

enough of their own. It seemed that generally advantageous patterns of cooperation were developing, with the socialist sector using its large land area and machine stock to concentrate on crop production and the peasantry applying itself to the more labour-intensive tasks associated with animal products. Such was the general ideological trend in the 1970s. It was held that peasant production could be increased without weakening the socialist sector, which on the contrary was expected actually to expand its area at the expense of weaker elements of the private sector. The policies did enjoy a limited success in increasing commodity production in Wisłok towards the end of the 1970s.

It must be emphasised that this upturn resulted from the efforts of a small proportion of the private sector, and that several of those who drew most assistance from the authorities implementing these policies did not repay the faith that was placed in them. Most individual farmers registered some expansion, but to break completely away from the old 6 hectare subsistence farms, dependent upon horses for draught power, was something which only the minority of specialists was permitted to achieve. The creation of such a privileged minority within the farming population constituted something of a political as well as an economic gamble by the Gierek regime. It might even be compared with the Czarist Minister Stoly-

47

pin's 'wager on the strong' in pre-Revolutionary Russia, which was also inspired by the hope that an agrarian problem could be solved by stimulating a minority of peasants to produce more and in effect polarising the different strata within the peasantry. The main problem in Poland in the 1970s was that the emergence of a robust, new, entrepreneurial class remained precluded by the official ideology. Farmers still could not prove themselves by competition on the open market, and there could be no guarantee at all that the socialist administrators would select 'the strong' or even enable the individuals favoured to consolidate their advantageous position in the long run. The lesson, that administrative methods are incapable of simulating market solutions, was one that was learned by the Polish economy as a whole in the 1970s. In agriculture little was done to help the majority of individual farmers, and the major change was perhaps that scarce resources were now made available to a privileged elite in the private sector as well as to the socialist sector. The combination of a run of bad harvests and the generally worsening economic climate led to grave difficulties at the end of the decade. By 1979, when fieldwork in Wisłok was begun, the flow of resources to the specialists had become a trickle. With the prices for their products judged to be too low and fundamental inputs (e.g. fuel) generally unavailable, the peasantry was again united in its hostility to the government. Some farmers, having failed to supply the quantities of output to which they had contracted themselves, did not know whether they were still regarded officially as specialists or not.[4]

The peasantry in the years of crisis

Almost every household in Wisłok is engaged in some subsistence production, though this is limited to a tiny vegetable garden in the case of some families employed in the socialist sector. Such production was always important in a village where supplies from outside were never reliable, but it became much more so when political crisis in the 1980s was followed not by an agricultural boom (as had been the case in the early 1970s), but by general shortages of foodstuffs. About half of the households in the village produce for subsistence purposes only. The number of active commodity-producing farms has fallen steadily over the last two decades, from fifty-seven in 1961 to little more than half of that number when fieldwork was conducted. Within these thirty households there are some which are no longer entirely dependent upon the farm for their cash incomes, and

6. Threshing with
an old machine
on hire from the
Agricultural
Circle (SKR).

this is one factor to be born in mind when analysing the present
resources of the peasantry. The detailed information presented
below was collected in the village and in the offices of the local
administration in Komańcza.[5] The reliability of the statistics
measuring farm output is enhanced by another piece of 1970s legis-
lation designed to encourage farmers to maximise their commodity
production: from 1978 the level of their future pension was closely
tied to the value of the produce they sold to the state over a specified
period before retirement. I shall begin by attempting to see if the size
of final output can be related to the various factors of production
already discussed — land, capital and labour — and then attempt to
summarise the present state of the private sector and offer a prog-
nosis for the future.

*   *   *   *

Table 2 divides the commodity-producing farms of Wisłok into five
groups according to the total area of land which they owned in 1981,
and shows the variation in size of area harvested (including hay-
fields) and in the value of production marketed. (Two annual aver-
ages are given, because of the very substantial price increases which
were introduced by the Jaruzelski government at the beginning of
1981; overall there is no significant increase in production in this
period; although, within each group, some individuals did expand
their output, others reduced it, and on the whole the larger sums

49

earned reflect only the inflation of purchasing prices; the 'average' farm of the early 1980s still made most of its money from a few hectares of grain production, supplemented by the delivery of just one head of cattle at the buying point; only a few specialists were regular suppliers of milk or fatteners of livestock.) The statistics give a reasonably accurate picture of the land actually used by the peasants: there is little lending or renting of land between them, and unofficial encroachment on State Farm lands is likewise insignificant nowadays. It can be seen that differentiation with respect to this factor of production has now become very significant. The average size for all farms taken together is 10 hectares, well above the national average. Each of the six farmers owning 15 hectares or more holds, or has held, a card proclaiming him to be a specialist; none of this group has any other source of regular household income. The largest holding is 38 hectares, and the average annual production of this farm over the entire six year period was in excess of 300,000 złoty.

Size of farm (hectares)	No. of farms	Average size /h/	Average size of harvested area /h/	Value of average annual output (in 000s of złoty)	
				1977–80	1981–83
0–5	7	3.5	2.1	36	70
5–7	7	6.2	3.9	50	133
7–10	6	8.3	4.5	62	145
10–15	5	11.0	5.0	78	198
15	5	22.9	9.1	149	252

Table 2: The Land Resources of the Private Sector

Farmers can also be readily differentiated according to the capital resources they own and the extent to which they make use of the facilities provided by the SKR. Clearly those who possess their own tractors and machinery are less dependent upon the latter institution, but several of the largest landowners are not in this happy position. Their bills for the hire of equipment may be large, but are normally still far below their larger incomes. Most peasants keep transactions with the SKR to a minimum. Some are willing to pay only for the services of a combine harvester, whilst a few consider even this to be an unnecessary extravagance: they harvest their grain by hand and pay only a small sum for use of an old-fashioned threshing machine. It would be misleading to present any figures, since the SKR has 'informal' competitors within the village in the shape of the private tractor owners. One tractor-owner also operates his own combine harvester, which he purchased second-hand from the socialist sector, but which is very difficult to maintain privately.

Investment credits obtained (000s of złoty)	No. of farms	No. owning tractors, 1981	Average value of annual output (000s of złoty)	
			1977–80	1981–3
0	8	1	52	94
5-50	8	0	43	116
51-150	6	2	82	149
151-300	4	2	93	272
301+	5	1	127	227

Table 3: Investment Credits to the Private Sector

As an admittedly imperfect measure of the capital resources of the private sector it is preferable to consider the investment credits awarded to individual farmers by the Agricultural Bank. The Bank has a complete record of such credits going back as far as the 1960s. The bulk of the credits taken up by Wisłok farmers have been drawn since the mid-1970s. They carry extremely advantageous terms for borrowers, with a low interest rate (typically 1 per cent) spread over a long repayment period (typically twenty-five years). Nevertheless, it can be seen in Table 3, which again divides the private sector into five groups, that some farmers have not profited from the opportunity for which almost all of them were theoretically eligible. Amongst those who have borrowed, the results in terms of output marketed are not as apparent as was the case with land. It can be seen that some of those who have borrowed most are still without tractors, though they may have erected imposing new buildings. As late as 1977 there were only two tractors owned by peasants in Wisłok, and the majority of households kept a team of horses. Later, in addition to the specialists who were supplied with new machines, a number of other peasants managed to acquire them second-hand from the socialist sector. Some of these continued to use and take great pride in their horses, of which there was an average of 1.5 per farm during fieldwork in 1981.

There are various ways of examining the effect of the family labour supply upon the level of independent commodity production, a relation which no synchronic study can hope to resolve. Table 4 shows no clear relation between the total size of the household (including infants and the infirm of all ages) and the value of output. It needs to be remembered that amongst these active commodity-producing farms there are some households which also have regular sources of wage income. In some instances unmarried children still resident in the village are the sole sources of such cash; but in others senior household members are employees of the socialist sector locally, or commute to an enterprise outside the village.

Size of household, 1981 (persons)	No. of farms	Average value of annual output (in 000s of złoty) 1980-81
2	3	27
3	4	98
4	8	54
5	6	191
6	6	90
7 or more	6	107

Table 4: Household Size and Commodity Production

About half of all active commodity-producing farms have some such source of outside income, which may influence agricultural production in various ways. It may remove the need to market produce at all when conditions are judged unfavourable, or at any rate cause families to reduce production targets significantly; and by removing members of the family from the private sector it also makes it that much more difficult for the family farm to function as efficiently as it would if all members were available all of the time. It was found, however, when looking at the production figures, that the value of output of many 'full-time farming' households (those closest to 'traditional peasantry') was not greater than that produced by households in which one or more members had some other employment. In both groups the range was wide, and it was clearly necessary to seek some more sophisticated means of examining the effect of the quality, as well as of the quantity, of labour available to the farm. The formulation of Table 5 was a simple step in this direction. It shows the number of persons resident (excluding children under the age of 16 and pensioners over 65) who were able to devote themselves fully to work on the individual farm. As might be anticipated output is much higher where a genuine family farm has persisted, with two members engaged full-time; but since no family has even a third member fully active on the farm the results fail to shed much light on the variations in levels of final output.

No. of able-bodied persons of working age available to work full time on the farm, 1981	No. of farms	Average age of the head of household	Average value of annual output in 000s of złoty. 1980–81
0	3	67	54
1	9	40	58
2	21	47	122

Table 5: Able-bodied persons available for full-time work on farm

The figures may also be set out from another angle, with all the components of production brought together and the active commodity-producing farms in the period 1981-3 divided into groups according to the value of output produced (Table 6). The imperfections and reservations noted in connection with Tables 2-5 apply with equal force; nevertheless, it is worth outlining the main characteristics of each of the three groups generated by this classification.

Average annual value of production 1981–83 in 000s of złoty	0–100	100–200	200+
No. of farms	9	18	6
Average size of land owned (hectares)	4	8.5	16
No. owning tractors	1	2	33
Average investment credits in 000s of złoty	32	100.5	267
Average size of household	4.8	4.5	5.4
Average no. of able-bodied adults, full-time	1	1.4	1.8
No. of farms with wage-labour income	6	11	1

Table 6: Selected resources of commodity producing farms, according to the value of their production in 1981–3

Beginning with the low income group, those farms which did not raise their production above the level of 100,000 złoty per year even after the substantial price increases of 1981, it can be seen from Table 6 that in terms of landholdings and capital assets their resources are indeed meagre. Most of them have supplementary sources of income, whilst the number of persons available for full-time work on the farm is significantly below that of the higher income groups. The families without other incomes are likely to depend on casual work in the forests and, at peak periods, on State Farms and even on the large new private farms; the first of these is by far the most important and will be discussed in more detail in the next chapter. Few farms in this group are likely to maintain even their present low levels of commodity production when the current head of the household retires; but because of its subsistence role the heirs are likely to retain the holding, or at least a part of it, for as long as they continue to reside in Wisłok. The general prospects for this group are bleak. Some of these farms are already 'marginal', in that they satisfy some domestic needs, but bring in much less cash than is earned in the socialist sector. Generally they are of no interest to the children of the first generation of worker-peasants, whose aspirations are set firmly on the town. Some provide subsistence for poor families without any regular source of outside income (except perhaps some welfare payments from the administration); but where little or no investment has taken place and the land area has not been expanded, there is little chance that these farms will remain viable commodity-producing enterprises. Legally, these farms can be inherited and the heirs become eligible for assistance in building up the scale of the farm; but few show any inclination to do so, and those who do remain in Wisłok are tending to become instead the nucleus of the permanent labour force in the socialist sector.

There is a large intermediate group, which may be regarded as the core of the surviving peasantry. Some members of this group increased production in the early 1980s, in response to higher money prices and the national propaganda campaign to overcome the food crisis. Yet so far, only a few have expanded their area significantly and only two have purchased tractors. Many continue to derive more money from grain production than from the special-ised stockbreeding or dairy production warranted by this environ-ment. Here also many have been tempted, especially members of the younger generation, the potential heirs, by opportunities to work in the socialist sector. In the absence of a tractor, these families have kept a team of horses, which they use to augment their incomes in the forests. Some of the household heads in this group have deliberately built houses rather than stables, for although they themselves have decided not to move away from Wisłok they doubt whether their children will wish to commit themselves to the farm. The future of the majority of the enterprises in this group must therefore be regarded as uncertain. The first immigrant generation has done just enough to keep open the option of staying on. Before the present crisis there seemed only little chance that many of them would. However, if a higher level of purchasing prices (in real terms) is maintained, if machines are made more widely available, as the government has promised, and if it is possible to expand acreage as well as to build and furnish new houses, then many farms in this group may remain viable and, indeed, expand the level of their commodity production.

This intermediate group also includes farmers who held specialist cards in the 1970s. These were the new arrivals of the 1970s, in whom the policy-makers placed their highest hopes, but who managed only intermediate levels of production. They began operations virtually from scratch on large new farms, entirely dependent upon the socialist sector for supplies and a continuing flow of credits. Their performance is frequently criticised by all other sections of the community (peasants, State Farm workers, even teachers), who level accusations of favouritism at the outside administration, and incompetence and laziness at the newcomers benefiting from its patronage. Some had no previous experience of independent farming, and all were clearly out of step with the traditional peasant labour process, preferring to rely on machine services from the SKR if at all possible. The average area of land actually sown by these farmers was lower than the average sown by other peasants in the intermediate group; most of their larger resources are used for hay, or simply as extensive grazing pasture. None of these newcomers lacking a background in peasant farming has lasted more than five years. Their performance over the short period of their stay has tended to be inconsistent; they too have tended to withdraw into subsistence production as soon as supplies from the socialist sector were no longer readily available.

It is equally true that there was some inconsistency amongst the specialists recruited from *within* the established community, and that some were deprived of their cards even before the scheme ceased to be of any practical consequence. However, a small number of specialists recruited from within the established peasantry constitutes the core of the high-income group. Between them they accounted for more than three-quarters of the total value of commodity production by the private sector in the early 1980s. Their output levels have been more than commensurate with the larger credits granted to them, and their increased acreage. It is clear that good performance owes as much to a favourable combination of traditional factors (a hardworking wife, and sons rather than daughters being the essential ingredients of the labour supply) as to help from the authorities. Such resources enabled a few peasants to maintain high levels of production during the crisis years, when some of the *parachuté* specialists virtually abandoned their farms. It is obvious that other peasants could follow this example, and that if supplies had not dwindled severely in the period when fieldwork was conducted, the performance of the peasant 'specialists' might have been still more impressive. Naturally, these farmers hope to find a successor from within the family. Some have concentrated their efforts on acquiring machinery and building stables, rather than houses in the first instance. They hope, naturally, that the latter will follow in due course, but even before the modern house is built these farms are much more attractive propositions for the younger generation.

*   *   *   *

The future of private farming in Poland, and the extent to which it retains its peasant character, will depend upon whether a wider stratum of the existing peasantry is given cause to adopt the attitudes of those whose performance hitherto shows what can be done, even in very adverse circumstances, with the traditional resources of the peasant household. The aspiration to prosper on one's own land, and then pass this on to one's children, is extremely strong. But equally rooted in peasant traditions is the desire to escape from the monotony of the old peasant labour process. Given the policies pursued in the first three decades of socialism, it is not surprising that many Polish peasants became pessimistic about their chances of ever becoming modern commercial farmers, and looked elsewhere for greater comfort and security. The policies of Gierek in the 1970s improved prospects for some, but they also exacerbated tension and led some to think that results might flow from taking on large credits alone, irrespective of experience on the land and inputs of human labour. These policies were not enough to overcome earlier neglect of the agricultural sector, and contributed to plunging the whole economy into crisis. Gierek's eventual successor, Jaruzelski, made an encouraging start by raising purchasing prices and by calling for a restructuring of socialist industry, that it might better satisfy all the demands of non-socialist as well as socialist agriculture. This, of course, will take time to achieve, and with little improvement visible on the markets and rapid inflation eroding the value of the price increases, commodity production in Wisłok was tending to fall again by 1984. At least the regime has remained faithful to one part of the agreements concluded with *Rural Solidarity*: it has constitutionally reaffirmed the inviolability of private property, and even put forward plans to permit dramatic increases in the permitted size of private holding (up to 250 hectares, more than the entire peasant sector in Wisłok combined).[6] Much must depend upon whether the peasant farms in the intermediate income bracket at present (see Table 6) can be induced to become more specialised, commodity-producing enterprises in the long run. There would then be less resentment within the private sector of an unduly narrow (and not exclusively peasant) elite enjoying the favours of the administration. Those households presently in the low income band would eventually cease producing for the market and become only part-time farmers, gainfully employed in the various branches of the socialist sector. In terms of the value of commodities marketed, society would not lose much from their metamorphosis. Jaruzelski's plan is not so different from that of Gierek: he has only promised more specifically that he will channel resources into agriculture, and thereby enable larger numbers of the peasantry to become 'strong'. But it is clear that many, perhaps the majority of the three million farms, cannot hope to carry on at all as significant enterprises. The inevitable polarisation will be contrary both to traditional communist doctrine and to the egalitarian spirit of the agreements with *Rural Solidarity*. Its implications for the rural class structure will be considered in Chapter Eight below.[7]

In this chapter we have outlined the main trends in the private sector of the farming economy of Wisłok since its reconstruction after 1947. The plundering and dissipation of the accumulated investments of the past were extreme (as elsewhere) in the Stalinist period in the early 1950s. This foreshadowed the general failure of successive socialist governments after 1956 to harness the potential of the private sector, of the traditional peasant economy, as an alternative to collectivisation and a basis for agricultural modernisation. In spite of the consequences of decades of neglect and discrimination, the recent performance of peasant 'specialists' shows that individual farming has retained much of its potential. If future governments can overcome the ideological difficulties, there is much scope for mutually rewarding cooperation between private and socialist sectors that would utilise to the full the advantages of the traditional family farm. This applies everywhere in Poland. It can apply also in countries in which collectivisation has deprived the private sector of its land resources, but where, given ideological flexibility, plot farming continues nevertheless to make a vital contribution. It applies with particular force to a mountain zone, where the elimination of restrictions on landholding and improved supplies from the socialist sector would do much to stimulate the animal production in which the private sector is best qualified to specialise. It is a question of enabling the traditional peasantry to transform itself into modern family farmers, a change which could only benefit farmers themselves and the society to which they belong. Those who doubt the enthusiasm of peasant smallholders to make this change, who emphasize conservatism, insensitivity to the profit motive, and even irrationality in peasant decision-taking, can draw no support from the Wisłok evidence. These peasants have showed a sound grasp of economic advantage in their dealings with the wider economy. As the state subsidy on bread increased in value during the 1970s, they found it more and more profitable to feed fresh loaves to their chickens and pigs; and they were quite prepared to stand in line to buy the extra loaves. They were at the same time fully aware of the irrationality of the *system* whereby this became a rational choice for them. Calculations of more complex kinds were demonstrated in the trading of ration coupons at the height of the crisis, and in the use of dollars, cigarettes and vodka as alternatives to the official currency. It can only be regretted that the opportunity to calculate and to gain advantage has seldom been properly put before the peasantry in the field of *production* in the socialist period. During the latest crisis there have again been signs that the authorities are genuinely concerned to arrest the decline of the commodity-producing family-labour farm (as opposed merely to staging another short-term boom for agriculture, such as followed earlier political crises). The absolute number of private farms must continue to fall, but to secure the future of non-collectivised agriculture in this socialist state it is now in the authorities' vital interest to build up the economic strength of those farms able to attract heirs and to produce the goods needed by society. Only when the new stratum (or class?) of strong, independent farmers is fully established will the Polish peasantry have been extinguished.

CHAPTER FOUR

The Public Sector

Every citizen of the Polish People's Republic has a duty to guard and to strengthen social property as the solid and firm base of the development of the state, the source of the wealth and strength of the Fatherland.
        Constitution of the People's Republic of Poland, Article 91

Peasant farming has survived in Poland because of the failure to implement collectivisation, but as we have seen it has been greatly handicapped by the failure to develop an adequate alternative programme of agricultural modernisation. In so far as any programme was implemented up to the mid-1970s, its cornerstone was a socialist sector organised along the same lines as in collectivised states. Even when the Gierek government began to pursue more constructive policies towards the private sector (or rather towards a small section of it) it did not abandon the ideological principle that the socialist sector was intrinsically superior and would ultimately expand until this superiority was as evident in Poland as in the fully collectivised states. This was precisely what angered so many individual farmers and inhibited them from investing. They also found themselves unfairly treated vis-à-vis the socialist sector in gaining access to capital goods and in many areas, including Wisłok, in the allocation of land as well. In addition to direct conflicts of interest between individual farmers and socialist institutions, which were consistently resolved in favour of the latter, there have also been more subtle processes through which the traditional base of the family farm has been undermined by the insidious rise of socialist wage-labour. This chapter will examine the leading socialist enterprises which operate in Wisłok and also certain other wage-labour opportunities which influence the local economy. Of course, this was not a 'closed' peasant community in the pre-socialist period, when migrant labour played an important role in the economy. Nowadays most village households have some regular, non-peasant source of income. But some have remained impervious to new opportunities — of these a few, as we have seen, may draw large incomes from their farms, and the others are forced to turn for casual work to the socialist sector.

The burden of proving the superiority of large-scale, socialist farming has proved onerous for the State Farms

Large private estates persisted in Poland long after the abolition of serfdom, but there was no precedent for the construction of a large-scale sector in agriculture along collectivist lines, as this was begun at the end of the Second World War. Large properties were confiscated, and although the Land Reform parcelled many of them out to smallholders, in some areas (particularly in Western Poland on the lands obtained from Germany) the solution preferred was to form State Farms. In Wisłok the only large holdings in private hands had been forest, but the evacuation of the indigenous population in 1947 left a vacuum. From 1948 the bulk of the farm lands of the village (everything apart from the plots in the centre of the valley granted to the new immigrants) was administered by a large State Farm with its centre at Jaśliska, about 15 km away. Communications were very bad and the farm was ill equipped to utilise the lands which it nominally controlled. Those lands not allocated to new immigrants served at best as additional reserves of pasture for a larger-scale version of the same economy of 'plunder' practised at this time by individual farmers. But whilst the new peasants were later forced to modify this mode of extensive exploitation, the State Farms have yet to do so. Hence, the remarkable contrast between public and private sectors in agriculture today.

In Wisłok large investments in the State Farms were made in the mid-1950s, some time before major improvements in local communications and in the community infrastructure. A major complex was constructed at each end of the long valley of the Wisłok, each containing stables, storehouses, workshops and units of accommodation for employees. Both continued to be administered from Jaśliska, and were to specialise in dairy production. Personnel were recruited from other farms in the socialist sector, some were perhaps attracted by the brand new accommodation. However, the main source of labour was a newly established penal colony, which brought a large, unskilled captive labour force to the area from the late 1950s (this too was part of the Development Plan for the Bieszczady region, though somewhat at variance with the simultaneously declared intention to encourage tourism). Later the centre of the State Farm was moved to the main site of the new penal colony in Moszczaniec, a village 6 km from Wisłok which had also been evacuated in 1947,

iew of State Farm buildings at the lower end of the Wisłok valley.

but where no attempt had been made to resettle peasants. In practice, control of the Wisłok farms throughout the 1960s and 1970s lay not at the centre of this State Farm in Moszczaniec but at higher levels of the national State Farm bureaucracy, which was effectively an integral part of the general system of state administration.[1]

The reputation of the State Farm in Wisłok amongst the individual farmers of the village is similar to the one they enjoy all over Poland. Even in the western territories, where the environment was a good deal more favourable than in Bieszczady, their performance appears to be greatly inferior to that of the private sector and to that of the socialist sector in neighbouring socialist states. Although it was not possible to obtain detailed information, in Wisłok they seemed to deserve their poor reputation. Milk production was low and fluctuated erratically throughout the year. Mortality rates amongst the animals were high, breeding records were poor, crop yields were low and both local units experienced the greatest difficulty in cutting and collecting the hay they owned and in harvesting crops sown. Some tracts of land were entirely neglected year after year. Wisłok peasants were also critical of the permanent civilian labour force, notably of high absenteeism, ill discipline and especially drunkeness, and of abuses of state property and the perks enjoyed by all employees, particularly foremen and directors. Although it is well

61

known that the Wisłok units regularly report large accounting deficits, until 1981 nothing was done to change this pattern. The director of the unit in the lower valley has lived adjacent to the depot in a state-owned flat for many years. During this period it is said that he has become a rich man, the owner of a house outside the mountain zone to which he will one day retire, as well as of the only private car in the village.

There are plenty of extenuating circumstances. Before 1981 the directors could justly claim that their hands were tied by the detailed instructions and plan targets passed down to them from above, and that the resources at their disposal were quite unsuited to the production profile demanded. It was asking a lot of a farm in the mountains to expect it to match lowland farms in its yield of crops. Yet the centralised planning system was reluctant to allow a more rational adaptation that would have permitted the provision of fodder supplies from outside, but only in order to allow the more efficient exploitation of Wisłok's abundant natural grassland. The director of the lower unit was also dissatisfied with the labour resources at his disposal, for though convicts receive only nominal wage payments they generally have no experience of farming and are unreliable in carrying out even the most menial tasks. Although the permanent civilian staff is recruited from local peasant families, because they continue to maintain individual farms they are often inclined to put their private interests before that of the large enterprise, e.g. by absenting themselves at peak periods. As the director sees it, it is necessary to invest much larger sums into the socialist sector, in order to make it fully independent of the penal colony and of the private peasantry. This would mean, first of all, an expansion of the stock of machinery and the workshops to maintain it, so that all lands might be exploited in the most efficient way possible; at present there are insufficient machines to do the job in the short agricultural season which prevails in the mountain environment. Secondly, it would be necessary to invest in more public sector accommodation, so that the State Farm units could attract skilled labour and not have to rely on prisoners and the less competent peasants (the more able prefer to farm on their own account if they can). To anyone familiar with agricultural conditions in other socialist states, such a diagnosis appears perfectly reasonable. This is not the place to pursue comparisons, but it would seem *a priori* insufficient in the Polish case to carry on pumping in larger quantities of capital, even if this were available. In other socialist states (except Yugoslavia) there is no alternative to the public sector for a skilled youth wishing to work on the land. As long as there is this option in Poland, and especially if it becomes more profitable, the State Farms will continue to have difficulty in recruiting skilled labour.

In practice, of course, the authorities are unlikely in the foreseeable future to be in a position to increase their financial subsidies to the State Farms. On the contrary, in an effort to reduce them in the current crisis they have gone some way towards eliminating the bureaucratic complications which previously constrained the local-level directors. From July 1981 the director was given much more freedom to decide what his unit would produce, and this did lead in Wisłok to some shift away from dairy farming towards the fattening of beef cattle. The director has always had far-reaching power over the local labour force, and the 1981 reforms can only strengthen his personal pre-eminence. However, continuing problems with the labour supply combined with the scarcity of key machines make it unlikely that there will be much improvement in overall economic performance.

One way forward for the State Farm in the present conjuncture would be to pursue possibilities for cooperation between public and private sectors. These have been little explored in the past, partly perhaps because of suspicions on the part of the peasantry, but also because of the predilections of State Farm directors. In the late 1970s, a few specialists contracted to raise calves bred initially in the socialist sector, and fattened them to the stipulated weight much more rapidly than the State Farm units could manage: the results were beneficial to both parties. However, the directors have remained reluctant to engage in such practices, whilst very few amongst the peasants have sufficient acreage to be able to take on additional animals during the grazing season. Patterns of cooperation could become much more rewarding if it were possible to transfer large resources of land away from the State Farm to the private sector, or at least to allow pasture to be temporarily leased by peasants. Such practices have become common in some parts of the country. The real difficulty in Wisłok is that the peasantry would like to expand on lands adjacent to those owned at present, which tend to be jealously guarded by the directors because their quality is superior to that of more remote fields. The inaccessibility of the latter renders them unattractive to the peasants. For these reasons there were few contacts between the two sectors at the time of fieldwork. Individual farmers could not obtain machinery or even transportation services from the State Farm units, but were obliged to travel to the SKR in Komańcza or Szczawne. The directors of the State Farm sometimes resorted to hiring peasant labour at peak periods, typically on a day to day basis to gather hay when supplies of convict labour were inadequate. Occasionally, too, they would dispose of equipment and old, unproductive animals to individual buyers. There is certainly scope for more constructive integration of the two sectors, and it would seem that a more flexible attitude to land leasing is the first step which might enable the State Farm to improve its balance sheet. Leasing would enable the facade of a strong socialist sector to be maintained and its advantages in terms of capital stock, breeding superior strains etc. to be realised, whilst the greater part of the increased value produced would flow from the peasantry, given the chance to prove its superiority in work that calls not merely for supplies of land and machines, but also traditional farming skills.

It was difficult to glean exact information about the State Farm units because they are so closely associated with the prisons (until 1978 they were administered not by the Ministry of Agriculture but by a division of the Ministry of Justice). The two units in Wisłok employed a total of twelve persons from eight peasant households, plus a further four persons from other, non-peasant, households for whom this employment was the sole source of regular income. The latter include the director and the two foremen of the unit at the lower end of the village. This unit farms about 1,000 hectares, of which 200 hectares are sown with the remainder providing hay and grazing pasture. The stables normally contain more than 300 head of cattle, rising to 450 during the main calving period. Average milk yield per cow is considerably less than 2,000 litres per year and has fallen steadily in recent years, because the feeds previously brought in from outside the community are no longer available. Apart from the director and foremen (one responsible for the stables, the other for the fields) there is a skilled mechanic in charge of the maintenance workshop and the remaining full-time civilian employees are mostly young tractor drivers. There is no accountant at the unit, nor is there the full-time agronomist the director would ideally like to see. The main work force is made up by a few dozen prisoners, who do most of the work inside the stables as well as performing such tasks on the land as are not at present susceptible to mechanisation.

The shortcomings of the new order in the forests are compounding inadequacies of the old order on the land

The large areas of forest on the periphery of Wisłok were for the most part privately owned before 1944. There were still some large holdings which belonged to outside individuals or institutions, but most village families had access to their own small plot. It provided them with fuel, and also with a reserve of capital. The total forest area had declined rapidly from the late nineteenth century, large quantities of timber being sold across the Hungarian border in order to alleviate increasingly difficult economic circumstances. The steepest parts were almost impossible to penetrate, but networks of paths permitted good access generally; between 1940 and 1944 German occupation forces augmented these by constructing a new retreat road to the south across the Slovakian border.

As with the agricultural land eventually taken over by the State Farms, there was a short lag before the forests confiscated and abandoned by 1947 were assigned to a new socialist Forestry Commission. A much longer lag ensued before this new body had the resources and manpower to take the job in hand. During this period the forests were neglected and many access routes were damaged or destroyed by natural causes. New growth impeded the exploitation of the older forests (where the *Rus* community had been used to grazing its animals) whilst the total forest area now began to expand again, thanks to unplanned and highly inefficient reforestation of areas previously utilised agriculturally. Most of the investments necessary to establish the new organisation were forthcoming in the 1960s and it was greatly facilitated by the opening of the asphalt main road. (Improvements in communications within the forests are still going ahead today, for the demands of the new sawmill enterprises require that very large quantities of wood be extracted.) In the 1950s forestry staff were given temporary quarters in surviving *Rus* dwellings. In the 1960s roughly a score of new flats was built to accommodate personnel, including large detached houses for the local directors. (Like the State Farm organisation there were two units of the Forestry Commission in operation in Wisłok, one with its centre near the source of the river and responsible for the forests in the border zone, the other with its centre at the lower end of the village and responsible for a slightly smaller area of just over 1,000 hectares in areas north-east of the main river valley.) Techniques were modified as better cutting equipment was provided, though the

8. Trouble in the forest as a peasant struggles to bring a single trunk to the roadside.

petroleum chain saws brought new safety and health hazards in their train. Exploitation of the forests was fully re-established on the new, socialist footing by the end of the 1960s. The two directors had secondary education and a professional qualification. There was a permanent labour force of about a dozen men, and also a small administrative staff to assist in carrying out the orders of the regional headquarters (at Rymanowa, 28 km by road through the mountains) and in maintaining meticulous records.

The 'permanent' labour force was a curious assortment and always highly fluid. They were all male, like the employees of the State Farm, and they were likewise attracted, some of them at least, by the promise of accommodation and above-average earnings in relation to days worked. Many chose this work in preference to the State Farm because they had been unable in the past to tolerate the discipline of the socialist enterprise. Others had failed to meet the new challenge of peasant farming, in Wisłok or elsewhere. Working for the Forestry Commission gave them a large degree of freedom to determine the time they would put in over any given period, and they were largely unsupervised on the job. Some men brought families with them and settled permanently in the state-owned accommodation provided. Those recruited from amongst the local peasantry were more likely to stay in the old dwellings and keep up some interest in the farms attached to them. Others arrived in the village individually or with an all-male gang, sometimes leaving a wife and children behind. Their living conditions were usually tough, for they would be offered a dilapidated *Rus* dwelling rather

66

than the modern flats available to others. Alcohol was always their main consolation. Mostly they stayed no longer than a year or two, but the local directors came to reckon with the high turnover and were able to build up their contacts in different parts of the country such that labour could usually be found when it was needed. When they were unsuccessful, prisoners or soldiers could be called in to help with particularly pressing tasks. The planting of new zones was one demanding task which required large amounts of seasonal labour. This need was met by female labour, recruited mainly from the more densely populated lowland villages. These peasant women came to the mountains of Bieszczady year after year, usually when the spring sowing was completed and they had a slack period on their own farms. Some of them found husbands and settled permanently in Wisłok and neighbouring villages.

The most important and unchanging feature of the present labour process in the forests has been the involvement of the peasants. The private sector has been integrated much more effectively into this part of the socialist sector than it has into the large-scale agricultural sector. The farmers' contribution is simple enough to describe. Trees are selectively felled by the full-time loggers, who usually work in pairs with a single power saw and should have undergone some basic course of instruction in how to use it (in the recent past even this work was done by individual farmers, without special training). The peasant then has to haul the fallen trunks with his team of horses from the recesses of the forest to the roadside, where they may be transferred to lorries and taken off to the sawmill. Less frequently smaller logs are cut and stacked in the forest and the farmer is asked to cart these to the roadside collection points. In the difficult conditions, horses are the only means by which the timber can be extracted. The only vehicle which might conceivably replace them is a helicopter. Thus, the owner of a team finds that the Forestry Commission can use his services throughout the year. Seventeen individual farmers keep two or more horses, though this is scarcely warranted by the scale of their farms, and most of the remainder have one, which is sufficient for less demanding work in the forests. They work largely at their own convenience, generally putting in more days during the winter, when for some it is almost the sole occupation. Large sums can be earned rapidly, but the work is strenuous for both men and animals. The amount of work undertaken is likely to vary according to current cash needs, and may change greatly from one year to the next. It is worth noting that some of the more successful farmers are also amongst the busiest in the forests. But it should also be recognised that the relative ease and speed with which cash can be obtained in the forests may remove the stimulus for peasants to develop their agricultural enterprise. It is a major distraction, which relieves short-term cash flow problems but does not generate large investment funds, and which leaves men and animals physically exhausted. This exploitation of peasant labour is perpetuating technological backwardness both in the forests and on the land. A peasant who keeps horses is keeping open the opportunity to use them in the forest, when he might otherwise be more inclined to replace them in agricultural work by modern machines. (Even those who have succeeded in acquiring tractors are often tempted by the availability of forest work to retain at least one of their horses.) There are also far-reaching consequences for family and social life. Peasants are removed from their homes, not merely from their farm work, sometimes camping out for days at a time when the job is too remote to return every evening. They are also more exposed to the full-time loggers and aspects of their behaviour — and in particular drinking habits — are inevitably transmitted.

The local directors and the foremen who work below them sometimes use arguments analogous to those advanced by the State Farm leadership, to the effect that the ultimate problem which handicaps the socialist sector is lack of investment. If more and better houses could be built for the labour force, if more and better access roads could be constructed, then it would be possible to attract and retain better quality labour and perhaps even to dispense with the peasant contribution. No-one considers this to be realistic, for the scale of the task would far exceed the sums required to modernise the State Farms. There has been some reorganisation in recent years, and there is no longer any clerical staff employed in Wisłok. But whereas the State Farm units obtained a measure of genuine autonomy in 1981, the two forestry units remain tightly constrained by the plans and quotas passed down to them from Rymanów. These in turn are determined by the requirements of the sawmills recently established in the Bieszczady region. It is widely feared that forests will be rapidly depleted if plans to expand production still further are fully implemented. One of the two foresters has been a Wisłok resident for more than twenty years and several of the foremen have been in the service since it was established. They have worked conscientiously, they are proud of the improvements they have attained. But they admit to being unable to compensate for the years of neglect after the war, and they are not optimistic about the prospects for more efficient exploitation of the forests in the future. The likelihood is therefore one of continued dependence upon an unstable body of unqualified, full-time workers and the marginal labour and horses of the peasants, with all that is implied by this combination for the economic future of the individual farms and for the general culture of the community.[2]

When fieldwork was conducted in 1981 the figures were as follows. Twelve men from twelve households were employed full-time by the different units of the Forestry Commission. All except one lived with their families in state-owned houses at the disposal of the Commission. The exception is a foreman who is of local *Rus* origin and who purchased his own house and farm when he returned to Wisłok after many years in the North. He is the only employee who is also registered as the owner of an individual farm, a small one of about 5 hectares. In fact several other employees also market agricultural commodities from the smaller plots allocated to them. Most have an allotment of 2 hectares, which is enough to meet much of their subsistence requirements. It is usually worked by the employee's wife. Apart from the two directors, four foremen and permanent workers domiciled with their families, there are also the temporary recruits. In 1981, apart from those who came for short periods only, there were three characters who shared an old *Rus* shack and worked in the same way as the permanent labour force. The charcoalburners were a similar group. They were installed in 1979 in caravans on the edge of the forest, just outside the residential boundaries of the valley, but were never properly drawn into its society in the eighteen months or so that they stayed. Finally, there are several ex-employees of the Forestry Commission or their descendants who are no longer active in production but continue to reside in state-owned houses. One is a widow of a former director, another is a retired clerk, the others are persons who draw special disability pensions. Amongst the active labour force there are also many persons who have enjoyed lengthy periods of sick leave, the usual reason being not specific accidents in the forest (though these are common enough) but cumulative chemical poisoning caused by the chain saws.

Convicts, commuters and other opportunities in the public sector

Apart from the units of the State Farm and the Forestry Commission the residents of Wisłok also have a few other openings locally within the public sector. Chief among them is the prison network, which was established in the region to provide labour for the State Farms from the late 1950s. In Wisłok itself there has been only a small establishment adjacent to the State Farm at the lower end of the village. It had a complement of about seventy convicts and a staff of fewer than a dozen uniformed warders. Three warders were accommodated in 1981 in flats built by the State Farm on which the convicts work. The administration of farm and prison remains essentially a single operation, even though the Ministry of Justice relinquished direct economic control in 1978. The establishment at Moszczaniec (6 km) is much larger: in addition to warders and other ancillary staff there were several hundred convicts. Formerly, there was a large penal colony, associated with the other State Farm unit in Wisłok, but this was abolished in 1977 (apparently because the unappealing spectacle in full view of travellers along the new road surprised an important foreign delegation — but this, like most of my information about these institutions, I was unable to verify adequately). At the head of the valley the buildings which formerly housed these convicts are now used as stables, and labour has to be bussed in from the remaining camps elsewhere. In 1981 there was an initiative from the *Solidarity* trade union to convert all of these into holiday camps. Surprisingly, the scheme was in large part implemented during the period of martial law: the camp in Wisłok was closed completely, and that in Moszczaniec run down so that numbers were barely sufficient to carry out essential work on the State Farms.

The prison service has much to offer prospective recruits. The pay is good, accommodation is provided very cheaply, retirement is early (normally after twenty-five years service) and the work is not strenuous. It is not therefore surprising that the service can recruit intelligent young staff, and is able to maintain reasonably high professional standards, buttressed by the strong Party organisation which exists at Moszczaniec. Nevertheless, there have also been abuses, and warders have been obliged to resign when these reached excessive proportions. Since many have no wish to settle in Wisłok and it is possible to request a transfer to other regions, the turnover is high. Their families may develop only tenuous links with other residents. The recurring complaint that peasants voice against them concerns the private exploitation of items of public property. Neither against forestry workers nor against State Farm employees is complaint so frequent as it is in the case of the warders. This may be because the latter are not obliged to perform any manual labour: they have comfortable white-collar jobs for which no professional qualifications are required and all that is demanded is stricter conformity and loyalty to their administrative superiors than is expected of low-level employees in other branches of the socialist sector.

Access to state owned housing, which generally includes access to a garden plot, is the factor which unites the three branches of the public sector in Wisłok we have looked at so far. The only other individual to enjoy this privilege was the headmaster of the village school (until 1979), a middle-aged bachelor who lived alone in the school building (before 1944 the Greek-Catholic presbytery). This is the only 'household' dependent upon a teacher's salary. The other teachers are women; only one is married to an individual farmer, and she gave up her job in 1982 in order to contribute more to the farm. There is one shop in the village, controlled by the commune cooperative in Komańcza. It is staffed by a lady who commutes to Wisłok from Rzepedź (14 km) because no local volunteer can be found; a similar problem has kept the kiosk in the lower part of the village permanently closed in recent years. There is a Postmaster, who has a part-time assistant-cum-postman; he is married to a teacher and therefore head of one of the few 'white-collar' households in this village — certainly they are the only owner-occupiers in Wisłok who earn their living by non-manual work. To complete this survey there are a few additional positions and part-time jobs which generate a small income. The post of village headman is not entirely honorific, for it involves a good deal of time-consuming administration in matters such as animal sales, tax collection etc. Apart from prestige it also confers the advantage of a telephone upon the household. The post of village librarian is much less demanding. Finally, the milk round is performed daily by a young farmer who uses his own cart, and the part-time post of school cleaner is filled by the nearest volunteer.

Outside the village job opportunities have multiplied in recent years, mainly in response to the opening of the new road and the sawmill at Rzepedź. There has always been a small group of long-distance commuters, usually young unmarried men who return irregularly to the village and settle as soon as possible in the town where they find work. There are two skilled workers who commute daily to Komańcza, where they are employed by the SKR. Everybody else commutes to Rzepedź. In 1981 there were eighteen persons from fourteen households making the daily journey, on buses

9. A commuter to the Rzepedz sawmill with family.

laid on by the enterprise. For about half of these households it was the major or sole source of income. Most employees do not become skilled workers. The younger ones (including a few unmarried women) generally do acquire a vocational qualification, but this is not essential for work at the sawmill. Those who expect to work at Rzepedź in the long term hope sooner or later to be able to move into one of the modern blocks which the enterprise is helping to construct. This also appeals to some of the older workers, but only those who have retained substantial farming interests in Wisłok can afford the very substantial downpayment needed for a new flat in Rzepedź. The existence of such a farm can also serve to dissuade families from giving up the advantages it confers, and the result is that during years of procrastination these worker-peasants straddle public and private sectors. As with forestry and the State Farms, it seems clear that as soon as peasants take up the factory-commuting option they begin inevitably to neglect their farms. Where the effects are highly deleterious it is nowadays possible that the Chief Executive in Komańcza will use his powers to confiscate and redistribute land. But often the owners of smaller plots are left in possession, even when their commodity production dries up altogether.

Work in the new sawmill is not regarded with much affection. Here too the labour turnover is high — many young persons try it for a year or two, before moving on to something else. They are lured

72

initially by the only large enterprise that is within comfortable, daily reach of the village. The plant exploits this advantage in recruiting from a large area of the surrounding countryside. Several further comments may be advanced. Firstly, were the prospects for peasant farming brighter, the sawmill would have more trouble in finding good quality labour. Secondly, its difficulties would be greater if it were easier for commuter workers from the countryside to settle in the urban environment. The housing shortage in the lowland cities is extreme, hence the sawmill in this socialist equivalent of a 'company town' is adopted as a second best. The survival of the old *Rus* dwellings in Wisłok and similar villages continues to assure the plant its captive labour force. Thirdly, a peasant who has once got himself a job in the factory is unlikely to consider full-time farming again, if only because he has begun now to qualify for a superior industrial pension. The progression runs, in the categories used by official statisticians, from peasant to 'peasant-worker' (the full farm is retained), to 'worker-peasant' (subsistence holding only — less than two hectares) and finally to 'worker', whenever permanent migration is possible. To whittle down the scale of one's farming until one produces only a part of one's subsistence requirements is easy enough; the opposite, gradually to build a farm up again, is a much rarer accomplishment. None of the households with members employed at Rzepedź figure amongst the more successful farming households, although eight of them maintain commodity producing farms (average size: 6 hectares). The accommodation and general living conditions of the few commuters without a farm are amongst the poorest in the village.[3]

Can public and private sectors co-exist in the long run?

Table 7 summarises the pattern of full-time manual employment outside peasant farming for 'permanent' inhabitants of Wisłok in the middle of 1981. The distinction between ordinary workers and 'foremen' is more significant as far as income is concerned than that between skilled and unskilled. Few of the foremen have any vocational qualifications — they owe their positions to many years of experience rather than to the short training courses they may be required to complete. On the other hand most young workers today are required to undergo some training before they earn full wages, even if this is no more than learning how to drive a tractor or to operate a simple machine. Few of them are properly skilled, for the genuinely skilled are unlikely to remain domiciled in Wisłok. It is common for peasant children to seek some form of off-farm employment near to home when they have completed their schooling, even if one or more of them is likely in later years to take up farming on his own account. Almost all the peasant farmers of Wisłok have had some experience of the public sector before they took over their present farms. Thus, the life-cycle of the household influences the extent of its participation in the socialist labour market. If such younger workers are omitted then one is left with a total of thirty-three adults (from twenty-seven households) active full time in the public sector (excluding teachers and the post-office staff). They include four women who work at the sawmill, one of them in the canteen.

	State Farm	Forestry Commission	Prison Service	Sawmill	Other
Foremen and above	4	6	1	1	1
Workers	6	8	2	17	3

Table 7: Employment in the Public Sector, 1981

The presence of full-time adult workers in the household does not necessarily indicate that the public sector is the main source of household income. In most cases it is, but in several instances it is fully matched by farm earnings. There is no case of an adult working full-time off the farm and farm income nevertheless clearly exceeding wage income. Households in which agricultural commodities bring in sums roughly comparable to income earned by household members in the public sector may be described as 'genuinely mixed'. There were eight such households in Wisłok in 1981, including two in which the wage-earners were members of the younger generation and both parents were fully engaged on the farm.

A further ten households could be classified as inactive in production, and dependent primarily upon pensions. The existence of such a group is a very recent phenomenon and testimony to the emergence of the socialist welfare state. Three of these pensions were earned by individual farmers and the majority of the remainder by former employees of the Forestry Commission.

The remaining forty-seven households could be divided into twenty-two which were *basically* active in peasant farming, and twenty-five active mainly or exclusively in the public sector. Some of those in the first group have junior members earning wages, and even adult members with part-time jobs outside the farm. Most of those in the second group maintain garden plots, which play an important role in the provisioning of the household and in some cases yield significant cash incomes. In a sense, then, almost every household is simultaneously involved in both sectors. The wage-earners (and also the pensioners) must be able to produce some food for themselves, for it has never been very easy to obtain everything needed with cash. Likewise, peasants cannot hope to be fully inde-pendent of the public sector. Those who sell few commodities will be obliged to supplement their incomes, typically by casual work in the state forests. Those who wish to increase agricultural production will inevitably be drawn into more intricate links with the public sector, which not only has a monopoly over their marketing but also con-trols the supplies of essential inputs.

If one disregards, amongst the twenty-two households basically active in peasant farming, those which in fact resort frequently to the forests or have some other non-agricultural income (e.g. teenagers working in the factory), then one is left with very few pure 'full-time farming' households. It might be argued that similar patterns are characteristic of many other peasant societies, and that the number of self-sufficient households in pre-socialist Wisłok would also have been small. That, however, was caused by more fundamental demographic pressures upon scarce natural resources. Today, under socialism, the pressures are different: they are caused by the creation and maintenance of the public sector in its present form.

It is not simply that the public sector owns most of the land in Wisłok, does not use it very efficiently, and would do better to allow the private sector to expand its area. In other parts of Poland the proportions of territory controlled by public and private sectors are the reverse of the ratio in Wisłok, but the effects of the public sector are no less strongly felt. Elsewhere the socialist sector in agriculture may be represented by a production cooperative rather than by State Farms, or solely by the Agricultural Circles. Elsewhere the forests may be exploited differently, the prisons entirely absent, and the number of factories within daily commuting range is likely to be greater. In most other villages the proportion of genuinely mixed or 'worker-peasant' households is likely to be greater than it is in Wisłok. These are differences of detail and the substance of the situation remains the same. The socialist sector in Poland has been developed in such a way as to subvert the private sector rather than to complement it;

and despite a lot of official rhetoric, in agriculture virtually nothing has been done to 'integrate' the private sector into the modern socialist sector. The expansion of the latter has been profoundly antagonistic to the former. The most distressing indications of the pressures to which the private sector has been subjected are the ageing of the population and the reluctance of the young, even if they do remain in the village, to inherit the patrimony. As farm modernisation is unrealistic, the potential heirs have preferred to take up one or other of the many options available in the socialist sector; or alternatively they have solved their cash needs by working in the forests — this is the particular illustration in the atypical mountain community of how the socialist sector has exploited the peasantry and denied it the incentive to modernise.

Viewed in a wider comparative and historical context it is easy to see how this pattern has come about. The decline of the self-sufficient rural community (and Wisłok was self-sufficient to a very high degree until the nineteenth century) has been documented all over Europe; and in the concomitant processes of agricultural modernisation the peasant has given way to the modern farmer. This transition has been difficult and protracted in many parts of Western Europe, where some of the problems experienced are similar to those which have affected Poland in the course of industrialisation. The crucial difference is that industrialisation in Poland has taken place in a well-defined socialist context, and it is with the other socialist states that the most revealing comparisons must be sought. In terms of the simple dichotomy used in these last two chapters, the independence of the 'private sector' in these other states was eliminated almost literally overnight by the forcible imposition of collectivisation. From that point onwards every household had to seek its livelihood in the 'public sector' — there was no alternative. Collectivisation was a tragedy almost everywhere. But at least the new public sector so brutally conceived had to be allocated sufficient resources to make the transition from the peasant labour-process to socialist wage-labour an economic reality. In practice, the most successful states were those which not only invested heavily in the new public sector but also continued to stimulate family labour in its newly defined sphere, based on the household plot. Poland failed to collectivise and failed to develop any alternative strategy for modernising the countryside and maintaining food supplies in a period when the population, and especially the industrial work-force, was increasing very rapidly. She fell between stools, neither encouraging individual

farmers with realistic, market-determined prices and the (ideologically unacceptable) long-run guarantees about private property
rights, nor moving decisively to establish a new, large-scale sector on
a socialist footing. It can be argued from the Right that quite enough
resources were wasted in attempting to build up the socialist sector in
agriculture, and, from the orthodox Left, that no socialist agricultural policy could succeed as long as a large, independent peasantry
was allowed to persist in any form. There is truth in both of these
claims, for the socialist sector has been developed sufficiently to
undermine the potential of the private sector in agriculture but has
not sufficed to create a satisfactory alternative perspective. In a
political context in which steps to eliminate the private sector by
coercive means remain precluded, it would appear that the only way
out of the impasse is to fashion real bonds of mutual interdepen-
dence between sectors in agriculture. Integration *could* be pursued in
such a way that both would benefit. This would require some modification of ideological positions. Ideally, it would be preferable to
transfer the *ownership* of resources away from the public sector, which
is incapable of using them efficiently, to the peasantry, for which
personal ownership undoubtedly provides a powerful economic
motivation. But, provided that the peasant is left with enough land
that he can call his own, leasing might be a way out of the impasse,
enabling an increase in production without any infringement of the
prime ideological taboo. Any reinforcement of the private sector in
agriculture might lead to a desirable *separation* of public and private
sectors in other spheres, i.e. to less exploitation of peasant labour in
the forests and in the factory.

*   *   *   *

In the last two chapters we have seen how public (socialist) and
private (peasant) sectors have coexisted in Poland throughout a
long period of transition, which has differed markedly from the
experience of other socialist countries (because of the failure to
collectivise) and from non-socialist experience (because of the decisive effects which socialist ideology has nonetheless had in constraining the development of the private sector). Scope for mutual cooperation between the two sectors in agriculture has not been realised.
Instead, the private peasantry has been rendered increasingly
dependent upon the socialist authorities, whilst the internal functioning of the household, the crucial productive unit, has been

undermined by the lure of the socialist sector. It may be that in future the farming population will become more differentiated, and that, if industrialisation proceeds more smoothly, there will be a clearer separation of the two sectors. The total number of commodity-producing farms will become smaller and the number of households fully committed to the socialist sector will increase. The authorities might then be able to retain the traditional economic advantages of peasant farming (and even regain some of those lost because of past discrimination against the private sector). However, the real problem is likely to be one of establishing a genuine market environment for agriculture, in which the remaining private farmers are not subject to close administrative controls and deprived of genuine productive incentives. The policies of the 1970s made the leadership very unpopular and ensured general support for the demands of *Rural Solidarity*. We must consider the impact of that movement, with its central plea for the reaffirmation of full, authentic, private property rights, in the light of the system of administration in the socialist village, which has subjected the nominally 'independent' peasantry to greatly increased bureaucratic controls.

CHAPTER FIVE

Administration and Politics

L'administration est tout ensemble une organisation, une science, une culture et un art. Aucun domaine ne lui demeure étranger: c'est là sa force, mais aussi un risque de faiblesse.

Janusz Letowski *Le Contrôle de l'administration en Pologne,*
CNRS (Paris 1978, p. 22)

The socialist characteristics of the political system have held firm enough to preclude an analysis of local politics in the familiar Western terms. Poland is not a pluralist society, and, although the church may constitute a countervailing power nowhere so strong in other socialist states, conflicts of interest cannot properly be expressed (let alone resolved) at any level of the formal political structure. In Wisłok this did not change even in 1980–1, when controls were substantially loosened and elsewhere the free trade union *Solidarity* flourished briefly. Where links between the rural community and the national society are overwhelmingly *administrative* in character, even the social anthropologist whose approach to political phenomena is not limited by the categories of Western pluralism may have difficulty in identifying such phenomena at the local level. The socialist system has always legitimised ties of vertical dependence in terms of a hierarchical theory, democratic centralism, and in Poland a series of reforms accomplished in the 1970s extended their scope down to the level of the peasant household. When horizontal contacts between households are inhibited, when each is like an atom with a common nucleus only in the administrative apparatus, then political activity in the peasant community effectively ceases. This chapter will describe how this has come about in Wisłok, and will give some examples of how the administrative mechanism works and of the corruption which it engenders.

The withering of pioneer democracy

In the aftermath of the deportation of the *Rus* population in 1947 the new immigrants to Wisłok had few doubts about the powers of the new socialist regime and its readiness to deploy them. Most of the newcomers were resettled by the administration directly: agreements were signed at District (*powiat*) level with regions in which rural overpopulation was particularly acute. Peasants, with appetites whetted by a concerted propaganda campaign (see the story of Jan Janicki, related in the Appendix), were then directed by officials to particular villages, sometimes even to specific farms. In the case of Wisłok the police and the military maintained a presence in the village long after the threat of Ukrainian terrorism had passed, because of the proximity of the state border with Slovakia.

In spite of these factors those who can remember the early days of the new community recall an open, democratic spirit and a high degree of self-administration. This situation may not have been typical of the Polish countryside generally in the last years of Stalin, for this was a time of bitter class struggle, when the authorities were actively committed to an unpopular collectivising strategy. The atmosphere differed in Wisłok, partly because of its poor communications (which made it difficult in practice for the authorities outside the village to interfere in day-to-day affairs), and partly because its new residents all hailed from the lowest strata of society and could scarcely be accused of harbouring members of the rural bourgeoisie. The immigrants could choose the leaders they wanted to represent their views to outsiders, whilst within the village they were allowed to allocate dwellings and settle disputes with minimal reference to the commune authorities in Komańcza (10 km), let alone the district authorities at Sanok (50 km). They were granted permission to use one of the surviving *Rus* churches, which a priest was able to visit once a month. They were encouraged and assisted to establish secular communal facilities, which included schoolhouses and a community-centre (*świetlica*) centrally located in the valley, where newspapers and books were available, entertainments were mounted, and assemblies of the whole community frequently held.

The apogee of this phase was the period 1954–8, when Wisłok enjoyed commune (*gromada*) status in its own right, i.e. it was independent of Komańcza in the administrative hierarchy. According to the rules of democratic-centralism as then practised (similar structures still form the framework of local government in most socialist countries) it was subordinate to the district authorities at Sanok, who were in turn subordinate to the voivodeship which had its centre at Rzeszów (125 km). This was the formal structure governing the organisation of both the state bureaucracy and the Communist Party: the two were intertwined at all levels.[1] In Wisłok the key figures in the running of the *gromada* were encouraged to affiliate to

10. Jan Janicki, village headman, 1948-1981, with medals for distinguished service. (See *Appendix* for personal history.)

the ruling party, but in practice their superior organs expected little more than this formality. Contacts with the outside world were relatively few in the years before the construction of the modern road, and peasants were able to arrange their private and collective lives with little pressure applied from outside. As indicated in previous chapters, the opportunities for economic expansion were severely constrained. But there was never any attempt to take back the lands that had served as the major incentive for migration to Wisłok in the first place. On the contrary immigrants were frequently reassured that they were the sovereign owners of their plots, and that the deported *Rusnaks* would never be permitted to reassert any claim. The political crises of 1956 left no mark on the village.

Wisłok ceased to be an independent *gromada* in 1958. Since this time it has elected a few members of the local council in Komańcza. Apparently it was considered too small to continue to manage its own affairs, though the population had in fact increased since 1954. This loss of control was mitigated in 1960 by the establishment of the Agricultural Circle, which, as described in Chapter Three, did give peasants some influence over the economic matters of greatest concern to them. In other spheres control was increasingly vested in outsiders. New shops were constructed under the aegis of the 'Peasants' Self-Help Cooperative', also based in Komańcza. The community-centre atrophied and was no longer in use by the end of the 1960s.

81

As in economic affairs, in administration too the Gierek years ushered in a new phase.[2] Centralisation and bureaucratisation were the main implications of the changes introduced into the system of local government. The district (*powiat*) was abolished and the new, 2-tier structure was made up of smaller counties (Wisłok currently belongs to that of Krosno, 55 km) and much larger communes, henceforth known as *gminas*. Komańcza soon became the seat of a commune covering about 550 km² and including several dozen villages. The new *gmina* was supposed to correspond to an economic microregion and to enable an expansion in autonomous decision-taking at the lowest levels of the administration. Accordingly, the party and state apparatus was now consolidated at *gmina* level. Executive power was removed from the presidium, the group which had previously managed the working of the local councils, and vested in an individual Chief Executive, the *naczelnik*. He was not to be elected, but was appointed by the county authorities. He did not have to reside in the *gmina* he administered, and the Komańcza Chief Executive commuted to his sprawling *gmina* from a small town outside the mountain zone. Simultaneously, the representative institutions were modified, without being essentially transformed. The new *gmina* council was a very large body, though the number of members from Wisłok remained at three — the village headman and two others, all of them in practice selected by the authorities. Sessions of the full council achieve nothing, in the opinion of the Wisłok councillors, and the general public nowadays takes no interest in them.

The reforms were implemented in several stages in the years 1972–5, and their import was not immediately understood. It was thought by some early commentators that they would lead to an expansion of representative and democratic forces in local government, at the expense of 'centralist' tendencies.[3] In the event the opposite came to pass and centralist forces extended their hold. Villages such as Wisłok were now subjected to more outside interference than they had known before, largely because of the new powers vested in the Chief Executive. The disappearance of the *powiat* became a source of regret, for in the past it had sometimes served peasants well, enabling them to redress grievances and counteract commune-level decisions. With the new county centre no more accessible than the old, citizens now felt more exposed to the vagaries of the state machine than before. The *powiat* had permitted more feedback within the administrative system than was possible within the new streamlined version.

In these circumstances it was predictable that the character of local government in rural areas would become a major issue when the political climate enabled contentious problems to be openly discussed in 1980–1. The apparatus was briefly forced onto the defensive and many officials lost their jobs. There was wide sympathy for *Rural Solidarity*'s demand that the village 'open meeting' should become an instrument of authentic self-administration, and not a mere talking-shop on a par for irrelevance with the *gmina* council. In Wisłok, as elsewhere, great attention was paid to convening such meetings in 1981, and the Chief Executive himself went out of his way to attend them. But participation was still poor compared to the early days of the new community, and hopes that open meetings might gradually upstage the elected councils and force the apparatus to respond to them were not fulfilled. Certainly in Wisłok and Komańcza nothing in the administrative structure established by Gierek was dismantled, and under martial law the old system came back into normal operation. If anything it has been operating with a vengeance since 1981 — against peasants as a whole, who are regularly accused of failing to meet their obligations to society, and more particularly, against anyone so unwise as to have raised his voice in protest against the local administration in 1981.

How the bureaucracy works — some examples

Administrative methods were most notoriously demonstrated in Komańcza in 1961. Wisłok was part of the Komańcza commune at this time, but this matter concerned mainly the large Ukrainian population in the commune centre. After the deportations of 1947 they possessed the only Greek Catholic (Uniate) church in active use in the entire mountain zone formerly inhabited by the *Rusnaks*. It was an exceptionally fine wooden edifice built in the early years of the nineteenth century and prominently located on a hilltop next to the village cemetery. All the property of this church was officially confiscated by the state in 1946, and the Greek Catholics have not been recognised by the authorities since this time.[4] However, in Komańcza, where Ukrainians survived in relatively large numbers (mainly thanks to the railway, which needed a labour force), the discreet approach of the local priest and tolerance on the part of the local authorities enabled the church to survive. After the death of this priest in 1961 the authorities in charge of religious matters at county level decided that this anomaly must be eliminated. They were prepared to let a successor hold Greek Catholic services, but only in the small chapel used by the Roman Catholics of the village. To ensure that the famous old church would no longer serve the Greek Catholic parish the keys were appropriated by a bureaucrat from Rzeszów, who obtained them from a priest by posing as a tourist. This action provoked vigorous protests from the Roman Catholic hierarchy as well as from the Ukrainians of Komańcza, who sent their petitions to Sanok, Rzeszów and ultimately to the First Secretary of the Communist Party in Warsaw. They protested their loyalty to socialism, cited the fact that many residents of Komańcza had fought in the Red Army and claimed that bereft of a church their community would disintegrate. It was all to no avail: Warsaw upheld the decisions taken in Rzeszów. It was asserted that there could be no legal basis for recognition of a Greek Catholic Church in People's Poland. Later the policy was modified and the old church in Komańcza was transferred to the Orthodox Church of Poland. Yet even a state-salaried Orthodox priest, when duly installed in the village, was unable to persuade significant numbers to abandon the Greek Catholic faith, as the price for being allowed to use their former building. The situation did not change in 1980–1, although many peasants hoped that political liberalisation would lead to formal recognition of the Greek Catholics, as it had in Czechoslovakia in 1968. They continue to share a small and much less distinguished chapel with the Roman Catholics and, with the protection and cooperation of the dominant church, to withstand the authorities' periodic attempts to obstruct and interfere.

This is a clear example of how the administrative apparatus implements a centrally determined policy. Representative institutions, the local councils, were never involved. The only way in which the population could express its views was to send off petitions to the higher echelons of the administration. The unofficial tolerance of the Greek Catholic Church in Komańcza, and of a few other parishes in former *Rus* areas, is extended because of the power of the Roman Catholic Church. In the absence of this countervailing power the Greek Catholic Church would have shared the fate of its counterpart in the Soviet Ukraine, where it has enjoyed only an underground existence since 1945.

In this context another example from Komańcza is revealing. This time it was a matter which directly affected all the inhabitants of the outlying villages, including Wisłok. There was a spate of public building in the commune centre in the early 1970s, much of it initiated by recent immigrants who were as talented in mobilising local resources as in deploying the energies of outsiders, notably student groups interested in touristic projects. The outstanding achievement was the construction of a well equipped, modern health centre. It was organised largely by one tireless young doctor, who had further ambitious plans to exploit natural mineral waters and develop the village as a health resort. This was too much for the local authorities, who were also concerned by the doctor's regular attendance at the Roman Catholic chapel. He was eventually transferred to another area, and the fine new facilities fell into rapid decline. For some time no doctor at all could be found to work in Komańcza, and patients who did not reside in the commune centre could never be sure when they might attend a surgery. In 1981 the only doctor resident was the same man who had built the health centre, but he was unable to work there. Since his popularity was undiminished, an open meeting was called to devise some way of reinstating him and also of assisting him in his schemes to develop local springs. The wishes of the population and of the doctor himself were clear enough; but administrative obstruction (which had earlier included deliberate attempts to impede the doctor's personal housebuilding in Komańcza) ensured that nothing issued from this meeting. The doctor is being required to continue his appointment in a sanatorium some distance away, whilst the people of his own commune remain badly served by the present organisation of the health centre. In the early days of the new community a nurse held a regular surgery in Wisłok itself and many complaints could be dealt with on the spot. Nowadays the nurses do not travel, and it is often necessary to make several trips to the surgery in order to consult a doctor, and to travel much further afield if the case is urgent.

Within Wisłok there have been no large-scale attempts to construct communal facilities by relying on voluntary 'social labour', at least not since the early years of pioneer democracy in the new community. The authorities continue to keep statistics of such activities, e.g. whenever a group of neighbours combine to improve a stretch of road. But when no pressure was applied in 1981 (because it was no longer necessary, for form's sake, to maintain such statistics), it transpired that communal self-help activities ceased entirely.

In day to day business and especially concerning less sensitive matters where religion is not involved, the hallmark of local administration is familiar bureaucratic incompetence. One might note, for example, how the authorities have implemented another aspect of a centrally determined programme, this time in the field of cultural policy. Since the 1950s there has been a library in Wisłok. Whilst the council was locally managed, and even afterwards for as long as the community-centre remained in active use, it apparently functioned quite well. When this building fell into decay the stock of about 5,000 books was transferred to the house of the local postmaster at the top end of the village. The demand for books proved to be low. When the library was again transferred, this time to the house of a popular peasant farmer in the centre of the village, there was a sharp increase in the number of readers and in the frequency of borrowing. However, the routine of this household was considerably disrupted by the popularity of the library. For nominal remuneration the peasant was required to keep a room open during long hours, to provide heating in winter, and — the most serious irritation — to attend classes in librarianship in a remote town and maintain a full statistical record of library use. When the authorities would not agree to modify these conditions the library had to be transferred again. This time it went to a house at the far, lower end of the village, where it was once again inaccessible and seldom frequented (in 1980 it counted only thirteen adult readers in the whole village). In 1981 it was moved back to a more central location, but the use made of this facility seems likely to remain small so long as the books are stored in a private home.

The administration is frequently criticised for its failure to replace the community-centre, which functioned well in the first decades of the new community in Wisłok. As a central meeting place it has to some extent been replaced by the new post office and main shop, but the club room which forms part of the latter building has never operated as planned. It is now used on one or two occasions in the year for village open meetings. Entertainments are extremely infrequent, though there are limited opportunities for amusement at weekends in Komańcza and at Rzepedź, where there is even a small cinema; but there is a problem for the young persons interested in such events: the last bus back to Wisłok leaves at nine o'clock.

There has never been any café or restaurant in Wisłok in the socialist period. Until quite recently it was possible to purchase alcoholic beverages in the village shops. Sales of vodka and beer were stopped by the cooperative which controls the shops after local women protested about the large sums squandered by their menfolk and the drunken scenes outside the shop where the liquor was consumed. Sales of a pernicious wine, allegedly produced from a mixture of fruits, continued after 1981, though drunkeness became less frequent. The shopkeeper declared that if alcohol sales ceased altogether she would give up the job, for her wages were related to turnover.

Although some responsibilities may be formally delegated by the authorities, e.g. to the *gmina* cooperative which runs the shop, in fact the peasants of Wisłok assign responsibility for all ills to a single, monolithic administration. The Gierek reforms concentrated bureaucratic competence in the person of the Chief Executive, and so it is, naturally, to him that people complain when there is no bread in the shop. Everything that is available is there by courtesy of the higher authorities, the woman in charge does not know what she will be able to sell the next day, or even when to expect deliveries. The inefficiencies of the administrative system were especially obvious during the grave food shortages of 1981. An official from Komańcza distributed ration tickets efficiently enough each month, and officials from Sanok made long journeys to ensure that sanitary conditions in the shop were up to standard; but the tickets could not often command goods, and on four days out of five the shopkeeper was idle and her shelves empty.

Bureaucratic discretion and corruption

The examples given above involved public institutions and items of collective consumption. Ration tickets, giving rights to goods for individual consumption, were allocated impersonally (though there was still broad discrimination between categories, e.g. between town and country residents, and this gave rise to criticism). On some local issues there is a real perception of collective discrimination; thus the inhabitants of Wisłok point to the higher levels of public investment in Komańcza, the commune centre. They would like funds to be diverted to the construction of a new school, of an animal purchasing point, and of a piped water supply. The authorities would like to accomplish these same objectives by means of 'social labour', and consequently a stalemate has existed for many years.

To Wisłok peasants the malign hand of the outside bureaucracy is even more apparent in the selective allocation of goods and services to particular households. This problem was touched upon in Chapter Three, where it was pointed out that peasants who wished to expand their production become highly dependent upon the administration for essential inputs. Even those with no ambition to improve farming techniques are in need of winter fuel, and everybody is likely at some stage to have to face the task of renovating dilapidated *Rus* dwellings or constructing modern ones to replace them. In these circumstances, the peasant must turn to the outside administration. For the hire of agricultural machinery it is necessary to turn to the SKR, in Komańcza or Szczawne. For financial help it is necessary to have recourse to the Agricultural Bank, which has a branch in Komańcza, though the matter may well need to be referred to senior staff in Sanok. Credits are almost automatically available for larger purchases, such as that of a tractor. The difficulty lies not in raising the money but in obtaining a paper authorising the purchase. Strict quotas are dictated by the government apparatus, with the Chief Executive able to control distribution within his *gmina*. Sometimes the decisions are badly received, as when one of the upstart specialists was awarded a tractor; but nobody considered complaining when a new van was offered to the Wisłok headman. Let us now suppose that a potential customer from Wisłok wants to buy some smaller item, one which is not allocated by committee, nor by ration tickets, nor by any other administrative regulations (e.g. coal is normally sold to peasants only when they have delivered a set quantity of commodities to the state), and that he has the money to do so. He will normally visit the main depot of the Peasants' Self-Help Cooperative, main source of building equipment, farm materials, fuel, — everything down to the kitchen sink. It is likely that an employee here will inform the peasant that the item required is unavailable, or that he may add his name to a long order list. Sometimes this information will be correct, and the would-be purchaser must either continue the search elsewhere (difficult, since many items are sold only to residents of the local commune) or try to obtain a guarantee that he will be able to purchase later, when supplies are available. But it transpires with great regularity that the goods *are* available all the time, or can be made so very rapidly, if certain steps are taken to wheedle them out.

The single most important step to take in this situation throughout Poland is to supply vodka. Depending on the scale of the favour or its urgency for the customer, it may be appropriate to offer a superior foreign product, such as cognac. Cash too may change hands. But the clients, at least the Wisłok peasants whom I knew and whose dealings with the administration were largely restricted to their own *gmina*, assured me that in most cases the half litre of vodka was sufficient. They said that the practice had not become endemic until the middle of the 1970s, when the new bureaucracy took shape in Komańcza. Some farmers despised the procedure and said they never enjoyed participating in the consumption of the spirit in the office of the bureaucrat. Some officials could not be bribed in this way. Others kept glasses hidden in the drawers of their desks and were squeamish enough to lock themselves in, while their secretaries carried on typing outside during the half an hour that it might take two men to down half a litre. Amongst would-be clients, not everyone could accustom himself to such new and unfamiliar patterns of behaviour. A favour obtained from a neighbour in the village commonly elicits a gift of vodka, usually in the form of shared consumption *after* a service has been performed and in addition to a monetary payment if costs are incurred. Some peasants tried simply to invite officials to the public restaurant for a drink, but somehow this was not as effective as the gift of a bottle. In 1981, when vodka went up sharply in price and for long periods was virtually unobtainable, it became less usual to drink it at once in the office and the client ceased to sample his gift. However, although many other items were in equally short supply (and *were* used as currency in other contexts) I never heard of anything other than vodka (or similar strong spirit) being used in transactions of this kind.

In the unusual atmosphere which prevailed in 1981 officials had to exercise greater caution. Yet, because of the severe shortages, the scope for bureaucratic discretion was greater than ever before. Journalists were not slow to expose the more colourful examples of corruption, for instance when the directors of a State Farm near Jaśliska (15 km) were accused of having accepted bribes to sell produce to farms across the state border in Slovakia. At the highest level the abuses committed by the First Secretary, the Prime Minister, and other cronies, became widely known. Rampant corruption at lower levels of the administration is popularly perceived as the specific product of the socialist period. It is the direct consequence of the genuine material advances that have been made in this period, which have brought isolated rural communities into intimate contact with the national economy and the national bureaucracy. The aspirations of most peasant households have increased, and particularist demands intensified in Wisłok after the first families began to mechanise farm production in the 1970s. However, supplies of the goods desired, whether for productive purposes or for consumption, were never sufficient. To the extent that the distribution problem was resolved by market instruments, prices were so extremely high that many peasants gave up their aspirations as unrealistic. To the extent that the problem was resolved by the monopolistic bureaucracy, it led inevitably to corruption. If the lower reaches of the bureaucracy became more degenerate in Poland than in other socialist states (a very uncertain proposition), this could be associated with the failure to extend the domain of socialist ownership in agriculture; for had peasants not been clamouring for the materials to maintain and expand their farms, the demands upon the bureaucracy would have been greatly reduced. Again, the point is not that collectivisation works well, but that in the given socialist framework, with the economy not producing sufficient of the goods which agriculture ideally needs, the pressures placed upon local officials are great enough, without the additional burden of distributing basic production inputs.

In Poland in the early 1980s the market principle was in some respects more completely subordinate to the administrative principle than it had been in Stalin's time. In addition to native Polish terms a new set of internationally derived words was in use in the villages to describe aspects of *korupcja*. Thus, a peasant is sometimes said to enjoy the *protekcja* of an official when he is able to approach him informally, not necessarily deferentially, make the usual gift and obtain the favour required. This relationship can develop into a bureaucratic variant of the tie between patrons and clients. The patron is an official who derives his power from his position in a well-defined bureaucratic hierarchy. Relationships may be less durable than patron-client ties elsewhere, for the bureaucrat is ultimately concerned more with his administrative superiors and in his work he does not need the allegiance or support of any client. The latter may well try to reinforce links once they are established (e.g. by pressing further gifts, such as farm produce, to which the official perhaps has no easy access) but he cannot be sure of succeeding. Comparisons with other socialist countries reveal striking common features, though there is much variation in the extent to which broadly similar systems of administration have allowed local officials to function as 'patrons'.[5]

The Polish system must be one of the more villainous of all the corrupt bureaucracies known to history, if only because all its wheels are lubricated by vodka or even neat spirit. It has a decisive impact on the local economy, distributing resources independently not only of market forces, but also of socialist or any other humane criteria (such as need). The responsibilities of the administration are all-embracing in every socialist country — this is indeed the hallmark of socialist government. But the new, local elite in the Polish countryside grew too quickly in the 1970s. It did not grasp the notion of social responsibility, but exaggerated the hierarchical essence of the previously established system. With bureaucratic controls extending over a very wide range of goods and services, each peasant household, in order to survive in a worsening economic conjuncture, sought to become separately enmeshed in corrupt links of vertical dependency.

Depoliticisation

Another word of Latin origin to enter the Polish language recently is an ugly verb — *kombinować*. This refers to the whole undignified, frequently underhand and devious, manoeuvres persons must make to accomplish anything, e.g. to assure their supplies of a particular product.[6] A peasant does not combine, either formally or informally, with other peasants to achieve his goals, though the goals of the others might be identical, and an observer could point out that the needs of each individual might be better satisfied if some collective pressure were applied. In practice there is very little cooperation in the economic field, outside a narrow circle of kin. The employees of the State Farm, the only substantial group with a common workplace, do not exhibit much group solidarity. This may be because several of them are also active as peasant farmers. Other public sector workers tend to be very dependent upon their employers, who also control their accommodation. For peasant farmers, who do not enjoy a number of public sector 'perks', such as fuel provision, the only choice is whether or not to beseech bureaucrats, to participate in the vertical scrambling process. In the circumstances it is perhaps not surprising that some households have kept their demands to a minimum, even though their farms have suffered in consequence.

Without 'horizontally' recruited interest groups of any kind to complicate matters, village politics in Wisłok exemplify the absence of pluralist possibilities in the national political process. Apart from the council structure, mass meetings are convened annually or, at most, bi-annually. These provide an opportunity for grievances to be aired, but no guarantee that the *gmina* officials in attendance will do anything about them. The candidates in local government elections have always been chosen and vetted by the apparatus, and past practice was formalised in 1975 when the right of nomination was restricted exclusively to a committee directly controlled by the apparatus.[7] No upsets have occurred to date. Elections were due to take place in 1982, and it might be suggested that the possibility of an organised opposition emerging at the local level was one factor precipitating the decision to introduce martial law at the end of 1981, and in particular to clamp down hard on the activities of *Rural Solidarity*.[8] The organisation which might appear to have exercised more real influence than any other in recent years is that of the women, the Circle of Rural Housewives. Meetings are rare and seldom well attended, but the efforts of a determined few have been instrumental in curtailing use of the club-room and sales of alcohol from the shop next door. Their views may not reflect the views of the majority of women, but their vigour has brought them success because it accorded with the views of the apparatus in Komańcza.

The only formally constituted political group is the village cell of the Polish United Workers Party (the Communist Party). This had six members, including two teachers, one of whom resigned after the imposition of martial law. Meetings are rare and the party has never seriously attempted to represent the interests of the village, either at higher levels of the party or in connexion with the local government apparatus. A few farmers have joined when it was put to them that it might be in their personal interest to do so. Only one such member had materialist convictions (he was the only one not seen regularly in church), and he too resigned at the end of 1981. Over most of the preceding decade the secretary of the village cell was the local headmaster. When he was transferred to Komańcza in 1979 (though he continued to live in Wisłok), a peasant was persuaded to take over as secretary. This man ceased to collect Party dues. In 1981 none of the nominal members was active in any political field, and nobody else took the slightest interest in the local Party. The situation was a little different in the commune centre, for wherever a large white-collar apparatus is employed the organisation cannot become so completely moribund. At *gmina* level there was much talk of how to rejuvenate the Party around the time of the Ninth Party Congress (July, 1981). No substantial changes took place in the Party in the *gmina* of Komańcza, either during the period of so-called 'renewal', or during the period of martial law which followed. There were, however, several resignations at the point when martial law was introduced.

The persons who enjoy above-average prestige and esteem in the village, apart from the teachers, are those who have demonstrated their competence as farmers. Normally, these will be the persons invited by the *gmina* officials to stand for the council, and one of them is likely to be vested wih the powers of village headman. They are invariably male — no woman has yet played any significant role, except within the circle of Housewives — and the policy is to persuade them all to join some formal organisation. The most likely one, in the case of a peasant who attends church regularly, and is either apathetic or downright contemptuous of politicians generally, is the United Peasants Party. Though this played no role in village affairs in Wisłok, if it were able to develop an active organisation at village level it might in principle attract more members — certainly more than the Communist Party. It can be argued that the potential for an authentic populist party must remain so long as there remain peasants,[9] and the Komańcza based committee was a little more active than usual in 1981. Grass roots dissatisfaction throughout the countryside with the policies pursued by national leaders, especially towards *Rural Solidarity*, resulted in sweeping changes at the top, but did not restore political credibility. Most peasants continue to feel that this party will never have much influence over the communist-controlled apparatus at any level.[10]

Peasants seldom try to obtain favours or to redress grievances through their elected councillors. If the latter are nevertheless frequently consulted, this is because of their general standing in the community. They are seldom able to intervene effectively with the administration for they are in no sense themselves 'patrons' with an autonomous power base. If they do succeed on occasion as political brokers, this will owe little or nothing to their elected office. For most tasks, the more promising strategy is directly to approach the local apparatus of government employees, and if this is not successful, to follow this up by further individual approaches to higher levels of the hierarchy. The articulate and the literate, if they should be unlucky at *gmina* level, are well advised to take the matter to county level. A Party member able to write to the county level of the Party apparatus is in a particularly strong position, and it is even possible nowadays for some kinds of business to be resolved speedily over the telephone (thus, a call to the appropriate office in Krosno can release supplies for a Wisłok farmer from stocks kept in Komańcza). Although collective petitions have been very rare in Wisłok, persistent letter writing has also paid off for a dozen or so households in the upper hamlet, who were regularly cut off from the world by atrocious road conditions. When Krosno failed to give satisfaction they appealed to

Warsaw and sought the attention of the national media. The *gmina* was eventually forced to act, but only when what should have been a routine piece of local business threatened to become a national scandal. The case, involving a degree of cooperation between households and pressure being applied on the authorities via the threat of media exposure, was highly exceptional.

In general it would appear that political activities in Wisłok have been greatly inhibited by the functioning of the state administration ever since the formation of the new community, and that the dominance of an apparatus based outside the village has become gradually more complete as more complex ties have developed between the village and the national society. In many parts of Poland in 1980–1 the emergence of *Rural Solidarity* democratised the character of the local political process and gave peasants the opportunity not only to make known their views but also to influence decisions. Sometimes this happened through mass meetings, sometimes initiatives were taken up by galvanised Communist Party cells or by a purged local apparatus. Within *Rural Solidarity* populist and syndicalist currents were strong. Many urged the dissolution of the new bureaucracies, and sought to place effective power in the hands of the open village meeting. One had the impression nevertheless that most was achieved where the new union evolved an active and militant bureaucracy of its own, that only such an organisation could force the apparatus to alter its policies, e.g. in allocating land or equipment to the private sector. The progress made by the new union in 1981 was very uneven across the country. In Komańcza the cause was taken up by persons whose general standing in the community was the opposite of the peasants appointed to the councils in the 1970s by intelligent bureaucrats. Thus, the union mustered little support locally, and none at all in Wisłok, although a few farmers were profoundly sympathetic to *Solidarity* as a national movement.

There are good reasons why *Rural Solidarity* did not achieve the well nigh universal backing which the workers' movement proper gained in its industrial constituency. There were organisational deficiencies, personal clashes within the national leadership and factional disputes over policy, all of which were readily exploited by the authorities in their efforts to discredit the new union.[11] In the case of Wisłok relative isolation from urban and industrial influences also contributed to the union's unpopularity — though it may be pointed out that militancy was high in other, equally isolated parts of the Bieszczady region, where the existence of an extravagant government hunting reserve was the touchstone. It has to be acknowledged that increased difficulties in obtaining supplies for the farm and consumer goods, combined with the anti-*Solidarity* propaganda of the media, turned many peasants against the new movement in the later months of its existence. The propaganda was not so easily countered in the countryside as it could be in the towns and factories. The *Solidarity* weekly newspaper devoted little attention to agriculture, and in any case did not attract any peasant subscriptions in Wisłok. The whole episode would seem to conform very well with the image of conservative passivity so often associated with peasantry. Yet the history of peasant political parties in Poland in the pre-socialist generations goes rather against this stereotype. Populist parties were extremely powerful, and some of them had a strong socialist orientation. Perhaps, therefore, we should explain the failure of *Rural Solidarity* not in terms of the generic handicaps of peasant movements,[12] but rather in terms of the consequences of several decades of debilitating socialist administration. Some farmers were deeply suspicious of *Solidarity* when it first emerged as a workers' movement, they were determined to have no truck with those setting themselves up as a political opposition to the authorities. Such fears were fully justified, both in view of the tragedies to which peasant activism had led in the past, and in view of what martial law was to bring to some activists in the 1980s.

To summarise: *Rural Solidarity* might well be seen as a continuation of the Polish peasantry's notable populist tradition, a gallant successor to the old peasant parties which had been irrevocably compromised under socialism. The threat to the dominance of the socialist administrative system was brief. In Wisłok and Komańcza the most respected peasants, who might have been its spearhead, had been neutralised by their partial recruitment to the administrative system. They held council positions which gave them little power, but compromised them sufficiently to remove their will to *oppose*. The apparatus was not everywhere so efficient in this respect, and of course eventually it needed to declare a 'state of war' to ensure the defeat of this populist revival.

Social control becomes bureaucratic control

Analysis of the political systems of even complex, modern societies can often be illuminated by enquiries into methods of dispute settlement and the maintenance of law and order. The local, informal sanctions of the rural community have everywhere declined with the expansion of the state, and been replaced by formalised legal institutions, intended to make standard codes of behaviour effective throughout a given territory. In countries where these institutions do not develop concomitant with the penetration of a market economy and the state remains weak, alternative linkages may appear in the form of clientelist political relations. The socialist political system, though a strong state system *par excellence*, permits the emergence of a special kind of clientelism, as indicated above, in which the individual farmer who wishes to expand his farm becomes dependent upon local bureaucrats. Increasing bureaucratisation of the machinery of local government is not the best way to aid the adoption of 'universalistic' legal norms. At the same time it has had some effect in the field of social control: the procedures commonly activated today are an adaptation to depoliticisation, and one further aspect of administrative hegemony.

Traditionally, in Wisłok as in other villages, especially those located so far into the mountains, local and informal sanctions were of decisive importance. We noted how, through several centuries, the nominal political rulers were unable to control the activities of bandits who enjoyed the support of the community. The power of the external authorities became stronger under Austrian rule, but it was not until Galicia returned to Poland in the inter-war period that a specialised institution for the maintenance of law and order was set up in the village — a police station manned by Poles. Its presence still had little effect on routine processes of dispute settlement, which continued to depend upon local sanctions and would seldom require a higher level of arbitration than that of the elected headman, a man of immense prestige in the village.

In the early post-war years when Wisłok was resettled by Polish immigrants, informal procedures were still of major importance. In the 1970s the village headman (in office continuously since 1948) insisted that he was always willing to mediate in disputes, to preserve harmony and goodwill between neighbours. In reality he enjoyed little prestige and his interventions were extremely rare. He was simply not consulted, and quarrels were taken at once to the commune centre, to the police station there (if an offence was alleged) or to the person of the Chief Executive in the case of more nebulous complaints. Within the *gminas* established in the 1970s there is a disciplinary institution known as the *kollegium*, a tribunal dominated by local bureaucrats which is empowered to adjudicate a wide range of minor offences and impose penalties (usually fines). In the last few years residents of every neighbourhood in Wisłok have entered formal accusations against their immediate neighbours and had their complaints upheld at the ensuing *kollegium*. The commonest offence was minor assault whilst under the influence of alcohol, and the usual punishment meted out to the offender is a fine (related to his means), sometimes supplemented by a specified number of hours of 'social work'. The latter punishment is not strictly enforced. An exceptional case witnessed in 1981 arose out of a long-standing dispute between peasant neighbours in the upper hamlet, which crystallised during the distribution of small plots of State Farm land, claimed by both families. Each attempted to graze his animals on the land, the tension mounted over a few weeks and eventually boiled over in the presence of witnesses favourable to one of the two parties. The other was accused of disturbing the peace and using obscene language in the presence of children, and fined 1,100 złoty. The land dispute itself was resolved when the Chief Executive came out in person and formed an ad hoc *komisja*, with the participation of neutral local residents as well as other members of the administration. This led to a compromise acceptable to all. The system, including the *kollegium*, is thought to work well by the local administrators, who say that by resolving minor disputes and dealing with petty crime at the *gmina* level it spares everyone the necessity of litigation at higher levels. However, it may also lead to the exaggeration of minor misdemeanours, and have a negative impact on neighbourhood relations. There is nowadays a tendency in the heat of an argument to rush to Komańcza to institute formal proceedings, when previously another neighbour or the headman might have been called in and a compromise reached without recourse to the administration.[13]

The *kollegium* is now widely accepted as an impartial regulator of inter-household disputes. But, as in the case of other administrative decisions, it is possible to appeal against a verdict. Here, too, the writing of letters (initially to the county centre, later possibly to Warsaw) has payed off for at least one Party member in recent years.

Disputes within the socialist enterprises operating in Wisłok are infrequent. One case at the State Farm in 1981 showed that the employee has little hope of succeeding with a complaint against the management. It involved an illiterate night watchman, who alleged pilfering by the Director. The accusation was taken to court at county level, where the plaintiff claimed he was not given even the semblance of a fair hearing. He received no compensation when he was dismissed from his job soon afterwards. Whatever the merits of his allegation, it was interesting that fellow workmen were critical of his pressing a formal complaint. They suggested that it was useless, even dangerous, to challenge the authority of the Director. It would seem that the formal methods of dispute settlement are appropriate to the resolution of conflicts with one's neighbours and equals, but are not recommended if one is in conflict with a socialist institution.

There is no 'law and order' problem in the contemporary village. For some time after Wisłok was resettled there was a resident policeman, but he was stationed here because of the village's proximity to the border and not in order to interfere in the affairs of the embryonic community. There was a higher level of violence in these years, mainly because of rivalry between youth gangs, formed according to regions of origin. Such patterns were very typical of the Polish countryside, and they still surface occasionally when the young men of Wisłok attend entertainments in other villages.[14] Within the villages no such groups have functioned in recent years, doubtless because few young men remain on the farms. Within certain families there is still a disconcerting incidence of violent behaviour when vodka is consumed; but the nearest regular policeman (as distinct from the prison warders and the frontier patrols which are quite frequently in evidence) is nowadays in Komańcza, and there is really no call for one in villages without a public bar.

*　　*　　*　　*

'Administration' is the term used loosely in this chapter to characterise the external organs and officials of the state and Party apparati who have power in Wisłok. The political process itself has become an *administrative* process, one which keeps each constituent household in relations of vertical dependence. It has not been conducive to the formation of alliances or pressure groups within the village, nor to any expression of village unity within the present system of large communes. Administration did not impinge thus on the *Rus* community, and 'local self-government' was a socialist ideal which had some reality in the first decade of resettlement in Wisłok. Lately, however, especially since the reforms introduced by the Gierek team in the 1970s, there has been an enormous expansion in the size and functions of an apparatus now entirely located outside the village. The power which it wields at local level has not been subject to effective legal controls: the formal introduction of martial law at the end of 1981 actually made hardly any difference to this peasantry.

There are risks in subverting local democracy so completely, as the quotation from Letowski at the head of this chapter reminds us. When hierarchical dependence is so great and basic features of the economy are not working properly, as they certainly were not in the early 1980s, it is the administration which will be held directly to blame. As Letowski puts it, thirty years ago it was still possible to blame the bakers whenever supplies of bread were deficient. Today everybody blames the appropriate administrative organ, and rightly so in an advanced socialist society. When the whole economy breaks down the official response, at least in the short term, is to intensify administrative controls and introduce rationing. The attitude of the population is one of cynical indignation towards all the representatives of the state, which may not remain passive if some novel organisation can mobilise the protests. Such a risk may exist potentially in other socialist countries, though none has yet devised such a lethal combination of economic incompetence and inflation of the bureaucracy. But the Polish case has further peculiarities. This variant of bureaucratic socialism does not in fact have anything like the total control to which it aspires. The countervailing power of the Roman Catholic Church cannot be expressed in political opposition; but it hardly needs this kind of demonstration, which might indeed conflict with its cultural and spiritual functions for the population. In the following chapters the strengths of contemporary Polish Catholicism will be compared and contrasted with those of secular culture and socialist ideology; we shall then be in a position to examine, in Chapter Eight, the full consequences for the social structure of the administrative mechanisms described here.

CHAPTER SIX

Religion

*. . . the moral-religious system not only retains almost all of its traditional power,
except in some limited circles, but is still growing as new conditions of communal life
arise and the old principle is applied to new problems.*
William I. Thomas and Florian Znaniecki (1918–20, p. 286)

The position of the Roman Catholic Church in Poland invites comparison with the other great Catholic nations of Europe. In the
second half of the twentieth century the spiritual hold of the church
appears to be greater in socialist Poland than in Italy or Spain, whilst
its political significance has no parallel in any other country (perhaps
the closest comparison would be with the position of the Irish church
before the achievement of independence). The distinctive characteristics of Polish Catholicism have been widely recognised, especially since Karol Wojtyla was elected Pope; but it is not always
appreciated how important a role religion played in the development of Polish national consciousness, especially from the latter half
of the nineteenth century, when this consciousness spread amongst
the rural population. In the case of the new community in Wisłok,
this background has an added significance because of the ethnic
troubles of the recent past and the physical reminders of the existence of another rite. This chapter begins by looking at the symbiosis
of church and nation produced by Polish history, for this can help us
to understand both the political role of the church today and the
private religiosity of individuals. We shall also note the particular
attention which the church pays to its rural constituency, and consider how this too has helped the parish to become the focus of a new
collective identity.

**The Roman Catholic Church is the national church of Poland and
has been compelled to play an increasingly complex political role
in the socialist period.**

A clear statement of how the Polish church sees its own position in
the history of the nation can be read in a public letter sent by the
Polish bishops to the German episcopate in the mid-1960s on the eve

of celebrations which, for the church, commemorated the mil-
lenium of Catholicism in Poland and, for the secular authorities, the
foundation of the Polish state. They wrote: 'The symbiosis of Christianity, Church, State has existed in Poland from the very beginning
and has never really been destroyed. In time it moulded the almost
universal political attitude: Polish has come to mean Catholic. From
this association there emerged, too, the Polish religious form, in
which the churchly and the political have been woven closely
together from the start, with all the positive as well as the negative
aspects of this problem . . .' (letter of November 18, 1965; translated
in *German Polish Dialogue*; Edition Atlantic-Forum, Bonn 1966)

   The secular authorities were incensed by this political initiative, as
in fact they often had been in the past, despite the Bishops' claims
concerning the fusion of church and state. A closer examination
reveals that relations between the two were actually rather turbulent
during several centuries of the Middle Ages (Saint Stanislaus being
the Polish Becket). In accounting for the unique strength of the
church in modern times, many historians attach the greatest importance to changes brought about by the Counter Reformation. It
should be noted, however, that in the seventeenth and eighteenth
centuries Poland remained on the whole a rare example of religious
tolerance in Europe, and a 'state without stakes'.[1] The accretion to
religious affiliation of an embryonic national identity was still
limited at this period to the educated classes, if indeed it had begun
at all. There is more widespread agreement that the institutional
survival of the church in long periods during which the state was
deprived of its independence (between 1794 and 1919; and again
under the Nazi occupation) helped to spread this confusion to all
social strata. Moreover, when it began to apply itself to the task in the
latter half of the nineteenth century, the church was able to play an
active role in the *creation* of national sentiment. In consequence, the
political emancipation of the Polish peasantry took place in such a
way as to bind them even more closely to their church. A new Polish
patriotism was indissoluble from their traditional commitment to
Catholicism.[2]

   For about the first decade of the socialist period relations between
the church and the new secular authorities were extremely bad. After
1956 both sides seemed to recognise the futility of direct confronta-
tion, and the relationship that has since developed has been subtle
and complex. It has been extensively studied, and the observers are
generally agreed that the church, in contrast to its performance in

101

other socialist states, has here held its ground if not actually enlarged it. However, it is also appreciated that statistical data, such as the figures which show high levels of participation in the life-cycle rituals of the church and the only slightly less impressive figures for those who attend mass regularly, cannot give a complete picture of religious commitment. They are not sufficient, for example, to refute the claim frequently made by the socialist authorities to the effect that Polish society is nevertheless undergoing profound secularisation.[3]

There is no doubt that the church is viewed by some Poles as a quasi-political institution, as the only possible vehicle for political opposition in a socialist system. Whatever the specifically religious meaning of a commitment to this church, which we shall consider below, Catholicism is for all a patriotic affirmation; whilst for some, affiliation is simultaneously a rejection of the communist order. One of the many paradoxes of this situation is that opposition to a doctrinaire establishment can only be expressed by allegiance to one of the more doctrinaire of religious creeds. It is fertile soil for a well-trained clergy, some of whom do not worry unduly about straying into territory that is controversial politically. In fact, there can be few countries where a priest is quite so free to lambast the establishment, secure in the knowledge that he himself cannot be identified by his congregation with the ruling classes. This is the regular pattern from country pulpits such as that of Wisłok. It is perhaps of equal significance in accounting for the continued religious commitment of the industrial working class. The church suffered so much in the Stalinist period, and is still frequently obstructed and harassed — thus, its priests can hardly be perceived as privileged, as a class enemy, though earlier generations of socialists may have tried to cast them in this light.[4]

One of the most graphic illustrations of the present power of the church has been in the unauthorised construction of new church buildings. The diocese of Przemyśl, to which Wisłok belongs, has been exceptionally prominent in this activity. It is a mainly rural diocese, and the proportion of practising Catholics ('*dominicantes*') is higher here than anywhere else in the country. A remarkable expansion in the number of vocations to the priesthood has enabled the diocese to mount an ambitious offensive to improve the quality of pastoral work. Smaller parishes have been created, and new churches constructed in outlying hamlets whose inhabitants formerly travelled elsewhere to attend mass. The authorities have the right to withhold planning permission and have often exercised this power to frustrate the building of churches, in both urban and rural parishes. However, in Przemyśl an exceptionally energetic Bishop has shrewdly encouraged the clergy to take matters into their own hands whenever unreasonable obstruction occurs. The latter have seized the opportunity to mobilise their congregations: building has invariably been accomplished not by professional firms but through self-help, in such a way as to reinforce group identity. Interference by the authorities and the fines imposed by the *kollegium* (see previous chapter) are taken in their stride. A notable example in which several Wisłok men participated was the establishment by the Komańcza parish priest of a new church (later to become an independent parish) in the village of Rzepedź, site of the sawmill and model socialist housing estates. It is typical too that this church was dedicated to Maximilian Kolbe, the Polish Franciscan who became a martyr at Auschwitz and was canonised by the Polish Pope, John Paul II.[5]

In political life at the national level the power of the church has been amply demonstrated in the successive crises of recent years. As the problems have worsened, the socialist politicians have looked to the church to restrain its followers, and have forged closer links with its leaders. For its part, the church has been wary of being drawn into unpopular compromise, but is keen to profit from a general relaxation of the previous climate of persecution. The emergence of *Solidarity* posed great dilemmas for the church. In spite of the sympathy and support given to the free trade union, the hierarchy was certainly mindful of the dangers. Its occasional efforts to curb militancy disappointed many intellectuals, and perhaps also some workers, who may have recognised at these moments that the church was principally concerned to ensure its own survival. The wisdom of its strategy would seem to be confirmed when *Solidarity* was duly repressed. The church was not treated in any way harshly in the period of martial law. It appears to have regained its optimal historical position as the exclusive institutional focus of opposition to the ruling power, and seems certain to remain a vital and generally respected mediator of the political process.

Traditional affectivity is supplemented by a social doctrine tailored especially for the peasantry

From 1980 to 1981 the Polish church was perceived to be, at every level, much more firmly committed to one wing of *Solidarity* than to any other. Its support at the highest level was instrumental in securing formal recognition in the courts for *Rural Solidarity* in May 1981, whilst at lower levels, the clergy vigorously encouraged the new syndicalism.[6] Under martial law the church was more cautious in most of its political statements, but did not hesitate to call for a revival of the peasants' independent union. This was not merely because workers were judged to be able to look after themselves. Behind the support for *Rural Solidarity* lies a more profound commitment on the part of the church to certain ideals and idealised notions of rural society. The Catholic Church has developed this theme in other countries, perhaps most successfully in Italy. There, as Guizzardi (1976) has shown, the myth of a 'rural civilization' based upon private property and the integrity of the family is manipulated by the church to preserve its own power and the legitimacy of Christian doctrine in the increasingly adverse conditions of industrial society. There is a comparable situation in Poland, in fact the circumstances here may be more propitious for such an ideology. In most parts of the Catholic countryside in Western Europe the peasant is rapidly disappearing in the course of modernisation; but in Poland the survival of the old agrarian structure has ensured that the configuration of social classes is still conducive to the propagation of this kind of ideology by the church. Thus, the failure to implement collectivisation, apart from its implications for the economy and for the political system, discussed in previous chapters, may also in this way have far-reaching effects upon consciousness. The persistence of peasant private property has helped the church to consolidate its position. This has obviously vexed socialist practitioners of 'religiology', whose scientific principles had led them to predict the opposite, i.e. a gradual weakening of religion.[7] Some have reacted by suggesting that support for the church in the present situation is not evidence of a genuine religious commitment, and they have accused the church of systematically adapting its religious package in order to maintain maximum social support. These claims are not entirely convincing. The church can fairly point out that in the inter-war period, when there was no realistic prospect that socialists would assume power, the Catholic hierarchy had already worked out a social doctrine similar in spirit to that propounded today, based upon a democracy of smallholders.[8]

It is nevertheless true that Polish Catholicism has changed considerably in the socialist period, and this can be interpreted as an accommodation by the church to new conditions, as successful an adaptation as that of the Counter Reformation in its day. The most conspicuous and frequently criticized features of pre-socialist Catholicism in Poland were those common in popular, charismatic religions elsewhere, and exemplified in Poland in Marian cults and pilgrimages to Częstochowa. The emphasis was placed upon 'the external, ritualistic aspect of worship unrelated to a moral and eucharistic life'.[9] William I. Thomas and Florian Znaniecki, in their classic account of the Polish peasantry (1918–20), reinforce this interpretation by playing down the significance of subjective, individualist interpretations of religious phenomena amongst the Polish peasantry, in contrast, for example, to the Russian peasantry under the Orthodox Church. It is possible that fundamental changes were taking place in this, the 'traditional religious culture' of the countryside, even before the socialist period. At any rate in recent decades secular pressure (e.g. preventing the church from organising public processions) has combined with reformist tendencies within the church itself (those which culminated at the second Vatican Council) to reduce the importance of external, 'ritualistic' aspects. The church which serves the new community in Wisłok illustrates the new situation. This small building is not the centre of a parish but a filial church of the Komańcza parish. It is used only on Sundays. Even on most holy days, apart from Christmas and All Saints, it remains closed. Sunday mass frequently brings together more than half the population. However, participation in other services and rituals is limited for most peasants to the major celebrations of the life-cycle (christenings, marriages and funerals), and to a child's first holy communion. Confessions are not held in Wisłok, and holy communion is usually made only by a few school children. At each mass the priest leads the congregation through a limited repertoire of hymns, of which by far the favourite is an invocation of the paramount national symbol, the Black Madonna of Częstochowa, hailed explicitly as the 'Queen of Poland'. About half a dozen young boys serve him at the altar. He encourages the congregation to bring objects to mass with them at specific times of the year for blessing — eggs at Easter tide and flowers a little later in the spring. He shows the church's readiness to modernise its ritual services by sprinkling holy water over private motor vehicles on Saint Christopher's Day (as yet there is no local demand for this service in Wisłok). The only occasion on which there is any procession or protracted ceremonial inside or outside the church is on the first of November, the eve of All Souls Day, when it is customary to sing and place candles beside the

11. Catholic priest blesses a visitor's motor-car on St. Christopher's Day.

12. Cemetery rituals on All Saints Day.

family graves. More elaborate rituals are organised in the main parish church in Komańcza, where it is possible to attend services daily, and also to prepare zealously for the major feasts (especially the Holy Week vigil, before Easter). In practice it is difficult for Wisłok residents to attend a church 10 km away, and only a few non-peasant women have time to do so. (Many hope that in time Wisłok itself will become a parish, with the services of a full-time priest.) I knew of nobody who had taken part in a major pilgrimage. However, many persons with relatives in villages outside the former *Rus* zone have experience of lesser patronal feasts (and choose this occasion each year to visit their relatives). Although the church in Komańcza has not held such celebrations on a significant scale, it is interesting that an attempt is being made to establish August 14 as a major holiday at the church of Maksymilian Kolbe in Rzepedź. The filial church in Wisłok does not have a patron saint at all. Pride in the first Polish Pope was universal amongst Poles. No one from Wisłok made the journey to Cracow to see him when he returned to his homeland in 1979, but many had a souvenir postcard prominently displayed in their home. A fine photograph of Pope John Paul II hangs inside the church, and in other alterations to this old Greek Catholic building, part of the surviving *Rus* iconostasis has been covered by two distinctively western portraits, one of Our Lord and the other of Our Lady (there was no female image previously), and by a large eagle, the Polish national symbol.

The strength of private religiosity in Wisłok was a matter into which I conducted no detailed enquiries, nor do I know of any method which would reliably reveal ultimate convictions. My own observations at Sunday mass and interviews in every household convince me that it is considerable, although it does not always influence behaviour in the way that might be expected.[10] The old emotional and ritualistic components have not disappeared entirely and religious images are conspicuous in almost every dwelling. Nevertheless, many traditional practices have been modified and the use since the second Vatican Council of the Polish vernacular in all services has perhaps done more than anything else to demystify religious ceremonies. The church has found more than adequate compensation through being able to encourage 'a more mature, intellectual approach to religious life' amongst large sections of the intelligentsia.[11] In the rural milieu it has developed its pre-socialist social doctrine, idealising all that the peasantry prizes most highly (and fears for constantly) under a socialist regime. In Wisłok

13. The surviving *Rus* church, used by the Roman Catholics since 1948.

ecclesiastical pomp and ceremony are minimal, but scarcely a Sunday passes without a reminder from the pulpit of God's hand (usually benevolent) at work in nature. Sermons are rich in agricultural metaphor, and the real shortages of food in 1981 gave them an added poignancy. The basic message was that God continually produces anew, whilst Poland's secular leaders had been sowing bad seed for nearly forty years. The wealth accumulated by past generations of peasants was being rapidly squandered. God was to be praised if the current harvest was good, but equally He should be praised for disasters such as the floods of 1980, if in this way those who have mismanaged the nation's inheritance may learn the errors of their ways. Like a majority of the clergy throughout the country, the priests who spoke in this vein in Wisłok were themselves of rural or small-town origin. One of them, an older man attached to the monastery in Komańcza who referred frequently to his extraction, was occasionally adjudged to overstep the mark in expressing his anti-communist sentiments. The parish priest himself was more discreet, preferring to expound more on the manifold, links between God and the natural environment, and to extol the historic legitimacy of the peasant family unit as tillers of the Polish soil. He thus eschews a dubious political role and never attempts to mobilise discontent collectively. He merely offers his congregation what they are ready overwhelmingly to accept as individuals, irrespective of whether or not they themselves own any land — a coherent system of values and an alternative ideology to communism.

The church can integrate diverse groups and create new patterns of social cooperation

So far we have noted that the Catholic Church in Poland is perceived as a bulwark of the national cause, and that in particular it supplies the peasantry with values more fundamental than any they have been offered by socialism. It still does what religion must do in simpler societies, where it '. . . establishes, fixes and enhances all valuable mental attitudes, such as reverence for tradition, harmony with environment, courage and confidence in the struggle with difficulties and at the prospect of death.'[12] However great the distance between the modern Polish village and the archetypal primitive community of the anthropologist, the functionalist approach still seems useful. I would contend, in some contrast to the account of traditional Polish religiosity put forward by Thomas and Znaniecki (1918–20), that the religiosity of individuals may now be stronger, whilst public performance of religious acts and ceremonial aspects tend to be less important today. However, I am in agreement with these authors on a more essential point: religion still functions to draw the community together, and the role of the church in stimulating new ties of solidarity has been of the greatest significance in a settlement composed of unusually diverse elements. Amongst the many ways in which a sense of community is fostered we shall look briefly at three: mass meetings of the congregation at the divine service, individual contacts with the parish priest, and neighbourhood ties and other forms of association called into being by the church.

The Sunday mass has always been the most important public occasion in the life of the rural community. In the *Rus* village the religious service was a transparent pretext for the social assembly: only the women entered the building at all during the warm summer months, whilst the men remained outside, chatted and played cards.[13] In the early stages of the new settlement the pioneer settlers strove to institute regular services and later to establish a new cemetery, separate from the old Greek Catholic burial grounds. Nowadays nobody remains outside during the service. But the men still aim to arrive early and their conversational groups do not disperse until the moment mass begins. Everybody dresses for the occasion, and it is common then to go on to visit family or friends in the afternoon. Attention is paid to church attendance, and regular non-attendance may well be a cause for reprobation. Most of those who incur this sanction earn their living in the socialist sector. The fact that seasonal workers in the forests seldom attend is explained by peasants in terms of irregularities in their domestic affairs, the presumed motive in most instances for their presence in the region. Such men do not become part of the community in any wider sense. On the other hand, most employees of the socialist sector who are long-term residents *do* attend church services, as do most of the teachers. As in other resettled areas of the Bieszczady region the peasants have a stronger identification with their parish than other groups, and this can be correlated with their stabilisation in the new environment and their loyalty to the region.[14]

The parish expresses the unity of the community, but the church building and adjacent cemetery are 'the visible symbol and the material instrument of this unity'.[15] This is no longer quite the case in Wisłok, for this village does not constitute a parish, and the Greek Catholic building probably does not satisfy the present Polish population aesthetically. It is one of only thirty-two filial churches in the 426 parishes of the diocese of Przemyśl. This makes the priest less accessible to his outlying parishioners, but it is recognised that in present circumstances Wisłok is still too small to warrant a resident priest. The present incumbent at Komańcza is a young man with considerable energy, who became personally acquainted with each family within a few years of his arrival. He is easy to approach and the congregation is regularly encouraged to use him as a pastor. He is respected as much for his personal qualities as for the prestige of his office, which cannot be said of many secular office-holders in the *gmina* of Komańcza. He is always extremely busy, but anyone reluctant to bother him with private matters has at least one opportunity in the year when he calls on them personally, 'in the carolling season'. This is an occasion for simple hospitality and a long chat in the deep of winter. The priest is welcomed into almost every home, both Polish and Ukrainian. Conversation may not touch upon religious matters at all. But the priest may use this opportunity to exert pressure, e.g. in households where a Catholic marriage has broken down or when a child is not participating regularly in catechism classes. In this way, through conscientious pastoral work, the influence of the church is better preserved than it would be, e.g. if the priest were to announce bluntly from the pulpit his intention to deny a religious funeral to anyone whose marital relations had not been validated by the church; this kind of sanction is never invoked in practice.

Thus, peasant families obtain a common identity in their parish, through the work of its attentive priest. Sunday assembly at the church and personal contacts are supplemented in a number of other ways. For example, in 1981 an association for Catholic women was launched, with around a dozen members initially participating in a series of prayer meetings. It soon atrophied, just as the secular Housewives' Circle had done earlier, simply because the peasant women had not the time to sustain their commitment when the agricultural season began. More important is the catechism for schoolchildren, normally taught by the priest himself in a peasant's farmhouse close to the village school. Attendance is almost universal, though the attitudes of some non-peasant parents are ambiguous, and their children may not participate beyond the completion of their first holy communion. As throughout Poland, there has been in the past acrimonious discussion over the priest's right to perform this instruction inside the school, or even within the official curriculum. In some areas he is able to use the school, but the Komańcza priest is satisfied with the present arrangements, which leave him complete control over the manner in which the faith is taught to future generations.

In 1980 I witnessed a rare occasion when religion brought together, outside the church itself, large social groups which would not otherwise have gathered. The circulation of replica effigies of the Black Madonna of Częstochowa is nowadays organised mainly at diocesan level, through national campaigns have been mounted in the past. Arrangements once the image has arrived in a parish are left very much in local hands. During her stay in Wisłok the Madonna spent twenty-four hours in each house, before being carried aloft in a procession to the next. She was invariably displayed in the best room in the house (if it contained more than one), often surrounded by lesser images and adorned with coloured lights. A few small pews were occupied by the old and infirm, whilst up to fifty or sixty persons stood nearby. These always included the immediate neighbours, those with whom the Madonna had lodged the previous night, and to whom she would go on the morrow. The composition of the rest of the crowd would depend upon the popularity of the family,

111

and the numbers of their kin in the village. Most families were keen to attract a respectable attendance, yet this was a holy occasion and hospitality was almost entirely precluded. Certainly there was no drinking of alcohol. Peasants and non-peasant families nonetheless did turn out, in the early hours of the evening, at a time of year when there was a great deal of work in the fields, and spend two or three hours singing hymns and reciting all the prayers that they knew in front of this holy image. Each family was anxious that nothing should be missed out in their house, and the best known hymns to the Virgin were sung many times over. Children were frequently called upon to read prayers. Many older persons were moved to tears. This was clearly a visceral experience which involved all three of the levels at which we have been discussing the functions of religion. This image of the 'national virgin' was a most potent symbol for the individuals who gathered before her, and the way in which she circulated helped to cement the social unity of the parish.[16]

The image visited almost every house in the village, including those of Ukrainian families (where it looked most at home, surrounded by icon reproductions). It was explicitly rejected by only one household of confirmed atheists, recent immigrants brought up in an urban environment (see Krzysztof Oltarzewski's own description of the problems he encountered in Wisłok, partly through failing to conform to peasant requirements in this respect, in the Appendix — 'Two Immigrants'). In the judgement of most villagers this was enough to place them beyond the pale of the community, and it does illustrate how very difficult it is in the Polish countryside to maintain even an agnostic position.[17] Peasants are more tolerant of common law marriages or still more flagrant breaches of the Catholic moral code than they are of a man who will work on Sunday if it suits him and makes a point of not sending his children to catechism. The priest, however, is tolerant of all wrongdoers, and he still regards this family as part of his flock. Under pressure from their own urban relatives they were obliged to turn to the priest the following year and *ask* him to baptize their younger son, then four years old. The priest was flexible enough to accede to this request, and the ceremony took place as usual in the course of a Sunday mass. There was great surprise in some quarters, and I heard some more favourable comments about this family afterwards.

Three contrasts

From both ethnic and religious standpoints Poland has been, since the end of the Second World War, one of the most homogeneous states in Europe. The Roman Catholic Poles of Wisłok are therefore in an unusual position in being bounded to the east, west and north by three very different types of community (to the south there is the state border with Czechoslovakia, where only a few Ukrainians have some family contacts). Although I am not at all sure to what extent the religious consciousness of Wisłok residents is affected by this diversity, some peasants do draw comparisons. Each of these neighbouring communities is a case worthy of consideration in its own right.

10 km to the east along the main road from Wisłok is the commune centre of Komańcza, where the same small wooden chapel which serves the Roman Catholic parish is also used by a Greek Catholic (Uniate) priest. His congregation comprises the descendants of the indigenous *Rus* population, nowadays widely dispersed and in most villages outnumbered by Poles. The largest concentration is in Komańcza itself, causing some Poles in Wisłok to describe their commune-centre mockingly as 'the capital of the Ukraine'. Despite the crass religious policies of the authorities, noted in the previous chapter, there is little tension between the two main congregations. Inter-marriage is common, and the trend regretfully acknowledged by the Greek Catholic priest himself is one of rapid assimilation into Polish society. One aspect of this is the younger generation's abandonment of the Byzantine rite. Relations between the two Catholic priests are very cordial; and with the firm allegiance of about eighty families (nearly half the population of the village) the Greek Catholics are still a force to be reckoned with in Komańcza.

Many Wisłok residents had been conditioned by anti-Ukrainian propaganda long before they migrated to the mountain zone and had any direct contact with a non-Polish ethnic group. This is as true of the first peasant immigrants who arrived after the liquidation of the guerilla bands in the 1940s as of the atheist immigrant from an urban background who arrived only in the 1970s. A good deal of prejudice extends to religious matters. Amongst the Ukrainian families in Wisłok there is not one which would refuse to welcome the Latin rite priest into the home; but most prefer to attend their own services in Komańcza whenever possible. They observe Polish religious holidays, but also those of their own calendar. There are a few old peasants who say that they find it painful to enter a church which they built (i.e. the church in Wisłok), but where they now hear a Latin rite service, in a language which they understand but cannot call their own. The presence of such a small group in the village, and the more conspicuous Ukrainian presence in Komańcza, has an unfortunate influence on some members of the new majority. The surviving roadside shrines, crosses and inscriptions in the churchyard, the church building itself — these are all tangible reminders that Wisłok once belonged to another religion and another people. Some Poles would gladly destroy all these traces. Official Roman Catholic policy is more restrained, but has not prevented the destruction of many Ukrainian churches in recent years.[18] So long as attitudes of deep mistrust persist the age-old identification of religious creed and national identity will be reinforced for the inhabitants of this village. To this extent the Ukrainian minority in Wisłok cannot be fully incorporated into the Roman Catholic parish.

Quite different conclusions may be drawn from the experience of the village of Wola Piotrowa, although this may be less prominent in the consciousness of Wisłok residents. This village is located about 10 km to the north, close to the road which leads from Wisłok to the small town of Bukowsko. This route over the mountains is nowadays used only by forestry workers. Like other villages of the region it was depopulated and destroyed in 1947. Unlike Wisłok it was not resettled until more than twenty years later, but the story which then began was one of the most remarkable of the entire Bieszczady region and a much publicised example of its very wide appeal. Poor peasants came to Bieszczady because they were promised land, foreign refugees (notably Greek communists) found asylum here, criminal offenders found a place where they could forget their past, and students found a place to drop out. Wola Piotrowa became the 'promised land' in a profoundly religious sense of a Protestant sect which originated in California in the early part of this century, spread to Poland via Germany in the inter-war period, and has continued to flourish under socialism. Indeed, they alone amongst peasant immigrants to this region have succeeded in transcending peasant status in socialist conditions. Although loosely associated with other tiny groups throughout the country, the three villages settled by the sect in the Bieszczady region (of which Wola Piotrowa is largest) are recognised collectively as an autonomous religious grouping by the secular authorities, who have registered them as the *Bieszczady Protestant Community*. Their own name for themselves is 'Union for a Resolute Christianity'.[19]

In 1981 the village contained thirty families, all residing in large modern houses, most of them owning cars, but all regulating their lives according to a strict moral code and denying themselves not only alcohol and tobacco but even television or the occasional cinema trip. Most of them are farmers, and they have been lauded in national agrarian publications for their diligence and innovations on the land. Their farms are not larger than farms in Wisłok, but, having sought and obtained larger credits, they are incomparably better equipped and it would no longer be appropriate, given the large surpluses which they market, to describe them as peasants. Each household modestly attributes its success to the help it has received, both from the state and also from neighbours and kin, especially in the period when they were building up their farms. Certainly the community is more tightly knit than the new community in Wisłok. It does not, however, have much room for communal principles in economic life. Their successes have been achieved by individual endeavour, they too are proud to be private owners of their land; when the outside authorities persuaded them to establish a produc- ers' cooperative, this venture was the first failure after many years of unmitigated prosperity. Observers from neighbouring villages explain their results not in terms of mutual support for each other, but in terms of individual diligence in application. (And they cer- tainly did not offer vodka as a bribe in order to obtain what they needed from the administration; it seems more reasonable to sug- gest that they succeeded in official quarters by dint of greater perse- verance; and it is possible there was discrimination in their favour, since it was clear that no credits or supplies would be wasted by these farmers: they wanted to market as much produce as possible to the state.) It is not to be concluded that it is religion which prevents Polish peasants from following this path — on the contrary, the more modern farmers in Wisłok also tended to be the more devout Catholics. It is simply that the religion-based zeal of this community was strong enough to transcend all the 'rational', economic factors outlined earlier, which are blocking modernisation for the peasantry as a whole.[20]

Two further perceptions, voiced by Poles from other villages nearby, are worthy of note. Firstly, it is considered as odd (though perhaps admirable) that one's faith should influence one's daily behaviour to such an extent. Thus, Catholics in Wisłok, whether Poles or Ukrainians, see little connection between their religion and gross over-indulgence in alcohol (though the church is nowadays trying hard to encourage temperance). It seems that Catholics are more oblivious to the bearing of the moral teaching of the church upon many aspects of personal behaviour, and this is why the strength of their religious commitment has been questioned. But to the outsiders it is the sect which makes such extreme demands upon the individual that is the puzzling phenomenon. A second revealing feature of local perceptions of the people of Wola Piotrowa is the way their otherness is sometimes classified. If, faced with basically the same existential situation, they have behaved so differently from the majority of Poles, it became natural to bestow upon them a different ethnic label. The group hailed from the Cieszyn (Teschen) area, near the border with Czechoslovakia, and a few actually originated from the other side of the state boundary. Although all were 'ethnic Poles' and few spoke any other language (some knew German), this was enough for some of their Bieszczady neighbours to christen them 'the Czechs', and in this way again to complement a different religion with foreign ethnicity.

The third and last contrasting community is Moszczaniec, about 6 km west of Wisłok along the main road. Since the late 1950s Moszczaniec has witnessed the construction of a large penal colony, with room for up to about 500 prisoners. Warders and other ancillary staff, including officials of the State Farm on which most of the prisoners work, are accommodated on a new housing estate in four-storeyed blocks of flats. It is a sort of garrison settlement, provisioned directly from Komańcza, without a shop, a school, or public institutions of any kind. It has no church, and relatively few inhabitants attend the services in Wisłok. For the peasants the settlement at Moszczaniec has represented something deeply disturbing. The staff there is as emphatically outside the community of civilised society as the prisoners themselves. Warders are looked upon with some contempt: their uniforms distinguish them from those who have to work honestly for a living, and although they enjoy prosperity and relative comfort in their state-owned accommodation, they have turned their backs on God. A few Wisłok families have relatives on the dechristianised estate, and these can be drawn into the Wisłok community (they are then unlikely to gain rapid promotion in the prison service). No ties are maintained with persons who do not attend church. The priest, who will not acknowledge the presence of a single atheist in Wisłok, allows that many workers in the socialised sector are permanently estranged from the church. A high proportion of these people have found their way to Bieszczady after coming into conflict with the church in their native regions. For such people, in contrast to the mass of peasant immigrants, a strong identity with the new region is possible without allegiance to the church. Their individual stories are not known and are of no interest in Wisłok. A free man who chooses not to go to church is as remote from their community as the shaven-headed convicts with whom they may mingle more readily (and to whom the local clergy has consistently been denied access). Nobody calls into question their ethnic identity, any more than they question the Polishness of the one atheist within their own farming ranks. In the same way that Komańcza represents the threat posed by the Ukrainian minority on a magnified scale, so Moszczaniec is the atheist threat writ large. It is the secularised community which has been prominent in socialist ideology since the new community in Wisłok was founded, though to peasants it is no more acceptable now than it was then. (We shall consider the effects of secular ideology and culture in more detail in the following chapter.)

The aspect of religion most clearly brought out by these brief sketches of contrasting communities is the *integrating* function. The 'new conditions of communal life' to which Thomas and Znaniecki refer in the quotation at the head of this chapter were in fact the conditions of emigrants in North America. But the 'old principle', according to which social unity was forged by the parish and allegiance to the church confused with allegiance to the nation, has still been of use in the construction of a new society in Wisłok. Atheists excluded themselves completely. The Ukrainians, Catholics of another rite, were less than fully incorporated. With these qualifications religion has still been the basis of what Thomas and Znaniecki term the 'moral unity' of the current peasant community in Wisłok. Malinowski, too, considered that one of the main functions of religion in primitive communities was the maintenance of moral standards. It is now time to turn to the secular context of an advanced socialist society in order to understand how religion can retain its 'moral' importance whilst having but little effect on individual behaviour.

CHAPTER SEVEN

Secular Ideology and Socialisation

. . . the educational ideal is to develop a type of new man, one who has internalized the moral values growing out of the Socialist belief system and, at the same time, continues the best of Polish traditional culture.

Joseph R. Fiszmann (1972, p. 106)

In ideal-type models of the totalitarian state great emphasis is always placed upon the role of ideology. Some have been tempted to argue that dogmatic Marxism-Leninism, despite its rationalist foundations, has become a religious system, though perhaps of a rather special kind.[1] Its coexistence with a strong, traditional church makes the Polish case much more complex than the 'totalitarian' model allows. In recent years the Communist Party has been struggling to maintain the illusion of 'hegemony' which its ideologues claim for it. To the outside observer it often seems that church and state are competing for the same ground — in particular, for custody of certain nationalist symbols, in which the deepest historical legitimacy is perceived to lie. Thus, the church is frequently to be seen taking initiatives outside the religious sphere, narrowly defined, whilst the state has been consciously encouraging new, secular patterns of ritual behaviour. Certainly, neither has been static over the years, and we have noted already, for example, major changes in emphasis in the position taken towards non-socialised agriculture. Yet Polish peasants themselves do not see any convergence. Early communist leaders may have sought to present socialism in the guise of a competing church. But we have noted already that aggressive anti-Catholic policies were counter-productive: they only increased the vitality of the traditional religion. The secular 'world-view' (*światopogląd, weltanschauung*) is weakly developed in all sections of Polish society, but especially amongst the rural section. But, given the general failures of secularisation policy, the aim of this chapter is to consider whether the socialist authorities have nevertheless succeeded in injecting a socialist character into certain other areas of consciousness. If we find but little evidence of 'new socialist man', the causes must be sought not in the vicissitudes of economic crises, but deeper in the processes of socialisation.

118

The gulf between the ideals of the system and its reality is nowhere greater than in an isolated village

The populist rhetoric which enticed immigrants to Wisłok after 1948 was calculated to appeal to the peasant's hankering for a viable, independent farm. These pioneers were led to expect a great deal from the 'new government of the workers and the peasants', and their later disillusionment was proportionately intense. Those who arrived at the height of the Stalinist period, influenced by success stories like the one related in the Appendix, found that although the ideology might still be populist (in propaganda brochures), the reality was already socialist. Their plots were barely sufficient for subsistence, the new peasants were not free to choose what crops they sowed, they were required to assist in the establishment of the State Farms, and they were often unable to repay the credits they obtained. Their general situation began to improve, though not substantially, after 1956. But the consciousness of the new peasant farmers was moulded irrevocably in the Stalinist years. Thus, they remained mistrustful of the Agricultural Circle, even when nominally under their control in the 1960s. Their attitudes towards the socialist sector of agriculture became more cynical in the 1970s, for reasons described in Chapter Three. So deeply rooted is the aversion of some peasants that they advise their children against a career in this part of the socialised sector in the strongest possible terms. Industrial work is popular, but even here some parents would prefer their children to remain as simple workers, lest they be tarnished by the responsibilities of any higher position. Such advice is based on their own experience of the socialised sector and their degrading contacts with the local administration. It is noteworthy that the policies of the 1970s, designed to permit a select minority of farmers to modernise and expand their enterprises, had to be accompanied by a significant ideological shift in the other direction, emphasising the inevitability of socialist sector dominance. It is not surprising, in these circumstances, that objective possibilities and intentions are confused; and if there is any doubt in the peasant's mind, his rule of thumb is to mistrust the authorities and to assume that Polish socialists are ultimately concerned to emulate all neighbouring socialist states and collectivise agriculture. Thus, new policies are interpreted with reference to this root paradigm of the socialist system, and the aggressive ideological stance of the Gierek years emphasised this tendency. It would have been different if a more revisionist leadership had tried to argue that socialism does not really require collectivisation at all, since the factor 'land' is not really one of the means of production. But dogged opposition to the registration of *Rural Solidarity* in 1981, lasting many months after the workers' movement obtained formal recognition, suggested that ideological rigidity towards the peasantry was continuing into the 1980s. Since the imposition of martial law no new unions have been permitted to form amongst the peasantry, in contrast to the considerable efforts to establish new unions for workers, and this too has been noted. Consequently, many peasants feel that they have been granted no more than a stay of execution as private owners. This uncertainty, which must adversely effect the effort they put into their farms, seems to arise from dogmas essential to the socialist system; and the instinct which makes peasants resist the confiscation of their lands makes them implacable enemies of everything which they can identify with this system.[2]

Peasants are strictly only one group in the village, not even the most numerous group, though it has been argued that they determine its ethos and provide its underlying stability. But resistance to socialist norms is equally evident amongst families which obtain their livelihood in the socialist sector. Poor labour discipline and the fact that some workers reserve their energies for work at home are the crucial problems here, as they are in other socialist systems where genuine opportunities to make money exist in the 'second' or 'informal' economy. Those employed at the State Farm or at the Agricultural Circle (now the SKR) do not suppose that these examples of socialist ownership have been conducive to economic efficiency and are in any way superior to peasant property.[3] The performance of the existing socialist institutions does not facilitate the acquisition of a socialist consciousness.

Of course, the style in which ideological campaigns are waged has changed greatly over the years, from mass agitation organised at the community centre in the 1950s to the more soft-sell approach in vogue in most of the socialist world today. In accounting for the patent lack of success, many are inclined to look at factors in the high culture of the nation before it encountered socialism, or to concentrate upon the historical traditions of the peasantry.[4] It needs also to be stressed that socialist ideals were contradicted by actual social and economic conditions at every stage, and this was particularly true in Wisłok, where the motivation to succeed as an independent peasant farmer had inspired migration in the first place. It is also difficult not to feel that the surfeit in the Stalinist period and again during the years of Gierek's 'propaganda of success' was deeply counter-productive. The principal channels nowadays are the broadcasting media and the press. Both of these have been, except briefly during 1981, under tight official control. Their influence is inestimable, but undoubtedly the effects are not always the ones intended. Very few persons subscribe to the party dailies, even to the regional variant covering the south-eastern counties. The papers most widely read are those produced for farmers, but the most popular of all is a weekly magazine for women. The demand for this exceeds the village's quota (thus, to obtain the papers one wants to read it is important to be on good terms with the postmaster, who controls this particular distributional problem). Television is an altogether more insidious weapon. It was a very social institution in the village until the 1970s, when almost all families finally bought their own. My impression was that some viewers were remarkably alert and do not hesitate to switch off when they sniff propaganda. Transmissions of interminable speeches by Gierek were seldom endured; there was equally great irritation in 1981, when films or other entertainment features were delayed or cancelled to permit newscasters to spin another anti-*Solidarity* yarn. The important point is that, however complete the controls which the authorities exercise over the media, the peasants are not easily duped. The greater the torrent of prop-aganda, the more glaring the contrast between media 'newspeak' and everyday reality in the village becomes.

The media may elicit a particularly negative response in the rural population, for they tend to heighten the feeling of relative depriva-tion vis-à-vis the towns. This can be found in more successful social-ist countries, but is more conspicuous in the country where collectiv-isation has not been achieved and overall public investment in the rural sector low.[5] The bias of the media reflects the commitment of the regime to urbanisation and industrialisation, with little attention paid to farming or forestry, etc. When the Wisłok peasant watches a clip about a new washing-machine factory on the television he is likely to be reminded that many village families still do their washing in the river because they have no piped water and the well is none too clean; and he will conceive of socialism as a system for the advance-ment of urban civilisation alone. The avowed intention of reducing the gap between town and countryside has not been a prominent feature of socialist ideology in recent years. In fact, in the crisis years the authorities frequently tried to exploit in urban dwellers resent-

ment of the outstanding advantage still enjoyed by the peasantry —
its ability to feed itself. In this way media manipulation was partially
successful in undermining the unity of the opposition movement.
Peasants were accused indiscriminately of hoarding and black market speculation, whilst rural society was inflamed by accounts of idle
coal mines and striking factories, at times when their products were
desperately needed in the countryside. Many Wisłok peasants have
worked in major industrial centres, typically living a marginal existence in workers' hostels from which they were glad to escape back to
the village. They have few illusions about the quality of life of those
who succeed in settling permanently in the town, but they also know
that the town offers a more comfortable home to a large white-collar
elite. Perceptions of this class became clearer with the revelations of
some notorious scandals in the early 1980s and must have increased
the estrangement of the peasantry from socialist ideals (though
without necessarily leading them actively to make common cause
with industrial workers).

Resentment, disillusionment and cynicism were widespread by
the end of the 1970s, and again in the wake of the repression of
Solidarity. After years of sterility Gierek had apparently promised a
new brand of socialism. The economy was indeed dynamic at first,
and the consumer benefited to a greater degree than ever before.
The progress (made possible largely by western credits) could not be
sustained, and only created a new problem of rising expectations. In
the early 1970s, only old socialists of the Gomulka vintage had
doubts about the policy instruments employed. In the early 1980s,
with the regime bankrupt in every sense, ordinary citizens unsym-
pathetic to communism could obtain ironic satisfaction by judging
their leaders according to socialist standards. A favourite case in
point was the black market in hard currency, which arose out of
deliberate policies to expand the network of dollar shops in Poland.
Whether one needed building materials for a house, spare parts for a
car, an acceptable gift to offer at a wedding or a safe means of
contraception, it became essential to have dollars. When the
debasement of the złoty reached its peak, even vodka, cigarettes
and basic toiletries were obtainable only for foreign currency (at this
point, in 1981, these goods were subjected to rationing, though
supplies were still often insufficient to meet the entitlement). Need-
less to say, dollars are not easily come by for peasants in Wisłok, few
of whom have relatives in the West. Those who have received help
from abroad are liable to be subjects of a fierce envy. Some peasants

tried to raise dollars in the towns of Sanok and Krosno, but despite their willingness to pay well in excess of the established black market rate they were often unsuccessful. Any visitor to these towns can walk into the 'Pewex' shops and inspect a range of goods he cannot hope to obtain unless he has hard currency. It must be no less galling to know that apartments and cars can also be obtained quickly and cheaply — if one pays in dollars. In the early 1980s many younger persons sought, often illegally, to work in the West. Older members of the family were happy to look after any young children they left behind, understood the temptation to remain permanently abroad and made ironic comparisons with migrant labour patterns in the pre-socialist period.[6] In this small village during the period that I was conducting fieldwork there were cases of both permanent and temporary migration abroad. The key factor in both cases was a prior family contact in the country of destination. There is no doubt that many more would leave if they saw any opportunity, and that they would have the sympathy and understanding of those they leave behind. The latter will continue to direct their bitterness and cynicism towards their socialist rulers, in whose hands socialist ideology has failed to satisfy the elementary dictates of distributive justice. It is perhaps remarkable that socialism is still popularly linked with ideals of social equality, and that cynicism is reserved for politicians who are falling short of their self-imposed standards. But it is appreciated that socialism is more successful in other countries (and, for example, that many of the items available only for dollars in Poland are available in neighbouring states for the national currency). The danger of the current situation is that some basic, lingering, normative perceptions of socialism as an egalitarian system will also disappear. It will in future be seen in the popular consciousness not only as a threat to individual property rights and as an economy of chronic shortage, but also as a system in which, outside the new intelligentsia, only those with windfall income from abroad can live tolerably well.

The educational system substitutes patriotism for the raising of socialist consciousness

It might be argued that the negative picture painted above is very much the product of the mismanagement of the 1970s, and that this does not reflect either upon other features of the Polish case (such as the failure to collectivise) or upon socialism as such. However, although recent crises have caused the system to be perceived in a worse light than before, I would contend that the consciousness of relative deprivation in rural areas has been a fairly constant feature, and one that is not peculiar to Poland. Let us now look more closely at how the authorities have sought to nurture minds that are too young to remember earlier crises in the construction of socialism in Poland. Adults may be to some extent immune to the manipulations of the mass media, but are the younger members of society nevertheless vulnerable through a state-controlled educational process?

A negative answer is suggested by Fiszmann (1972), who concentrates on the inability of the teachers themselves to perform the tasks expected of them. This author collected his data in the 1960s, but recent evidence from Wisłok supports his analysis. The staff at the village school is now entirely female (though the two headmasters of the 1970s were male). The complement is only four, the same as the number of diminutive classrooms available in the old building that once served as a Greek Catholic presbytery. The number of grades is theoretically eight, and is soon to be increased to ten. In practice the numbers of children are no longer great enough to warrant creating a fresh class each year, so that some children may either start late or be bussed to the larger school in Komańcza, to which Wisłok is subordinated. The staff is not highly trained. Several of those who have taught there in recent years have been fresh from their own studies at secondary level, although they should, in theory, have completed at least a two-year teacher-training course. Those who do possess this latter qualification are aware that it is substantially inferior to a university degree and to certain other pedagogical qualifications. If a school head has only this qualification he is encouraged to supplement it through correspondence courses. The prestige of the teacher is seriously diminished by their low salaries. As in other rural areas of Poland, these teachers are in the village only because their husbands are working there (none of them as peasants). Few have the 'secular world view' that is ideally expected of them. The present headmistress is not afraid to be seen in church on Sundays. It is her responsibility to teach civics (*wychowanie obywatelskie*) in the school, for which the syllabus includes the diffusion of information about the construction of socialism and the socio-economic and political system of the People's Republic.

The teachers to whom I talked in 1981 had very mixed feelings about the socialist achievement in the field of education. Items such as paper and chalk were unavailable at the time. The new building

The current school, with exhortations 'to build the new Poland' on playground poster, foreground.

which they had been promised for years seemed as far off as ever. Yet it was possible to excuse such material shortcomings, and it was pointed out that schooling was still less adequate in the pre-war countryside. Today at least all children do attend school, and since 1966 the eight grades have been compulsory (starting at around the age of seven). Moreover, most children nowadays proceed to some kind of secondary school, of which there are several main types. The majority of children from Wisłok go on to basic vocational schools. Local teachers feel that they are greatly handicapped compared to urban children, firstly in not being able to develop special high-prestige interests (such as drama or ballet) at secondary school level; secondly, in gaining access to higher education.[7] Some teachers even considered that more opportunities were open to the most talented rural children in the pre-war system. The teaching staff is dissatisfied with the policy that all children should, if at all possible, complete the eight grades, so that the statistics will look healthy when forwarded to the county authorities. They are thus discouraged from making pupils repeat grades, whilst if they dare to suggest remedial training they will be condemned by parents and by their administrative superiors alike. The nearest facilities are in Sanok (50 km), and quite apart from any deeper feelings of indignity, peasant families will

125

have difficulty in bearing the costs of hostel accommodation. To an outside observer these costs are not particularly high at all, but to the peasant, unaccustomed to spending anything on educational outlays, they often seem excessive. Hence, this factor has enormous bearing upon whether children continue their education at all beyond the age at which they may start earning (normally fifteen years; there are restrictions for certain types of work, such as forestry, where the minimum age is theoretically eighteen years, but these are not very effective).

The Wisłok teachers are prone to complain that parents take little interest in their children's progress at school and do not turn up to the meetings to which they are occasionally invited. Some parents certainly are indifferent, particularly those who are illiterate themselves, or experienced only a few years primary education. But others have complained about falling standards in the transmission of basic literacy and numeracy, and also criticised the failure to encourage any extra-curricular activities, such as excursions. For children who have little opportunity to travel outside their region, the prospect of a day-trip to Cracow or to Zakopane is thrilling; but it very seldom happens. The village school does not participate regularly in county or regional competitions called *olimpiady*, which are both sporting and academic in character. It makes no use of equipment which is available to it, for instance, to put on film-shows in the village. The teachers no longer organise adult evening classes, as they did formerly. In short the school is not a popular community institution. The only festive occasion is a party held at the end of the academic year for those graduating, to which parents are normally invited. Neither teachers nor parents have responded to suggestions from the Komańcza officials that the community should take some initiative in the construction of a new school, of the sort frequently taken, as we have seen, in the construction of new churches.

Given the conditions in which the teachers work and the demands made upon them it is scarcely surprising that they are nowadays rather reluctant to become social activists in the traditions of the rural intelligentsia of the past.[8] It would be even more remarkable if they were capable of nurturing a 'new man' committed to socialist ideology. But there is one rich vein which socialist educators have not been slow to mine, the vein of patriotism. Once again the 1970s were a most significant decade, for they witnessed a determined attempt by the secular authorities to substitute the socialist state for the Catholic Church as the prime focus of national sentiment. As an illustration, let us peer into the scrapbook compiled by the form teacher for the class enrolled in 1979. It contained ten pupils, aged around seven years, most of whom had already had at least one year of nursery school at the Moszczaniec complex (this is a recent innovation; formerly there were no facilities of any kind before school began at the age of seven). Here is the 'oath' recited by each child on his first day at school:

Akt Mianowania
I, the youngest pupil at the primary school at Wisłok, pledge my oath on the banner of my fatherland that I will be a good Pole. I shall be careful to preserve the good name of my class and school. I shall learn how to love my fatherland and how to work for it when I am grown up.

10 signatures, September 1979.

This sort of declaration at this age might leave no stronger mark than religious instruction leaves upon most schoolchildren in the West. But in Poland the strong emphasis placed upon the inculcation of national pride intensifies during the pupil's later years. A hint of the atmosphere is conveyed by the school's festive calendar, which is promulgated not by the local headmistress but by her superiors in Komańcza, who are in turn obeying instructions from the county. The glorious evocation of the exploits of Polish soldiers (and Polish socialists in particular) during the Second World War is one conspicuous feature of the centrally laid-down syllabus. Pupils in the eighth grade are supposed to receive eighteen hours of instruction on this topic, including such sensitive matters as 'the political causes of the outbreak of the Warsaw Uprising'. Teachers do not necessarily present the material in the crude, one-sided way in which it is presented by the text-book. I was told of an occasion when an old local forester, a veteran of the Battle of Monte Cassino, was invited to the school to give children a true impression of the role played by the Polish Army commanded by the London government in exile. However, it is extremely unlikely that any local person would be allowed to present the Ukrainian justification for the resistance struggle waged by UPA in this mountain region when the war was over. Nationalist opposition, and other forms of opposition to the early socialist regime, have been consistently associated with the horrors of Nazism. The lurid stereotypes of popular films and fiction concerning the last war and its terrorist aftermath no doubt offer greater distortions than the school textbooks. But the very fact that such attention is devoted to these events to them in school must reinforce the impact of the media in this respect: such films are extremely popular, whilst books about the resistance of Poles during the war and the crushing of Ukrainian resistance after it are the books in most demand, by all age-groups, from the village library. This may have little to do with socialism, but such accounts of recent history may serve the authorities well in legitimising the socialist state to the younger generation.[9]

SCHOOL CALENDAR 1980–81

DATE	EVENT	NOTES (format of the celebration etc.)
1st September	Opening of school year; meeting with parents; 41st anniversary of the outbreak of Second World War	Festive Celebration
12th October	Polish Army Day	Visit of locally-stationed soldiers
14th October	Teachers' Day	Festive Celebration
7th November	63rd anniversary of the Great Socialist October Revolution	Festive Celebration
4th December	Miners' Day	Talk
early January	Christmas and New Year celebration	Party
17th January	36th anniversary of the Liberation of Warsaw	Assembly and Parade
8th March	Ladies' Day	Festive Celebration (presents for teachers)
April (entire month)	Month of National Remembrance	Talk
1st May	Labour Day [*Not in fact observed* — author's note]	
9th May	Victory Day	Festive Celebration
May	Days of Culture and Education, Books and the Press	
1st June	Children's Day	Party
10th June	Graduation Ceremony; end of the school year	Evening party for graduating pupils, parents and staff
added later:	[*For the first and only time under socialism* —author's note]	
3rd May	190th anniversary of proclamation of liberal constitution	Festive Celebration

Alcohol is a consolation, but also an illustration of how the total responsibilities claimed by the secular authorities may rebound against them

Patriotism may be the most important area of social consciousness susceptible to socialist infiltration, especially for those excluded from the high culture of the nation in the past and now exposed for the first time to a more formalised and systematic educational process. However, even this must not be exaggerated, since many pupils seem to acquire little more in this regard than a smattering of military history and a passing acquaintance with the more romantic heroes of the novelist Henryk Sienkiewicz. Studies have shown that their image of the 'Polish national character' is not altogether flattering, and one of the most prominent negative features is an excessive penchant for drink.[10] Alcohol is used by virtually the entire adult population of Wisłok (there may be one or two elderly ladies who would decline a tot, or to whom it is never offered), and imbibed in excessive quantities, with great frequency, by a high proportion. Irrespective of the age at which young persons themselves begin to drink — some of them begin whilst still attending primary school in the village[11] — alcohol is so conspicuous that it must be presumed to play a major part in socialisation.

Vodka is the staple. Since the Circle of Rural Housewives protested a few years ago (see pp. 86, 92) it has not been available at the village store. The nearest shop is in Komańcza, and the cafe in the commune centre is the nearest place where Wisłok residents may drink vodka in public. Per capita spirit consumption in Poland rose sharply in the 1970s, to reach one of the highest levels in Europe. After 1978 there were several sharp price increases, but, as other socialist countries have also discovered, these had virtually no effect in restraining consumption.[12] When the crisis deepened in the 1980s, availability became the sole relevant factor. Readiness to stand in line for a product which (theoretically) could be stored for long periods was high. Eventually vodka was added to the list of items distributed through ration tickets, with an allocation of half a litre to each adult per month.

Beer might be able to compete more effectively with vodka if it were of higher quality and were consistently available. Since it does not meet these criteria, the only alternative is cheap wine. This is the only alcoholic beverage still retailed from the Wisłok store. It is a sweet concoction, very cheap compared to vodka, and considered by peasants to be greatly inferior though not inherently dangerous (condemnation on health grounds is restricted to the consumption of commercial alcohol, *denaturat*, which has been used by at least one individual in the village). Cheap fruit wine as a substitute for vodka is especially popular with forestry workers, who gather at the local shop whenever it is in stock. Their drinking bouts on the grass outside usually last several hours, sometimes provoke minor outrage amongst other customers at the store, but never serious affray. This is the only opportunity for public drinking in the village, i.e. for men to drink away from the often reproachful eyes of their families.

When alcohol (usually vodka) is consumed in small quantities in the home to mark some special occasion, it is usual for women to partake. (Because of the supply difficulties at the time of fieldwork, consumption was restricted in many families to major occasions, usually life-cycle transitions; it is likely that this was a distortion of the previously established and preferred pattern). Excessive consumption by women is considered distasteful by most peasants, but several families seem not to acknowledge this norm. Most women are poured half measures. They are never pressurised to drink more than they wish, whilst males in the company are expected to consume at the same rate until the stock is exhausted. (This might take several days.) The rate will depend upon the nature of the occasion. Bottles can be emptied rapidly in perfunctory manner, e.g. when one party has brought a gift to seal an economic transaction. The tot is normally downed by men in a single gulp; but an older man may sit calmly, chatting over a full glass for an hour or more, before draining it to the health of the person seated next to him and refilling the glass for the neighbour to drink in turn. Sharing the same small glass is sometimes declared to be a traditional expression of conviviality; but some families today are embarrassed if they cannot provide two separate glasses for each person in the company, a small one for the spirit and a larger one for the tea or soft drink which is sipped as a chaser.

Alcohol is considered proper, indeed essential, at every kind of celebration. It has to be stockpiled in large quantities for weddings. An effort is usually made to obtain some for men's name-day festivities, when family and neighbours may be invited for the evening, and also at the major holidays of the year, particularly around Christmas and the New Year. Parties are also thrown to mark most events of the life-cycle, including the birth of a child, its christening, and the occasion of its first holy communion. The church is very critical of families which celebrate important religious occasions in this way, particularly because of their impact upon children. Some peasants were reputed to add special colouring to the vodka consumed at first holy communion celebrations, so that their children would not betray them if questioned later by the priest!

The numerous individuals and families where dependence upon alcohol and alcohol abuse must be recognised do not need the special occasion for a pretext. Peasants, who have no work-group in which to seek companionship, do much of their drinking in the cafe in Komańcza. Sometimes they go there at the end of a strenuous period of work, sometimes when they have suffered some setback (such as the death of an animal), sometimes simply when the weather is bad and they have no work to do. Very often they visit the cafe when they have been in Komańcza on other business, and have been frustrated by the administration there. There are also some families, in both peasant and socialist sectors, which regularly pursue intoxication at home. These households are roundly condemned by public opinion, which is no less emphatic in deploring the activities of the wife of a forestry worker, who has endeavoured to cater for their needs by selling vodka at inflated prices from her own private store. Only in 1982 did the supply problem become so acute that, when even the ration entitlement was not available, a number of families began distilling spirit themselves. Some older peasants, themselves regular, but moderate, consumers of alcohol, believe that drinking behaviour has changed in recent years. They may hazard comparisons with the pre-socialist period, either for the Polish villages of the plains or for the *Rus* village in Wisłok. It is agreed that there was always a minority which drank to excess, and whose families were ruined in consequence. However, Poles and Ukrainians also agree that the spree drinking observable in recent years was less prevalent in the past, if only because the economic situation totally ruled this out. Today the cash is more easily obtained, but there is still not a great deal one can do with it. Land has lost its pre-eminence as a store of value, and other desired goods, which might be expected to stimulate savings, are either pitched at extremely high prices, or they are available only for dollars, or they are not available through market channels at all. The social consequences must be roughly the same now as in the past, and it should not be supposed that the socialist welfare services do much to alleviate the problems. Women certainly are abused, and many children must be permanently affected.[13]

Alcohol can also induce aggression in other contexts, e.g. it usually causes every village dance to end in a brawl. Young men go to dances in neighbouring villages in full and even eager expectation of this outcome. Its ubiquity in the workplaces of the socialist sector has been responsible for many accidents, including an incident at one of the State Farm depots in 1980 in which a foreman was beheaded by the blades of one of the Farm's helicopters. Forestry is widely

131

regarded as a kind of rural skid row.

I have no theory to explain why some persons in all occupational groups abuse alcohol, or why it dominates leisure patterns generally.[14] Amongst the peasants it is clear that the most economically successful are relatively sober, whilst excessive consumption is usually associated with an unproductive farm and substantial dependence upon casual work in the forests. This work is so demanding that some women are inclined to offer this as an excuse for their husbands' indulgence when flush after payday. Heavy consumption is also associated with occupation of old wooden dwellings and larger than average families. The teenagers who begin their drinking early belong to such families, whilst those who are slow to start are more likely to leave the village after completing their education. The contrast resembles that found in parts of the Irish countryside, where heavy drinking can be understood as a product of a disintegrating and demoralised community, and at the same time as an expression of the continued need for human contacts and conviviality.[15] Alcohol does sustain the latter, and cases of despondent, solitary drinking are not common in Wisłok. Moreover, in important respects the community is united in its opinions on this subject. Moderate consumption is approved, and even considered medically desirable, whilst only excess and profiteering incur disapproval. The unfortunate consequences of alcohol abuse can be conveniently blamed nowadays upon a power external to the community, namely the secular authorities. Formerly, it might not have occurred to villagers that families living in conditions of abject misery because of alcohol had anyone other than themselves to blame; at most they might have criticised profiteering by local shop-keepers. But it seems to be in the nature of a socialist regime that full responsibility can now be attributed to the authorities. Recent price hikes have intensified this propensity, the fiscal attractions of this policy for the government being transparent to all. With most households spending a high proportion of their income on alcohol, the government responsible can be blamed for the evils of drink much more completely than the Jews or the landlord's agents were blamed by earlier generations.[16] The church reinforces this attitude by playing a prominent part in anti-alcoholism campaigns and attributing the drunkenness which everyone deplores to the general moral degradation of socialist society. Again we see the opportunities open to the traditional church in this totalitarian system. For all the negative phenomena observable in everyday life: corruption, subversion of private property rights, lack of respect for public property, over-indulgence in alcohol etc., irrespective of whether the offenders might be in contravention of Christian moral teaching, primary responsibility can be assigned not to them as individuals but to the 'omnicompetent' socialist state. The more flagrant the breaches of the Christian code of behaviour by individuals, the more justified the church's fundamental moral opposition to socialism is perceived to be and the stronger a peasant's religious commitment may become. I would guess that most people in Wisłok, including some of the heavier drinkers, find the church's explanation of current drinking patterns convincing. Surely only a very dogmatic Marxist could contradict them and insist that religion, rather than alcohol, was the opiate of this community.

CHAPTER EIGHT

Family, Neighbourhood and Village

The family is practically the only organised social group to which the peasant primarily belongs as an active member
William I. Thomas and Florian Znaniecki (1918–20, p. 140)

It has been shown in previous chapters that the peasants of Wisłok share a common predicament in the politico-administrative setting, that they remain overwhelmingly loyal to their traditional religion and have failed to acquire a new socialist/secular consciousness. To the extent that any overriding principle of unity can be identified at all, this is provided by the established church and is in opposition to the established state authorities. However, it should not be assumed from this that the village is in any way a homogenous entity, and I wish now to look in more detail at its sociological diversity. Much of this can be related to the economic diversity described in earlier chapters. We can begin by considering the demographic factors which influence the composition of the family and household, and then proceed to consider social relations at neighbourhood and village levels.

Households consist mainly of nuclear families, which vary considerably in their reproductive capacity

The importance of the family as an economic unit and in socialisation has already been pointed out. To understand its role in the rural social structure it is necessary first to look in more detail at the demographic background. The Polish case is again unusual in Europe. High rates of fertility in Galicia before the socialist period generated severe pressures, only partially relieved by emigration. After the Second World War a high birth rate was required to make good heavy demographic losses. This was nowhere more obviously desirable than in a village such as Wisłok, where the population never reached more than a small fraction of its pre-war level. The birth rate reached its post-war peak (over 30 births per 1000 population) in the mid-1950s, after which there was a sharp decline. It began to rise again more gradually in the 1970s and appeared to be stable at the level of 19.5 in the early 1980s. This was higher than that of any other East European country. A closer inspection reveals that this is mainly attributable to the larger size of families in the countryside. The proportion with four children or more living at home is 9.1 per cent of the total number of rural households, but only 2.6 per cent in the cities.[1] The proportion has probably been consistently higher again in Wisłok, where most of the immigrant Polish families which arrived in the 1950s and 1960s and settled permanently had six children or more. This pattern, with minimal interval between births, is continued by numerous households in the village today, including younger couples.

Various reasons may be adduced to explain why family size in Wisłok and the Polish countryside in general should be significantly larger than elsewhere. Apart from the usual correlations with education level and employment opportunities, it can also be maintained that the teaching of the church has helped to maintain traditional rates of fertility, and that in the matter of contraception practice there has been a happy coincidence of views between the church and the pro-natalist socialist state.[2] (It is something of a puzzle why the state has not done more to accelerate the gradual decline in the birth rate which has taken place since the early 1950s. At that period the high rates could be justified in relation to wartime losses and the need to provide labour for ambitious industrial programmes; however, the reality of disguised unemployment has become increasingly transparent in the crisis of the 1980s.) Church policy is implemented by the local priests, who organise classes of instruction for couples engaged to be married, in the course of which Catholic doctors advise on methods of contraception approved by the church. Theoretically, fuller information is transmitted in the schools. However, should persons wish to adopt safer methods than those endorsed by the church, they will not find it easy to do so, particularly in an isolated rural area. Thus, although in Wisłok today some peasants may already be deliberately limiting the size of their families (none of the high-income farmers has more than three children), either because of the teaching of the church or because of practical barriers (not, incidentally, specific to rural areas) few are likely to be employing modern methods of contraception.

An alternative hypothesis that might be advanced is that most peasant families have sound economic motivation for wanting large numbers of children. Such a pattern is, after all, common to many

peasant societies, where, in addition to satisfying labour requirements, it is expected that children will guarantee their parents'
security in old age.[3] Several families in Wisłok would appear to
demonstrate such a pattern. A widow who lives in one of the Forestry
Commision's houses has raised sixteen healthy children, and
although not one of them is likely to settle in Wisłok, most are
assiduous in their visiting and she will always have a home to go to if
she needs one. The Stasiowskis were poor immigrants from a
densely populated area just outside the mountain zone, who settled
in a house in the upper hamlet and stayed until it began literally to
fall to pieces around them. By this time four of the five sons they
raised in Wisłok were bringing in some cash from the local State
Farm, and through strenuous joint efforts the sons were able to
construct an adequate modern dwelling for their ageing parents.
Other families anxious about the condition of their own dwellings
may draw the conclusion that it is in their interest to maximise the
number of offspring. It would be rational to behave differently only
if they had found some alternative security for the future, something
in which it was more worthwhile to invest, but, as we have seen in
Chapter Three, few individual farmers have any such perspective
and it is only very recently that a rudimentary pension scheme has
been established for them.

Sons are preferred to daughters. There is still the old desire to
keep property in a male line, whilst daughters may involve more
expense and are unlikely to be able to come up with the requisite
combination of physical and financial resources to be able to tackle
housebuilding. It is perhaps because employment opportunities for
women are so restricted here that the largest families today are those
of persons committed to the socialist sector. The wives of the loggers,
the State Farm workers and the warders, have nothing else to do, as a
few peasants sneer.[4] Only a few unmarried women commute to the
Rzepedź sawmill. Others migrate temporarily when their school
years are over, and permanently as soon as they marry — the desire
to marry outside the peasant class appears to be strong. Marriage is
seldom delayed beyond the early twenties for women; those who
marry locally seldom see any reason to delay starting a family;
pregnancy remains a common reason for getting married.

The boys and girls bred in Wisłok *have* gone forth to man the
mines and machines of the socialist sector: this kind of mobility is
more in evidence here than in most established lowland villages.
Considerable numbers have moved several hundred kilometres to

15. The wife of a State Farm foreman, with a few of her children.

the west, to the Silesian coal-mining region. Until quite recently recruiting teams used to come to the village to arrange for the transfer of likely lads to special mining schools, even before the completion of primary school. Nowadays it is more usual to complete vocational school within the county of Krosno before considering a move further afield. Peasants have little reason to stay. Numerous farms have reverted to the State because no son could be persuaded to inherit; and though extra land and separate buildings can be made available by *gmina* authorities if more than one son wishes to remain farming in the private sector, such circumstances very seldom arise in Wisłok. The proportion of youth remaining in the village is higher in the peasant group than among the workers of the socialist sector. But many of the sons who stay will inherit the least successful farms — they may continue to occupy the buildings, but abandon the fields and gravitate towards employment in the socialist sector. I know of only one case in which a farm has been inherited by a daughter, after her marriage to a former logger; formal ownership of the farm was transferred to him a short time later.

Contacts with emigrants, like those with relatives in the village of origin, are maintained by almost all families but with varying degrees of intensity. Most Ukrainian families have close ties with relatives in the northern and western territories, and also with relatives abroad. Economic factors certainly influence the maintenance of these contacts. For example, any protracted visit to a peasant family is likely to be made at a time when help may be needed, particularly during haymaking. I have heard of more complex arrangements between the son who remains on the farm and the siblings who migrate in other parts of Poland, where the land has retained more value; but these do not arise in Wisłok. Remittances from children who have left for industrial workplaces within Poland tend to be less significant than the contributions of kin resident outside the country. In particular, some new housebuilding has owed much to the influx of foreign currency. Trips abroad are almost unknown, and only those in the socialist sector not tied to a farm travel much outside the village. They visit others much more frequently than they themselves are visited, especially at holiday periods. The Ukrainians are the group most regularly visited at home (by their relatives from the north and west).

The majority of households in Wisłok today are composed of nuclear families. This seems to have been the case in many parts of Europe over a very long period, but it may be quite a new phenomenon in at least some parts of the Polish countryside. We have noted that groups of families may have worked the land jointly in the eighteenth-century *Rus* village (p. 23) but there is no reason to suppose that complex households were also common at this time. In the nineteenth and early twentieth centuries, however, demographic pressures (parents living longer, more children surviving) must have made the establishment of new households very difficult. Consequently the emphasis placed by Thomas and Znaniecki upon the role of the extended family in Polish peasant society may be entirely justified for that period.

The situation in the new community in Wisłok can be sketched as follows. Few people live alone. It is not unusual for the widowed to remarry very late in life, particularly if they have no family to take them in. Of the six solitaries whom I recorded in 1981 only two could be said to experience isolation. One was a retired clerk of the Forestry Commission, estranged from his family in the city. The other was a lady of local (Ukrainian) origin with a history of mental illness that evoked conflicting explanations. Apart from these two there was the schoolmaster (a bachelor who stayed on in his flat in the local school after his transfer to Komańcza), a retired forestry worker (who in fact spends much of his time outside the village in the house where he has settled his wife and children) and finally two old ladies recently widowed, one of whom was about to move to stay with her daughter in another village.

A further four households could be described as 'extended upwards'. In each of these cases an aged or infirm parent was no longer capable of supporting himself or herself. The moral duty to look after one's parents is generally acknowledged, and the old will normally carry on making a productive contribution as long as is physically possible. All of the households in this group are peasant, since the ageing dependents of those employed in the socialist sector are more likely to have other homes to welcome them in their native region. There is only one case of 'horizontal extension', in which a bachelor now in his late thirties has stayed on with his married brother. This will break up soon when the couple migrates to the new housing estate at Rzepedź, where they both work. Most of the five cases of multiple family households are also unlikely to last more than a few years. The younger couple endeavours to set up an independent household as soon as possible. In Wisłok it is relatively easy for them to do so, either because they will be considered for state-owned accommodation as soon as they have children, or because they will be able to purchase old *Rus* dwellings privately for relatively small sums. In some cases the ideal is more difficult to achieve, e.g. when both parents are in need of care. If such parents have a married son who is keen to retain the farm the property can be transferred to him, and it is possible that the living quarters will be formally divided until the death of the parents or until a new dwelling is built. Gradually, it is becoming necessary to replace all the pre-war timber dwellings. In the relatively few cases to date where the first immigrant generation has erected a new house, it has usually been conceived on a scale more than large enough to accommodate multiple family households. Such peasants say they are building to keep their families together, but none has yet obtained an heir through provision of this kind of facility.

The availability of accommodation is one of the few incentives to young people to stay in the village. The reasons why so few of them want to stay were partly discussed in Chapter Three. However, by the 1980s more new households were being formed by families of the second generation who had decided to stay than by fresh immigrants. Recently, there have been several marriages between persons whose parents came from very different backgrounds, but who grew up together in the same hamlet and attended the same class at school. Young persons who wish to stay in farming will receive some help from their parents, and if they wish to expand they can turn at once to the state for more land and financial assistance. The value of the state's contribution is likely to exceed that of the family. Resources accumulated from outside the immediate family in the course of wedding festivities tend to be meagre and may not even exceed the cost of the party (generally born by the family of the bride). None of the more substantial achievements of the new community to date (the few new houses, the stables, tractors and substantial tracts of ameliorated land, mostly the accomplishments of the specialists of the 1970s) have yet been inherited. Many have doubts whether they will be, but it is upon the transmission of this new wealth that both the economic future of the peasant sector and the class structure of the village must depend.

Neighbourhood links are not uniformly strong, even between close kin

The distance along the main road between the two State Farm depots at each end of Wisłok is about 7 km. Houses are located at irregular intervals along its entire length, but most inhabitants agree that three separate 'hamlets' can be distinguished in the upper, central and lower parts of the valley, each one of them served by a bus stop. There are two additional clusters situated some distance away from the main road, one at each end of the valley. The higher of the two owes its relative isolation to the fact that the new road was built in a straight line where the river makes a short meander. Ever since the opening of this road in 1972, members of this clearly defined group of ten households have sought to improve the condition of the dirt track which leads to their homes. It is frequently difficult to traverse, especially after rainfall, and residents claim that they must endure danger as well as inconvenience, since the track cannot be negotiated by ambulances in emergencies. When I first heard about their predicament (after moving in at the other end of the village) I was also told that these residents were united in their determination to secure an improvement, that they were sending their collectively drafted petitions to the highest authorities in the land (see pp.93-4). Later I thought this would be a promising context in which to look for further examples of neighbourly cooperation, but in this I was mistaken.

My initial information was substantially correct, except that the petitions had not been drafted collectively but were the work of a single young newcomer to the village (a man who was allocated a farm situated only about ½ km from the main road, but which was nonetheless cut off by terrain negotiable only by horse or tractor). However, relations between the households in this cluster were not generally good. The real reason why some of them needed access to the main road was that they could not rely on their neighbours to help them out if they were in trouble. One family was the object of general enmity. It was of mixed Polish-Ukrainian ethnic composition, and it managed one of the most productive farms in the village. Other successful households contrived to be generally popular, nor did anyone harbour any grievance against the other ethnically mixed household in this cluster. But anti-Ukrainian prejudice did make itself felt in perceptions of two further families. One of these contained an elderly couple who had returned to a small farm in their native village. The other comprised a young family planning to migrate to their place of employment, the Rzepedź sawmill (they found themselves in Wisłok because the man's parents had contemplated returning to their native village, bought a farm and a small plot of land, but then eventually decided that it was preferable to stay in the north-west; they then settled their son on it instead, but he has never shown any interest in utilising the land). There are no strong ties between these Ukrainian families, nor do the Ukrainian individuals in mixed households have close contacts with any other Ukrainians. In fact, the only close ties maintained by any of these families, inside or outside the cluster, are between families closely related to each other. Two in this group are regular recipients of economic aid from relatives who live a short distance away, whilst two others extend such help to their own ageing kin. Three more are drawn from time to time into less one-sided cooperative arrangements with other families in the village, including non-kin, whilst one manages to be almost entirely self-reliant. Finally, two peasant families of this cluster are related by two sisters, who each married in their native Jaśliska area and migrated with their husbands in the early 1960s. Their houses are barely 50 m apart and the children seem to have grown up feeling equally at home in both. Meals are regularly taken together, equipment and horses are always readily lent, the men often work together in the forests and even on the land numerous tasks are performed jointly (e.g. the grazing of animals throughout the summer).

These two women have two more sisters who followed them to Wisłok, married, and settled in the upper hamlet a short distance away. Only one of the two families here is engaged in farming, and although relations between all four sisters (and all four families) are extremely cordial, there is no pattern of close daily interaction such as that which proximity of residence and similarity of economic enterprise combine to produce in the cluster described above. There is a strong Ukrainian presence in the upper hamlet. Relations with the Poles living there are for the most part very good, but, curiously, the only families here that are closely related — two Ukrainian brothers — are not on speaking terms. This conflict arose out of a squabble over land. When the elder brother retired from farming he was deeply upset that his brother, who had also retired after many years working on State Farms, should successfully claim (ostensibly on his son's behalf, in fact at his wife's behest) the plots which the elder brother had secretly hoped he would carry on using.[5]

Other hamlets, or clusters within them, reveal similar patterns of cooperation and conflict. In one neighbourhood both kin and affinal links are very strong and the intensity of contact does not seem to be weakened by the fact that members of these households earn their living in three quite different fields of the economy. Two other farmers in this same cluster, both of them with exceptionally large acreages, do not get along well either with each other or with their neighbours, and neither has any relatives anywhere in the region. Their example shows that there is no necessity for a high level of inter-household cooperation in agriculture, and (at least since the demise of the locally based Agricultural Circle in the early 1970s) it would appear that the most successful farmers have also been the most self-reliant. The implications of this can be studied more closely in another cluster in the centre of the village, where a few relatively unproductive households cooperate quite intensively and a highly successful farmer has had to face tension between his own family and those of his brothers. All of the brothers are employed in the socialist sector. Two of them own their own houses and live nearby, whilst two live on the new estates at Moszczaniec. The successful farmer did not inherit either his farm or his land, but was assisted by the authorities after abandoning a previous job in the Silesian mines, became a specialist farmer in the 1970s, and village headman in the 1980s. He is dismayed to realise that his success is making it hard for him to maintain close ties with his own family (who seem to maintain much closer ties with each other than he is able to, even with those who are his near neighbours) and may also distort his relations with other villagers. He protested to me that he had no desire to become a *Pan* ('Lord') in the community, but complained that some people now saw him in this light. This might suggest that progress in farming requires that a family detach itself to some extent from the kin group as well as from its neighbours. Certainly those in the village who maintain kin or affinal links most actively are not amongst the more productive farming households.

A more uniform neighbourhood in some respects, since all are employed in the socialist sector, and a highly differentiated one in others, since senior staff may reside next door to the most junior employees, is to be found in the lower hamlet. The families here are not related to each other, and few have kin in other parts of the village. Rivalries and quarrels are not unknown, particularly where one or two strong female personalities are involved, but the general atmosphere, both on the State Farm estate and in the cluster built up by the Forestry Commission, is convivial. Contacts between these two main components of the socialist sector are not frequent. The women in all of these households have considerably more 'spare time' than any other group in the community, and they are perhaps the most overtly sociable of all the groups it contains.

Summing up this discussion it can be said that, whilst chronic isolation is not a problem in Wisłok (families are large, few persons live alone and the old are taken care of by their families), neighbourhood contacts work much better for some than for others. The factors which encourage strong ties are: firstly, relatedness (whether by blood or by marriage); secondly, comparability of social and economic standing in the village (rather than similarity of economic activities pursued); these seem to be more important in stimulating interaction than residence in itself, but all three factors reinforce each other in some neighbourhoods. Two factors which may have the opposite effect and produce sour neighbourly relations are *a*) ethnicity, and *b*) the emergence of a clearly differentiated group of households concerned to modernise their own farms, and no longer maintaining traditional reciprocal ties in the neighbourhood, even when the neighbours should happen to be kin. We shall now consider each of these factors in more detail, for they may be creating new primary groups at village level.

The Ukrainian minority group is slowly going the same way as Polish regional groups

The conflicts which the presence of a large Ukrainian minority helped to create in inter-war Poland were noted in Chapter Two. Events during the war, and the population transfers effected immediately after it, embittered relations further. Only after 1956 was a more conciliatory line adopted by the authorities. The Ukrainians no longer formed a compact territorial mass but they were still the country's largest minority group, with a total population of about 300,000. A Ukrainian Socio-Cultural Society was founded in 1956; its weekly newspaper and other publications are widely circulated. The official position, which is formally expressed in the Constitution of the People's Republic, is that citizens who belong to minority nationalities have the same rights and obligations as ethnic Poles. It is claimed that all minorities 'have every opportunity to develop their own cultural life', and that although 'a process of gradual assimilation is inevitably occurring, owing to the relatively small and dispersed nature of these minorities, it is one which is following an absolutely natural course, every citizen having complete freedom of choice as regards nationality, without any pressure or even encouragement on the part of the state'.[6]

The situation of the Ukrainian minority in practice is somewhat different. To begin with, those who are old enough to remember the events of the 1940s cannot forget the injustices done to them. No-one supposes that the former *Rus* homeland can be recreated, but at least a reappraisal of *Operation Vistula* might put an end to the more absurd misrepresentations of the struggle against Ukrainian terrorist groups still perpetrated by Polish authors. Those Ukrainians who did return to their homelands when the political climate improved in the 1950s encountered the deepest hostility, both from the new administration and from the Polish immigrants who had occupied their farms. Some were forced to return to the north and succeeded in settling only at the second or third time of trying. Unlike Polish settlers at this time, they were not given any assistance or credits to help them reestablish farms. On the contrary they usually had to pay twice over to acquire what had been forcibly wrested from them a decade or so earlier: first of all a bribe to persuade the Polish occupant to depart, and, secondly, an official payment in order that the administration ratify their presence. Until residence permission was granted, usually many months after their surreptitious arrival, the returning Ukrainians lived in dread of eviction. Long after their return they were hampered in the expansion of their farms because, not being officially classified as 'settlers', there was a range of economic benefits for which they were not considered eligible. This was despite the fact that they demonstrably cared about their farms, knew the conditions so much better than other settlers, and even without official assistance were easily capable of outstripping them in performance.

Discrimination against the Uniate or Greek Catholic Church was discussed in Chapter Five (pp. 83-4). It remains extremely important to the Ukrainians that this church should be allowed to function openly, like all other religious groups in Poland. Some Ukrainians have accepted the Orthodox Church, on the grounds that this was their original church, and adherence to this distinguishes them clearly from Poles, who also call themselves Catholics. The survival of the Greek Catholic parish in nearby Komańcza has restricted the number of conversions to Orthodoxy in this area. Some peasants deeply attached to this church declare their ethnic identity in religious terms: they do not say that they are Ukrainians (although they do not deny this, nor the terms *'Rusnak'* and *'Lemko'*), but they confess themselves first of all to be 'Greeks'.

Ukrainians in Poland experienced crude discrimination in the 1970s. It was an unfortunate time of cultural vandalism in the Bieszczady region, when some of the finest wooden churches were pulled down and scores of place names of Ukrainian origin were replaced by purer Polish forms. Entirely different names were dreamed up for several hamlets near Wisłok, but even Polish immigrants for the most part carried on using the old ones. The traditional names were officially restored during 1981, in response to pressure from Polish intellectuals as well as Ukrainian groups. There were other signs at this time, notably in the *Solidarity* newspaper, that a fuller understanding of Ukrainian grievances might lead to a long-term improvement in their position. Students were particularly active, and a Ukrainian Students' Union was officially registered a few months before the imposition of martial law. Although nothing may come of it for the time being — even if *Solidarity* could be revived as a workers' trade-union it seems unlikely that independent student groupings will be allowed to flourish as they did in 1981 — its appearance on the scene provided confirmation that some young Ukrainians in Poland were conscious of their separate identity.

More difficult to isolate than the Gierek cultural policies, but of greater significance, is the way in which a highly negative stereotype of the Ukrainian has been constructed in the past and is actively propagated today. The literature on the anti-terrorist struggle was referred to in the preceding chapter. The prejudice is not new, and it was particularly strong amongst repatriates from regions such as Eastern Galicia, where Poles had been outnumbered by the Ukrainian population. The old prejudices have in some ways been strengthened under socialism by indiscriminate application of the 'Nazi allies' smear; feelings towards Ukrainians remain unambiguously negative, i.e. there is not the mixture of antipathy and (at some deeper level) respect which many Poles feel towards their Western neighbours.[7]

The Ukrainian minority in Wisłok is heavily outnumbered by the Polish immigrants and much more self-conscious ethnically (though the Poles who settled in the 1940s may have been more conscious of their Polish identity than the *Rusnaks* whom they replaced were *at that time* of their Ukrainian identity). Many of its members have experienced discrimination in its practical forms, and had to fight hard in order to return to their native village. One man is still deprived of various rights as a citizen, including the right to vote, because of offences for which he was convicted in the 1940s. Blanket prejudice against Ukrainians is rare in the two neighbourhoods of the upper hamlet where the eight purely Ukrainian households are to be found. Their Polish neighbours find some better company than others, and are aware that relations between these eight families are far from harmonious. Those who get to know the individuals may well be on good terms with a man whose connection with the terrorist movement was proven in court, whilst Poles in other neighbourhoods continue to revile him as a public enemy. It is the Polish population in hamlets where no Ukrainians reside who are most prone to curse a Ukrainian conspiracy whenever they fail to obtain the item they require in Komańcza. The attitude of local Ukrainians towards Poles can be described as tolerant and resigned. They frequently comment upon the economic incompetence of those who have usurped their lands, and have a habit of pointing up negative characteristics in their neighbours as national traits (this applies particularly to current drinking patterns). Ukrainians were vociferous in their condemnation of the regime when the full extent of the country's economic crisis became apparent in 1981. It must also be said that one or two families entertained illusions at this time of changes more far-reaching than those to which a *Solidarity* inspired democratisation of the country might have led. Their regard for German efficiency is high (several experienced it at first hand as forced labourers during the war), whilst their respect for Soviet power is mingled with an awareness that this is where many of their kin reside (deportees of 1944–5) and that ethnically they stand closer to Russians than they do to Poles. I was seriously told on occasion that an intervention from either or both of these parties would be the best way to ensure a permanent improvement in the status of Ukrainians within Poland.

These are the sentiments of a few Ukrainians who recall the experience of war and deportation. What disturbs the older generation most is not that the small Ukrainian community in the hamlets of Wisłok is divided by various personal conflicts as well as by political disagreements, but that a process of assimilation (whether following a 'natural course' or not) is threatening their group with extinction. Signs of this can be detected even in villages such as Komańcza, where the Ukrainian minority is large and has a church as its focal point. As was pointed out in Chapter Six, interethnic marriages are common and the children of these marriages tend to grow up speaking only Polish and attending Roman Catholic services. Relatively few children receive instruction in the Ukrainian language at the village school in Komańcza (which would be much more popular if it were an alternative to compulsory Russian and not an extra burden for the pupil). In Wisłok there is no Ukrainian teaching and there are now very few Ukrainian children. Several sons have emigrated to North America after finishing school, other sons and daughters have gone to live in nearby villages where Ukrainians are more numerous. Some new houses have been built, but no farms have so far been inherited and one has already reverted to the state, for the want of an heir. A recent marriage, between the son of a Polish immigrant and a daughter of the Ukrainian viewed with the most suspicion by many Poles in the village because of his activities in the 1940s, highlights the problems faced by the minority. They are the only such young couple in the village (other mixed couples are much older, the partners did not grow up together in the same village), and both families have constructed modern homes. Since the only son in the Ukrainian family was permanently domiciled in the USA and there were other potential heirs in the Polish household, the new couple took up residence with the Ukrainian parents. It was rumoured that the head of this household had initially opposed the marriage, but I never saw any sign of this. Two children

were born within a few years, and they have brought the two households even closer together. Both sides declare that the infants will be
brought up to speak both languages, but it is difficult to see how this
can happen — the parents speak Polish most of the time, Polish will
be the only language the children will use in the Wisłok school, and
there will be no other children speaking Ukrainian dialects in the
village. The only other Ukrainian family with young children is
committed to a move to Rzepedź; and in this family, though both
parents know the local dialect, they do not use it; their children, too,
are acquiring only Polish.

Thus, it seems probable that the Ukrainian ethnic identity finally
assumed by the indigenous inhabitants of Wisłok will die out within
a single generation in the village to which a few of them succeeded,
against considerable odds, in returning. If present trends continue it
might not survive much longer even in settlements such as
Komańcza, where the size of the group is much larger and considerably greater interest is taken in its cultural traditions. As this happens
ethnicity will gradually lose its importance as a criterion for group
identity. I have mentioned that conflicts have emerged within the
present small autochthonous group (leaders of the Ukrainian community elsewhere informed me that such patterns are very common
and are often deliberately manipulated by the Polish authorities).
Yet any observer at the present time is also impressed by the tight
links which exist between them. They do look to each other for
economic assistance, even when Polish neighbours might be closer.
They observe their own religious holidays when Polish neighbours
may be working (but, not wishing to cause offence, they also observe
the Polish holidays). They feel more comfortable in each others'
houses than they do in a Polish milieu, and visit frequently. Curiously, the successful farmer and current village headman introduced
at the end of the previous section, whose prosperity was tending to
isolate him from his kin and neighbours further down the valley, has
sought instead to develop closer ties with the Ukrainians. He is the
child of a pre-war interethnic marriage, whose command of the local
dialect is imperfect, and he has no economic motivation for seeking
Ukrainian company in another neighbourhood. Yet this is where he
sometimes chooses to go at holiday periods, eschewing the company
of his kin, his neighbours, and others in the village of comparable
standing as farmers. His children know nothing of the language, and
very little about the history of their family and their village. All traces
of the *Rus* community will pass eventually: but at present the iden-

16. Ukrainian neighbours in the upper hamlet.

tification lingers, a source of pride still to some, and of irritation to numerous Poles.

No comparable sentiment exists within the Polish majority, although the presence of the Ukrainians may focus their own ethnic pride in ways unfamiliar in homogeneous Polish villages elsewhere. When the first waves of Polish immigrants arrived in Wisłok they brought with them conflicting regional identities, some of them as strongly felt as their national identification. The highlanders from the Tatra Mountains region were particularly proud of their traditions and frequently dominated the new areas they settled. In Wisłok they were greatly outnumbered by poor smallholders from the lowlands and also by former manorial workers, who retained their own group traditions and regional loyalties in the new village. With high turnover of the immigrant population and considerable intermarriage these distinctions have lost their practical significance. As we shall see, there is no evidence that they have been replaced by any strong attachments to the new region.

Polarisation of public and private occupational fields determines the new class divisions

When a successful farmer of local, but mixed Polish-Ukrainian ancestry, makes a deliberate attempt to cultivate Ukrainian company outside his own neighbourhood, it is worth examining more closely the factors causing this degree of estrangement from the kin and neighbours with whom he interacted previously. The present headman became, in less than a decade, the most prosperous peasant in his predominantly Polish neighbourhood. He was proud of the medals awarded for his achievements, and was respected throughout the village; at the same time he resented the suggestion that he might ever behave other than according to traditional peasant norms. Like most other heads of households in the private sector he would describe himself as a *rolnik*, meaning farmer, but he would also affirm that he was a *chlop*, a peasant like everyone else, and attribute his own success to traditional peasant virtues, above all to hard work and thrift. Notwithstanding his personal disclaimers, we must now consider what types of social differentiation are appearing at the level of the village, and whether in any sense they can be said to generate new class divisions.

On this issue, as in the case of ethnicity, one may derive something like an official line from the works of Polish sociologists.[8] It is commonly held that class divisions are present to a minimal extent if at all in the village. It is implied that social relations are no less completely socialist in Poland than in other socialist states which have acted more decisively to collectivise agriculture. The argument put forward is that legal relationship to the means of production is no longer an appropriate criterion by which to identify class relations. Although smallholders may technically be the owners of their means of production, in practice, the determining factor is the socialist context in which such farms operate. Rather than attempt to apply Leninist criteria and identify rich, middle and poor classes within the peasantry, it is considered that the peasantry as a whole can be seen as a relatively unified 'stratum', and that various status groups, based primarily upon occupation, can be distinguished within the aggregate rural population. The most important distinction is taken to be that between families which continue to devote themselves entirely to individual farming and those which combine farming with socialist wage-labour, the peasant-workers.

In earlier chapters it was quite easy to locate such occupational groups in Wisłok. In a village that is relatively isolated from industrial centres of employment the proportion of commuter peasant-workers is quite small, and most households are firmly committed either to peasant farming or to one or other field of the socialised sector. Within the latter several groups may be identified. The loggers are clearly a low-status occupational group, whose members spend a lot of time together during their leisure hours (especially when drinking wine outside the village shop). Less clearly defined is the group composed of State Farm employees. Some of these belong to households which maintain their own farms and their primary allegiance is still to the peasantry. Others, who do not farm and live on the separate housing estate, see each other more frequently outside work and obviously have different attitudes. In the eyes of the local peasantry they merge with the group formed by the prison warders, for the latter share the same housing estate and are often seen on the State Farm (since this is where the convicts work). Even if the two groups could be disentangled it would be difficult to say that one carried higher prestige. One occupation which does command greater prestige (though it has fallen in the socialist period) is that of teaching. However, the Wisłok teachers display little *esprit de corps* and play no active role in the community, either as a group or individually.

The general approach followed by Polish sociologists may seem perfectly sensible in the light of what has previously been said about the private sector. It was shown in Chapter Three that the conditions in which Wisłok was repopulated were highly egalitarian, and that until the later 1970s there was very little differentiation in the size of landholding, the type of machinery owned, and indeed in the pattern of final output. By the end of the 1970s differentiation was more apparent, and the scale of farming was doubtless affected also by the extent to which the household was attracted by increasing opportunities in the socialist sector. Yet observable income differentials could not be explained adequately in traditional Marxist-Leninist terms, i.e. by the relationship of the household to the means of production. As we saw in Table 3, some owners of tractors had quite low levels of commodity output, whilst some of the largest producers did not own tractors at all. In many cases the size of landholding was a very poor guide to a farm's productive performance. It was noted that all peasants, whatever their incomes, were greatly circumscribed by the socialist administrative framework. Whatever they might formally *own*, they remain dependent upon the administration for numerous essential inputs, for mechanical services, and an outlet for their final product. Yet, granted that the socialist authorities have built up an arsenal of discretionary powers, which they use in determining which farmers will be allowed to expand their holdings and

151

to take possession of new equipment, it is still possible to detect the seeds of a new type of class differentiation in the policies pursued by Edward Gierek in the 1970s and revived in their broad essentials in the 1980s. A minority of specialists did emerge as a privileged elite, and might be a more clearly defined post-peasant group in the village today, were it not for the general economic crisis and the levelling that has been induced by chronic shortage. When the situation improves, one might suggest that the fate of the inter-mediate group of producers identified in Table 6, whose production was averaging between 100,000 and 200,000 złoty in the early 1980s, will be crucial. Either the household must commit itself to a future in individual farming and invest resources in land and machinery as well as modern housing (all three will be necessary to persuade the next generation to remain on the land), or its commod-ity production will decline and its members gravitate towards the socialist sector. With other households (those producing at higher levels at present) also looking for more land and machinery, the competition may be fierce. It goes without saying that it will not be 'pure competition', arbitrated solely by the forces of the market. The greatest influence will be exercised by the authorities. For example, if a *Rus* dwelling or stable is disintegrating a family may be denied the credits to replace them if it is felt that their farm enterprise has no viable future; in this way the weaker farms will fade away and some peasants will drift into the socialist sector.

In the early period of the new community in Wisłok there was considerable movement from the socialist sector into peasant farm-ing, as men with a background on the land and an aptitude for independent operations grasped the opportunities available. Nowa-days, this is outweighed by the general movement in the opposite direction and the children of the more populous but less successful peasant households have come to form the mainstay of the local socialist sector. One should beware of exaggerating the speed with which such a polarisation of the two sectors could be completed. But it is possible to imagine a private sector in Wisłok under the domi-nance of small number of households — specialised, highly self-reliant and owning most of the important means of production, residing in large modern houses, not wasting their time in the forest and not encouraging their children to seek employment locally in the State Farm or the sawmill. The concomitant public sector would be manned by the tenants of state-owned flats concentrated at the lower end of the village, comprising a small directorate and a work-

17. The new
headman.

force that might appropriately be classified as a rural proletariat. At present the directorate in the various fields of the socialist sector has few contacts with successful individual farmers. An example of the power exercised by the directors was given in Chapter Five (pp. 97-8). If these projections are not altogether fanciful one might in twenty or thirty years see the post-peasant village more clearly divided into public and private sectors, and internal class divisions, at present faintly observable within the private sector, would by that time be more conspicuous within the public sector. The surviving farmers of the private sector, no longer pleased to be described as peasants, would present a more homogeneous picture than they do today.

They might or might not build the closer bridges with directors of the socialist sector which are absent in the community today.

Let us close this section in a less speculative manner by illustrating the developments already demonstrably under way in the private sector. A young student of the Agricultural College in Rzeszów was sent to Wisłok in the summer of 1981 to collect some data from farmers in the private sector as part of a large-scale investigation of the region conducted by staff at his College. Using the questionnaire techniques which I eschewed he found that most farmers in Wisłok considered the new headman, mentioned several times already in this chapter, to possess more *autorytet* (authority, prestige) than any other individual in the village. He represents the ideal to which other peasants aspire. Unlike others who have prospered, he is not only admired, he is positively *liked* by the vast majority. They come to him from all parts of the village and ask him to assist them with his tractor. If he can afford the time he will do so, and in payment, though he may grumble when he returns home and feel that he has been exploited, he often accepts some symbolic vodka or wine when the task is performed. Other farmers understand his position well, and many now have misgivings about approaching him. They cannot reciprocate the services he provides in the same direct way that inter-household aid could be reciprocated in the past. A few families, including relatives, have paid him in the form of labour services (e.g. sending their children to help him during haymaking); but such solutions are awkward and have not been welcomed by either party. Increasingly, private tractor owners demand payment in cash for the help which they give to others; but they charge considerably less than the SKR, the public sector alternative, and certainly this headman's relations with other households are not regulated by profit maximising. But nor can they be regulated by charity or altruism, and so in the long run the economic ties between the successful manager of a mechanised enterprise and peasants who do not modernise at all must crumble. As this happens, so their social links will also weaken. This does not yet lead the successful farmer to seek instead to strengthen economic or social links with others like himself. On the contrary the households which are the most dynamic producers of agricultural commodities are extremely self-reliant and maintain few close contacts of any kind with any other households. They may not yet constitute a new class, but in a sense they are already detached from the community. These farmers are admired for the advances they have made. Yet the reproach of traditional peasant egalitarianism is an embarrassment which keeps some of them (and especially the only one of local origin) continually on the defensive about their achievements. Their wives are more likely to feel the sting. Several of the most hard-working women in the village (whose contribution to the running of the successful family farms is so vital that one hesitates to say that these have fully lost their peasant character) are distinctly unpopular. Although the student's questionnaire did not ask about them, I often heard them described as *chytre*, meaning crafty and keen on material gain. It is they who are more isolated, who must pay the penalty for breaking with traditional values, while their husbands may gain in prestige.

CHAPTER NINE

Conclusion

The manifestation of a different type of authority, the institutional authority of the National Councils, is a new phenomenon in Bieszczady. This sort of authority is closely linked to the appearance of symptoms of integration amongst the settlers in all of the pioneer villages in consequence of the progressive crystallisation of the factors of economic cooperation, social activity and also participation in culture. Such integration is proceeding not only in particular neighbourhood circles but is progressively encompassing all the inhabitants of the pioneer villages.

Henryk Jadam *(Bieszczadzianie — tworzywo osadnicze in Młodość i Tradycja regionu krośnieńskiego*, ed. H. Jadam; *Rzeszów*, 1979, p. 158)

A New Community in Wisłok?

The method used in the closing sections of the previous chapter was to note an orthodox or widely accepted view in the Polish literature, and then to see whether or not the evidence from Wisłok confirmed that interpretation. It was found that the Ukrainian ethnic minority is by no means as satisfactorily integrated as official sources claim, although there are signs that in the long run the ethnic cleavages will weaken, as regional differences within the Polish population have weakened already. It was also suggested that new cleavages might appear in village society as a result of recent economic policies; the present divisions between occupational groups and a potential for class differentiation within the private sector could be followed by a polarisation of sectors and a situation in which class distinctions were more conspicuous within the socialist sector than amongst the successors to the peasantry.

Adhering to the same method we may now turn in this final chapter to consider the question of a new community in Wisłok. This concept, too, is problematic in Western sociology, though there have been efforts to adopt an unromantic and value-free approach.[1] Polish authors in the socialist period have tended to regard the formation of a new community unambiguously as a normative goal. Generally, they have reported that this desirable objective can be attained in socialist conditions. For example, in the general context of the weakening of ethnic and regional differences, a leading sociologist and ideologue has written of 'the new reality of an integrated national community being formed in the crucible of socialist change'.[2] He and many others have devoted particular attention to the achievement of this goal in areas where mass resettlement was organised after the Second World War, principally in the western and northern territories acquired from Germany. An official or orthodox position may also be derived without difficulty from the published works of sociologists and ethnographers on the Bieszczady region. I have relied primarily upon two authors who conducted empirical investigations, the sociologist Henryk Jadam (1976) and the ethnographer Maria Biernacka (1974).[3] The term 'community' does not appear in the titles of these studies, for it has no exact equivalent in Polish. The word *wspólnota* is occasionally used by Jadam but it does not have quite the same range (some would say vacuity) that community possesses in English. Instead, these writers use the concept of social and cultural *integration*, and they purport to analyse the 'formation of a new society', founded on these patterns of integration. Their conclusions can be fairly summarised as follows: in Bieszczady in the socialist period new social relations have come into existence which have permitted the formation of integrated communities in at least two senses, firstly within each rural locality, and secondly at the level of the region. Let us begin the empirical evaluation at the lower of these two levels, and consider first of all the economic transformation, which the Polish authors agree has been fundamental in creating the conditions in which integration could proceed.

As we saw in Chapter Three, it is difficult to maintain that the peasants of Wisłok are integrated in an economic sense. They do not interact constructively with the public sector. Most keep their demands for services from the SKR to a minimum, few have any contacts with the State Farms, and few have responded significantly to the authorities' attempts to increase production by a system of long term contracting. Even peasants who took up specialist cards (see Chapter Three, pp. 44-8) were soon disenchanted, as the state reneged upon many of its promises of assistance. The entire peasantry remains deeply suspicious of the intentions of the socialist authorities in agriculture, and is above all sensitive to any dilution of their private ownership rights. It will take more than slogans to persuade peasants to change their mentality of resistance for one of enthusiastic economic cooperation with the socialist sector; and for long periods, including the 1970s, even the slogans were far from reassuring.

Mistrustful of the state, the Wisłok farmers are also mistrustful of each other. Only in the first years of the new settlement was there substantial pooling of equipment and mutual aid between households. In recent years the latter has declined to negligible proportions, except for a few close kin who happen also to be neighbours. Farmers in most neighbourhoods cannot even agree to graze the few head of cattle they possess on any joint basis. Help is not extended in non-agricultural activities either (such as house-building). It might be supposed that the poor quality of the support and extension services offered by the public sector would be an incentive to high levels of cooperation, e.g. in the passing of information as well as in lending equipment. This is not in fact the case. An example of extreme self-reliance is being set by the most productive farmers, who find themselves increasingly isolated and unable to maintain close relations even with their kin. Nor are the less productive much more inclined to cooperate with other households to overcome their problems. When the prospects for the peasant farm are judged bleak, then not only the younger generation but also heads of households are likely to turn instead to the socialist sector.

Some of the consequences of central policies towards the peasantry in the Bieszczady context are noted by Jadam and Biernacka. They state that some immigrants did not settle because their farms did not prosper, and that some were unable to repay the initial credits which they received from the Agricultural Bank. They note that great importance was attached to the ownership of land, but that there were many who did not use their new resources efficiently. The deployment of credits to erect new residential buildings, rather than to build stables and attempt to mechanise the farm, is seen as a positive virtue by Jadam. It reveals (in his opinion) not the failure of the authorities to provide economic incentives, but a lack of commercial orientation on the part of immigrants which amounts to a break with the capitalist past: '. . . the farmers who came to Bieszczady did not represent the orientation of an enterprise, of an owner of capital. Rather they were characterised by the spontaneity of their economic actions . . .'[4] Attractive though this idea of non-capitalistic farming may be, it did not solve the problems of the settlers. It left most of them both unable to persuade their children to inherit, and obliged to supplement their incomes in the socialist sector.

Only if integration is taken to mean greater involvement on the part of immigrant families with wage-labour in the socialist sector can a high proportion of households in Wisłok be called integrated.

Centrally approved plans for the development of the region have consolidated this sector. Within the village, employment may be sought with the Forestry Commission or the State Farms. Outside it, but within daily commuting range, the socialist sector has constructed major new enterprises, such as the sawmill at Rzepedź. Those who work in this sector must accept (though to varying degrees) the labour discipline of the factory. Their pensions and social security rights are superior to those of the peasants, and in this sense it might be said that they are more completely integrated into the new socialist society. However, there is an inverse relation between integration of this sort and the stabilisation of a new community in the village. Those employed in the socialist sector discourage their children from remaining in the village, many of these workers aspire to leave themselves eventually and prefer to distance themselves from the local society. Most of the daily commuters hope to migrate to the new housing estates in Rzepedź itself. It is no more than a large village at present, but perhaps there a new socialist community may be formed. The implications for the several dozen settlements from which workers presently commute to the sawmill are rather different. Expansion of the socialist sector results in the presence of a number of distinct occupational groups, none of which has any commitment to the village's future. At the same time, some of the peasants who might develop such a commitment through building up their own farms are tempted to opt instead for a more regular cash flow and improved long-term security. Such peasants will hang on to their land as long as possible, for this continues to provide them with another kind of security. This group falls midway between the minority of peasants which has managed to improve its perspectives and whose farms should remain viable, and those families whose commitment is solely to the socialist sector. If more and more peasants drift 'spontaneously' towards the latter, Jadam might infer that socialist economic integration was advancing to a higher stage. But only the remaining family farmers will retain any commitment to the village, and it is difficult to envisage what feelings of solidarity can develop if they are heavily outnumbered by short-term residents working for wages in the different branches of the socialist sector. The fundamental contrasts between these two sectors of the economy seem certain to polarise the village even further. It is possible that in the future closer bonds will develop *within* each, but the tendency at present seems to be in the opposite direction.

18. Queuing outside the village shop in 1981.

Socialist integration is also alleged to have proceeded apace through education and culture. However, we saw in Chapter Seven that many factors continue to handicap children in rural areas. Although most children nowadays go on to some form of secondary education, this is usually of a very limited kind; and of the several hundred children who have graduated from the primary school in Wisłok over the entire post-war period, not a single pupil was admitted to university, and only a tiny fraction gained entrance to other forms of higher education (teacher-training etc.). We noted that in certain respects, particularly concerning the inculcation of patriotic sentiment, the system may work quite efficiently for the authorities. However, attempts to encourage 'participation in culture' have not been successful, for either youth or adults, since the closure of the community-centre in the 1960s. The active programmes allegedly organised by Socialist Youth Groups and the Housewives' Circles in other parts of Bieszczady are entirely absent in Wisłok. None of the new socialist public holidays are celebrated, as they are said to be in other places. The library is little used, except by a few non-peasants with voracious appetites for war thrillers (some of the most popular being full of anti-Ukrainian prejudice). There are no dances at weekends, as in other villages. There is no place where people can gather, apart from the post office, the bus-stops and the shop. How-

160

ever, for women standing in line at the shop and using the buses more frequently to search for supplies, the economic crisis brought about a dramatic increase in the amount of time spent in company. A true spirit of solidarity developed during the hours (sometimes days) they spent waiting at the shop for the delivery truck to arrive.

'Social activity' (*dzialalność spoleczna*) is another, related area in which our Polish authors (particularly Jadam) claim that the course of integration in the new communities of Bieszczady can be scientifically verified. Again it cannot be supported from contemporary Wisłok. In earlier years teachers did organise evening classes for illiterate peasants, and certain small jobs (such as the maintenance of public buildings and road verges) were carried out collectively, though at the instigation of the authorities. This ceased entirely during the 1970s. It is still expected that the population will pull together in building the new school; but the headman, despite his considerable prestige and some years of effort, has so far been unable to overcome the inertia. It has not been possible to persuade peasants to collaborate in their direct material interest, e.g. in laying on a water supply from a local spring; it was difficult to cajole small neighbourhood groups into working together to improve their joint access road.

The complete lack of social and cultural activities of the sort described by the Polish investigators can perhaps be explained by the absence of the organisations or individuals to stimulate them. It can be suggested that this may be related to changes which took place in the 1970s, after the fieldwork of Biernacka and Jadam was completed. The bureaucratisation of local government at a commune centre several kilometres away, and the development of new relations of vertical dependence between the administration and peasant households, had unfortunate consequences. It might be argued, from a purely formal standpoint, that more households were being drawn into contacts of a socialist kind; but the cost was total petrification of contacts within the village. Depoliticisation was carried so far that, with complete apathy in some quarters and perhaps shrewd calculations in others, not even *Rural Solidarity* could muster support.

The expansion of the socialist sector and of the sphere of responsibility of the administration at all levels is cast, particularly by Henryk Jadam, as the driving force behind the creation of new communities in Bieszczady. Hence, he is led to argue, in the passage quoted at the beginning of this chapter, that the official organs of

161

public administration enjoy great *autorytet* on the basis of the constructive tasks they carry out. He supports the claim with detailed empirical data.[5] On this issue the evidence from Wisłok is in such flagrant contradiction with the sociologist's generalisations about the region that I am compelled to suspect an error. The loan word *autorytet* has an ambiguity in Polish similar to that which it possesses in other languages. Jadam clearly intends to suggest that the new villagers of Bieszczady attach more *prestige* to the councils, the administrative organs and the village headman, than they do, for example, to the priest and the teachers. But only if it was *power* that his informants thought they were talking about in their interviews do their answers become consistent with my own findings.

Sharp practice of this sort is characteristic of Jadam's work, less so of Biernacka's. Both also contain abundant material that is corroberated by the evidence from Wisłok. They stress the importance of the nuclear family in socialisation, in contrast to the large, multi-family households which they claim were the norm in this region in the pre-socialist period. Both recognise the importance of the auto-chthonous group in many villages, find this to be a stabilising element and in the forefront both socially and in economic cooperation between households. Jadam writes occasionally of a 'homogeneous' population, which is clearly premature. However, the general picture of ethnic and regional differences being broken down is one that the Polish authors document very well, e.g. in describing the constantly widening circles within which marriages take place. This is certainly undermining the Ukrainian minority in the whole of the Komańcza area, whilst within Wisłok itself the diverse regional origins of the immigrants have left little mark upon their children. Current marriage patterns generally support the proposition that in the special conditions of resettled villages regional and ethnic cleavages can quite rapidly be broken down. However, with a high proportion marrying outside the region and many of those who marry locally also anxious to get away as soon as possible, integration of this sort should not be confused with the *stabilisation* of a new community.

In the early 1970s, when the fieldwork on which the Polish authors base their works was being completed, it might have seemed reasonable to assume that the breaking down of the most obvious barriers within the new population would lead eventually to stable communities. The turnover of farms in the private sector, though still considerable, was lower than it had been in the 1950s and 1960s, whilst some personnel in the socialist sector were residing for longer than they had in the past. However, the general effects of policies pursued in the 1970s combined to smother self-administration, to increase the unpopularity of the authorities, and to make the objective of the 'integrated community' more elusive than ever. Consequently, the evidence which I found in Wisłok does not affect the validity of the accounts I have been discussing, prepared almost ten years earlier. A further reservation should be entered in defence of Maria Biernacka. Whilst she generally implies, like Jadam, that integration is something more than an analytical category, that a new community is something which can be observed 'out there', she nevertheless confesses that in certain villages an opposite tendency is to be found.[6] We are not told how many such villages there are, or how they came into being. Instead, Biernacka goes on to discuss the processes of integration at higher levels, where her findings are again largely, though not entirely, congruent with those of Jadam. In the main the immigrants to Bieszczady have become increasingly attached to their *region*, and simultaneously they have been more fully incorporated into the new national community. Of the two authors, it is Jadam who places the greater emphasis on a new regional consciousness, which he claims was fully fashioned by the 1970s, and articulated in various ways by the new inhabitants. I would contend that, on the contrary, to the extent that Wisłok peasants do consider themselves to belong to Bieszczady, this is the consequence of sustained myth-making in the regional and national media, but is still far from deeply 'internalised'. The name which immigrants use (according to Jadam) in describing themselves — *Bieszczadzianie* — was never used in Wisłok, where even the term *Wisloczanie* to denote the members of the local community is very seldom heard. However, a researcher who made no systematic enquiries of his own throughout the region is in no position to dispute the more general claim. Upon reading Biernacka and Jadam, when my work in Wisłok was already at an advanced stage, I felt for some time that I was in an awkward position. Either I had to suppose that the entire situation had been transformed in the relatively short time — scarcely a full decade — which had elapsed between their fieldwork and mine, or I should face the fact that Wisłok was a quite exceptional village, from which it would be unsafe to draw any conclusions about the region to which it belonged, let alone the nation.

As already indicated, there is some truth in the first of these possibilities. The discovery of another reliable empirical study of the region, prepared by a young researcher with a particular interest in the sociology of religion, enables me confidently to reject the second proposition. Unfortunately, this work had not been deemed suitable for publication. Andrejz Potocki's thesis, entitled 'The link with the Roman-Catholic Parish and the link with the region of settlement; a sociological study based on the example of Bieszczady', was submitted at the Warsaw Theological College in 1974. The author conducted his fieldwork at approximately the same period as Biernacka and Jadam, and based his study on similar questionnaire techniques. Unlike them, however, he did all the detailed interviewing himself, tramping around the villages for more than a year in order to do so. Potocki distinguishes three socio-occupational groups amongst the new immigrants to the region: individual farmers, workers in the new socialist sector in agriculture and forestry, and finally those who earn their living outside of agriculture altogether (commuters etc.). High levels of satisfaction with their conditions in the Bieszczady region are expressed only by the members of a fourth group, the autochthonous population. Farmers in full ownership of their land were found to display more positive attitudes towards the region than the other Polish immigrant groups. However, Potocki is successful in bringing out the ambiguities of a concept of 'regional patriotism'. It transpires that some of those who have most sympathy for the region are also the ones least anxious that their children should remain there. Only in the autochthonous group was a majority of respondents keen that at least one child should remain in the region. Farmers were adjudged to be the most 'stabilised' of the three immigrant groups, but even here, the rates of re-emigration were high. In response to detailed questioning 34 per cent of individual farmers said that they had 'no social contacts' in their new community (the reasons commonly cited being 'lack of a suitable partner' or 'feelings of personal self-sufficiency'); 47 per cent declared that they possessed 'no friends'. Here was confirmatory evidence that I had not been spending my time in such an unusual community after all. The main sociology-of-religion themes in Potocki's dissertation were also most interesting. He found that the church generally played a very constructive role in fostering a new local and regional identification, but that there was considerable variation across the different groups. For farmers in the private sector, strong ties with the parish were positively related to the intensity of their ties with the region. However, in the case of those committed to the socialist sector a strong attachment to the region was compatible with weak linkages to the parish, and Potocki offers a plausible explanation for this. This group contains many individuals who have come to Bieszczady because they have infringed the Christian moral code elsewhere, most frequently in the course of the breakdown of their marriages. For such persons the new parish 'reminds them of duties which they prefer not to think about'[7] and they neither know their priest as well as other immigrants, nor do they attend mass so often. However, a large majority of persons in all of the groups examined by Potocki still described themselves as 'believers' (the range was from 85 per cent of those working outside agriculture to 95 per cent of individual farmers). The fact that the Bieszczady region offered asylum to some individuals seeking to escape from previous bonds of family and community did not prevent some of these from eventually forging new ties with the parish. For the large majority, the parish served from the outset as the major force promoting community in the new environment.

The role of religion and of the Roman Catholic parish in particular are subjects conspicuously ignored by the authors previously considered.[8] Yet if anything can be said to integrate the people of Wisłok it is their church. There is only one atheist family, and even they could not escape the church's monopoly of the rites of the life-cycle. Most families attend services regularly in the Wisłok building, even those working in the socialist sector whose ties with the village are so weak that neither they nor their children are likely to remain there permanently. The traditional ritualistic character of Polish Catholicism has been modified of late but the range of the church's functions remains wide. Its role in the past of the nation ensures that it cannot lose from any upsurge in patriotic sentiment. It has appeared to go out of its way to maintain its appeal to its rural constituency: the emphasis it places upon the family and the virtues of small holdings is intensely satisfying to peasants who struggle in a socialist environment. In the welding of a new local community in Wisłok the church has contributed a great deal. It might have done even more, had it been permitted to do so. Perhaps it would be more correct to say that people might have managed to do more for themselves had they been allowed greater freedom to express their religion. For example, the youth club might have functioned more smoothly if it had been organised under the auspices of the church rather than those of the Communist Party. There was also the sorry fate of a theatrical group which flourished in the village in the 1950s and early 1960s. Although not directly sponsored by the church, the most popular pieces put on by this troupe (and performed by them in many other villages in the area) were invariably religious in character. Eventually a performance was proscribed by the administration, and scripts confiscated. With the church unable to play any prominent role outside a narrowly defined 'religious sphere', cultural life has been needlessly impoverished in recent years. Nowadays there is really only the Sunday mass to bring the village together.

It is conceivable that the church could also succeed one day in creating a new regional identity for Bieszczady, as effectively as it already embodies the national identity, provides solace for the individual and the cement which unites the village. Although Latin Catholicism did not predominate in this mountain zone before the socialist period, the development of a new pilgrimage centre at Jasień is an illustration of what the church can do to create a new sense of belonging. It is hard to imagine that any other institution is capable of doing this. The attempts of certain Polish authors and the media to construct a new regional mythology seem likely to be less successful than the efforts of an earlier generation of Polish scholars to fabricate a regional identity for indigenous inhabitants of the mountain zone, who called themselves *Rusnaks*. The so-called *Lemkos* in the more westerly parts of the zone (to whom this name was indiscriminately applied only after the First World War) could at least be distinguished from their fellow *Rusnaks* in other parts of the mountains and from neighbouring Poles by any number of ethnographical and linguistic criteria. This is hardly the case in Bieszczady (a name not taken up until after the Second World War), where the diverse immigrant and autochthonous groups which make up the present population have been rapidly losing their distinctive identities in the course of the advances of the socialist economy and the homogenisation of the new national community.

To an even greater extent than other territories resettled in the socialist period, Bieszczady has stood out as a melting pot. However, the region has also been an instructive setting in which to consider the implementation of general socialist policies. Researchers have recognised the interest of the experiment, but from published studies it would appear that the village which I studied has no representative significance. Only the unpublished work of a young Catholic sociologist, bringing out the importance of religion as a factor promoting integration, convinced me that my results were not highly unusual. Whatever the general merits of the community study, a special defence can perhaps be made out for the foreigner when circumstances do not permit the publication of solid, truthful empirical studies by native investigators. Would I have done better to have translated Potocki's thesis in its entirety, or to have sought to emulate his methods in covering a much wider area? Had I done so I might be in a position to generalise more confidently, but I am not sure that this would have produced results more worthwhile than those of my 'massive immersion' in Wisłok. No doubt Biernacka, and most certainly Jadam, also feel that they have grasped a deep sociological truth when they write about processes of integration in the new communities which have taken shape in Bieszczady. They are native researchers from the towns who, like Potocki, applied sociological techniques in studying a large area; whereas I have relied on the oldest established technique of empirical anthropology to describe a single locality. On some issues I think our studies may complement each other, on some we may arrive at very similar conclusions. On some of the most crucial we are fundamentally at odds, and the reader must make up his mind. In my opinion, the complete absence of 'integrated communities' is highly relevant to the crisis besetting the socialist state in Poland. The causes must be sought *a*) in features common to many other societies undergoing rapid industrialisation, but also in *b*) features peculiar to socialist, centrally-planned, but non-collectivised Poland. Let us turn finally to consider again the latter, and the contradictory persistence of this peasantry.

The worse the better

Nobody can deny that the interests of Polish farmers are better protected than under any other East European government, even though they could always be improved.
Olga A. Narkiewicz (1976, p. 284)

The sub-title is a pithy encapsulation of communist policy towards the peasantry in the Stalinist years.[9] According to this principle the worse the position of the peasants became, the better the prospects for socialism and transcendence of the old class structures. Although these policies were ostensibly abandoned after 1956, in practice there have been important elements of continuity. The socialist sector has retained ideological priority inside as well as outside of agriculture. The inability to pursue collectivisation and the unwillingness to allow independent farmers to prosper along a 'capitalist road' has enabled the peasantry to survive.[10] It is important now to ask if this sterile conjunction was unique to Poland, and to assess how these peasants compare with rural dwellers in other socialist states.

First of all it is important to clarify in what sense the peasantry has been preserved. 'Traditional' peasant farming was extinguished in the 1950s, as elsewhere in Eastern Europe. This was a consequence of rapid industrialisation, and perhaps an inevitable one, given the political context in which this was pursued. In many parts of the country there was pressure to join cooperatives. The free market was effectively suppressed and the private sector (in which agriculture now dominated, after sweeping nationalisation in all other sectors) was denied the possibility of accumulation. Hence, many farmers were willing recruits for industry and the peasantry has become incomparably more open to the wider society. Some migrated permanently, but others worked as commuters because of the lack of urban housing. Peasant workers, like those who remained fully engaged in private farming, had their legal rights as private landowners reaffirmed after 1956. The extent to which the reality of *control* has been retained is debateable; it seemed to peasants that the constraints of the socialist environment tightened intolerably in the 1970s, when Gierek's policies enabled a minority of peasants, selected by the administration, to achieve long overdue modernisation. These policies seem likely to be resumed in the rest of the century, as the upheavals of the early 1980s recede. In the meantime the essentials of the peasant labour process have remained in place for the large number of rural households who have neither been elevated to 'specialist' status and expanded commodity production nor wished to rely solely upon wage income from the national labour market. The survival of the group of 'full-time farmers', albeit a minority in many villages today, has facilitated the survival of a 'peasant ethos' amongst other groups. This was strengthened by the effects of the economic crisis of the early 1980s, when the poor food situation forced a general re-evaluation of the subsistence plot. Farmers able to market a large surplus were reluctant to do so as the currency in which they were paid ceased to command any goods whatsoever. There resulted a burgeoning of 'informal' links between town and countryside (via kin, worker-peasants etc.), and these circuits permitted more realistic exchanges to take place, often by barter. After martial law the campaign against 'speculators' increased and government controls became more effective once again. All the old problems in persuading peasants to expand their production remain.

Politically, these years of crisis may perhaps be seen in retrospect as a late flowering of peasant populism. Government resistance in 1981 was on no issue so clearly in evidence as over the issue of allowing peasants to replace the defunct populist party and form their own free trade union. Central to the programme of *Rural Solidarity* throughout its brief existence was the demand for full and genuine recognition of the peasant's private ownership rights. There were significant conflicts within the movement. It was symbolic that one of the earlier designations of the union, '*Peasant Solidarity*' was dropped in favour of '*Individual Farmers' Solidarity*'. Some activists were well aware that reiterating the inviolability of two hectare parcels of private property was not conducive to solving the agrarian problem; but it was felt that without these basic guarantees the government could not win the trust of any peasants. Leaders had no convincing alternative to the 'Stolypinist' polarisation strategy of the government. Their egalitarian spirit was plainly incompatible with economic efficiency (except insofar as they demanded parity with the socialist sector of agriculture). In other words, in the technological conditions of the 1980s populism was even less viable than it had been fifty years earlier: it was unrealistic to suggest that all peasants could have access to the optimal size of holding, and the industrial sector was no better placed to absorb redundant rural labour than it had been in the capitalist period. In such circumstances, the similarities with the fate of earlier populist protests are striking. There were pockets of militancy, of which Bieszczady was one of the most notable, but altogether (perhaps because of the accumulated effects of socialist administration) the peasantry has been passive. If it is finally to disappear, it seems likely to acquiesce to its fate. It is not clear what kind of populism, if any, can be preserved by the modernised family farmers who replace them.

But in other socialist countries the authentic peasant representative bodies have long since vanished from the scene, and farmers no longer have the direct control over their labour process which enables *them* to determine production, and gives *them* the power to deepen a crisis such as that of 1981. The contrasts with the other socialist states of Eastern Europe are the most revealing, though they are not entirely straightforward. Poland's immediate neighbours are East Germany and Czechoslovakia. Both of these states were already developed industrially before they became socialist and embarked upon the collectivisation of agriculture. Although by Western standards productivity in agriculture may still leave a lot to be desired, output has expanded, the populations are well nourished, and the numbers employed in this sector have fallen to a relatively low proportion of the national labour force. Perhaps the most significant statistical indicator is one that was reported in the Polish press in 1981 (and noticed by peasants in Wisłok). It was stated that the proportion of industry's aggregate product going to meet the needs of agriculture in these neighbouring states was 12 per cent, compared to a figure of only 4 per cent in Poland.[11] In other words the failure to collectivise in Poland seems to have led not just to discrimination against the mass of peasant producers, but to discrimination against the agricultural sector as a whole.

A comparison with the two Balkan states collectivised along the Soviet lines suggests that it is the nature of the industrialisation strategy (rather than starting position, natural endowment, commitment to collectivist principles etc.) which is the crucial variable. Romania and Bulgaria started from an extremely underdeveloped industrial base, nearer to that of pre-revolutionary Russia than to the East German or the Czech position. Each still has a large proportion of the workforce in the agrarian sector (though this proportion has declined more rapidly than it has in Poland, where it has stabilised at about 30 per cent). The difference seems to be that Bulgaria, with a more centralised structure, has invested heavily and consistently to make the most of a favourable natural endowment, resulting in plentiful food supplies at home and useful surpluses for export, whilst the Romanian drive to attain a higher measure of industrial self-sufficiency has produced strains comparable to those encountered by the USSR when it embarked on a similar course. Thus, in Romania the proportion of investment resources going to agriculture began to decline once the collectivised sector was established, and without supplies of basic inputs (above all adequate fertiliser) productivity remained far below the potential. By the 1980s the food crisis was profound, and rationing had to be introduced almost on the Polish scale. The short-term solution has been to *require* the rural population to make good the inadequacies of the socialist sector by producing more on the private plots.

At this point we enter a potential minefield, for the role of plot farming in socialist states is easily misrepresented. It is best approached as one aspect of overall integration in this sector, important in every state, but particularly so where urbanisation and industrialisation are not advanced and there is the potential to mobilise labour in high-value, labour intensive branches of production. Hun-

gary is the clearest case in point. Her overall success with collectivisation results both from high levels of investment in socialist agriculture and from stimulating (using market prices as incentives, rather
than relying on exhortation and political pressure) high levels of
production on small, family-managed plots. The comparison with
Poland may be especially instructive, as the social structures of these
states were fairly similar at the onset of the socialist period. In
Hungary the proportion of workers employed in agriculture has
fallen much more rapidly, to below 20 per cent, and it might even be
maintained that the structure and performance of the urban labour
force have been decisively influenced in consequence.[12] But does
not the survival of the peasant labour process on these private plots
imply that peasantry is still alive here too? Apparently not, at least
not according to these petty commodity producers themselves, nor
to most outside observers. The inequalities between town and countryside are certainly there: lower wage rates, differential access to
state housing, to culture etc. But where there is enough flexibility to
permit material incentives to function in plot farming, the rural
population can actually acquire larger incomes (by giving up leisure)
and compensate handsomely for its inferior access to the benefits of
socialist redistribution. Because the socialist sector in agriculture is ·
strong and efficient in the conduct of large-scale operations, this
solution does not have the negative consequences for the agrarian
structure implied by the large worker-peasant population in Poland.
Where genuine 'market socialism' is put into operation, where rural
dwellers can build large houses, purchase cars in their own currency,
and have all that they need for production laid on by well equipped
socialist farms, then it is possible to speak of integration both within
the agricultural sector and at societal level. Exploitation through a
market mechanism seems preferable to the complete blockage which
the Polish peasant has experienced. In Hungary the peasant has
been 'captured', the old ethos is almost dead (it may survive in a few
isolated areas, amongst the most senior age groups only), and there
is no desire to turn the clock back to the days of private peasant
ownership.

Finally, if we omit consistently Stalinist Albania from this brief
review, there is the other outstanding representative of 'market
socialism', Yugoslavia, which from a number of angles would seem to
be most suitable for comparison with Poland. Not only is the size of
the agricultural labour force rather similar, but some 85 per cent of
the cultivated area is in private ownership and, as in Poland, given

the large numbers engaged in commuting who wish to retain their smallholdings, the structural problems of agriculture are serious. They are accentuated by a limit of 10 hectares upon the area to which a private farmer may expand (a restriction it has never been necessary to enforce in Poland, which had perhaps more effective means of forestalling progress in 'capitalist' directions), and by policies giving the socialist sector priority in investment programmes. It can be argued that these contradictions will bring agriculture to a critical point at which effective modernisation must be introduced, either in socialist ways (expanding the public sector) or by permitting the private sector to expand production. The similarity with the Polish predicament is obvious. It would seem also that we have greater likelihood of encountering peasantry in this context. However in Yogoslavia the decentralised and self-managed economy has not been excessively biased towards industry, and rural dwellers have been drawn in much more, both as producers and consumers, to the national market. The availability of more capital equipment to the private sector than in Poland, and the possibilities for intensification of production in many areas (not present to the same degree in Poland) have meant that in practice the Yugoslav peasant has not been trapped in the same way as the Pole. Above all perhaps, he has been given greater security of private ownership. Thus, the constraints deriving from self-management socialism are not the same as those of central planning within the Soviet bloc: the failure to collectivise need not have the consequences it has had in Poland.[13]

The comparative framework could be broadened further, to include the changes which have occurred recently in agriculture in other European states, with very different economic and political organisation. Exodus from the countryside and the consolidation of farms have been widespread phenomena, with peasantry surviving tenaciously only in conspicuously underdeveloped regions. The most impressive concentrations of peasants are now to be found where contradictions between socialist ideology and the economic requirement that a genuine market permit individuals to accumulate have prolonged the transition to a modern agrarian structure: notably in Poland, and to a lesser extent in Yugoslavia. In the latter it can be maintained that a more balanced industrialisation strategy and the relative adequacy of the market mechanism have permitted the assimilation of peasantry into that federal socialist society to advance more rapidly than has been the case in the national society of Poland. In relation to the collectivised socialist states the proportion of the workforce remaining in agriculture seems likely to remain high; it seems likely too that the traditional cultural stereotype of the 'peasant' will remain stronger in these countries. In the event of an economic crisis, such as that of the 1980s in Poland, the traditional versatility of the small farm may be reaffirmed, 'peasantry' may again become prominent both in the self-image of farmers and also in the attitudes of townspeople, incited to be jealous of peasant self-sufficiency by the propaganda of the politicians. However, in spite of these factors, when even the non-collectivised states of Eastern Europe are compared with other European states it can still be claimed that there has been continuous high mobility out of the rural sector, and indeed high rates of mobility in society as a whole. Peasant youth, though perhaps not everywhere to the same degree as in Wisłok, has preferred the towns and industrial employment. When one takes account further of all those who are drawn into socialist wage-labour without migrating from the village, it must be concluded that in the very broad sociological sense (the first aspect of our 'working definition' of peasantry), the peasantry in Poland has been a casualty of the policy of imposed industrialisation. In this basic sense socialist goals have been realised as fully as in the collectivised states: an antagonistic class has been incorporated, and its continued ownership of the land has not been the foundation for continued wealth and income differentiation of the kind found in capitalist class societies. On the contrary, in spite of official policies aiming to equalise incomes in rural and urban sectors, it seems certain that most rural dwellers in Poland are further from attaining such parity than the farmers of a collectivised state able to participate in a lucrative 'private sector'.

Whatever satisfaction the authorities might have gleaned from the social consequences of their policies towards the peasantry, they have fallen short of their own ideological standards, and for this reason persisted in dealing with peasants as a hostile, anachronistic element in the system. Proof that they were not in fact accepted as just another occupational group came with the protracted efforts to deny them the right to form a trade union in 1981, when this right had already been conceded to industrial workers. The authorities have also had to recognise that their policies have had disastrous economic consequences. In the absence of a coherent plan for the sector, only small numbers of individual farmers (not necessarily the most able) have been able to mechanise significantly, and to expand their acreage. It has been proven that forced expansion of the socialist sector in agriculture has been costly and inefficient, and detrimental not merely in direct material terms to the private sector (fertiliser diverted etc.) but even more importantly to the latter's sense of security. Consequently, many aspects of the old, labour-intensive, non-specialised peasant farm have remained in place, or re-emerged at times of crisis. In the current efforts to stimulate the private sector to move away from this pattern of farming and towards more modern types of production which will permit the marketing of larger surpluses, it remains to be seen if the necessary sense of security can be created. Experience would suggest that it might best be provided by a general switching from administrative methods to reliance upon the forces of the market, in the context of a far-reaching reform of the whole economic mechanism. For the fortunes of the private sector to improve, even for a minority, and to motivate youth to remain engaged in farming, it would appear essential that the land which they work also be subjected to the market, and thereby restored to its traditional role in the peasant community, the focus not merely of sentiment but of the most fundamental economic values. Here we are back once again with the dilemma of explaining just how important a factor land ownership has been in the persistence of peasantry, and the related issue of the extent to which the persistence of private property in land modifies the class structure of a socialist society.

An orthodox socialist response might be to agree that the deficiencies of agriculture were crucial to the productive system as a whole and so to political breakdown in the 1980s, and to insist that the persistence of peasant private property is the anomalous element in the socialist relations of production, responsible for the malfunctioning of the whole system. But does his ownership of land make the class position of the Polish peasant any different from, say, that of a cooperative farmer in Hungary? Hungary has much less private property, but makes much fuller use of market incentives, lacking in Poland: is Poland then less of a socialist society than Hungary? It might seem that the private ownership of land is not very important in practice, when it is very difficult to obtain, even to hire from socialist enterprises, the other 'means of production' without which the land cannot be efficiently worked; and when the controls vested in the state apparatus seriously qualify those ownership rights; and when the peasant has no representative body to help ensure that his legal ownership gives him the practical power to do things with his basic resource. When the socialist sector is as dominant as it is in

Poland (with only 22 per cent of the land but owning more than half of the machine stock and making about 70 per cent of new investment) then it seems ridiculous to pretend that Poland is on the 'capitalist road'. The social relations of production, in the broad Marxian sense, as opposed to superficial property relations, have been as socialist here as anywhere else in Eastern Europe, perhaps more so.

Rural dwellers are discriminated against in the other socialist states. In Poland many have remained private landowners and *resisted* incorporation into the national market; in other words, they could *choose* to remain peasants. It is a moot point whether the advantages they have gained in this process outweigh the disadvantages. If a very positive evaluation is placed on private ownership, small-scale production and the occasional surfacing of the peasant ethos in populist outbursts in the political arena, then the assertion by Narkiewicz quoted at the head of this section is unchallengeable. If, however, one takes due account of the aspirations of the people living as peasants, the desire above all to improve their living standards, then the Polish solution is no longer self-evidently superior. If one accepts as given, as previous generations of populists usually did, the 'framework of harsh political realities',[14] then it was, perhaps, a mistake to insist on the continued private ownership of land. Polish peasants may remain proud to be owners of their land, and many may have built large modern houses. But they also look enviously at the conditions enjoyed by cooperative members and employees in Hungary, where vastly superior market opportunities have more than compensated for the loss of private ownership of land. Collectivisation of land in the 1950s might, given that Poland was to remain firmly within socialist constraints, have led to more rapid improvements in the living standards of the rural population and more general satisfaction than is found today. On the other hand, if collectivisation had been pursued along the anti-market, industry-first lines followed in Romania, then the Polish peasantry would not have even legal ownership as a consolation today.

Collectivisation does not in practice bring about a modern agrarian structure 'overnight'. In their continued reliance upon the private sector it may be said that almost all of the socialist states are exploiting elements of the old peasant economy. The conditions of rural families are in certain respects almost everywhere inferior to those in the cities, the latter having far easier access to the rewards of the system. Yet, particularly where there are opportunities to redress this balance in material ways through activities in the 'informal sector' (including plots), where market criteria are effective, the old peasant ethos and self-image would seem to be on the wane. In the severing of links with traditional agrarian society, that of private land ownership seems to be the most important. In circumstances where the old agrarian class cannot be assimilated into society by either socialist or capitalist methods, legal ownership of land is sufficient to ensure the survival of peasantry long into the industrial age.

No doubt this stalemate, the barriers to modernisation, cannot endure indefinitely. The immediate impact of crises such as that of the 1980s is to reinforce small-scale production and to highlight the resilience and self-sufficiency of the peasantry. Yet, given developments in agriculture in other countries, the logic seems ineluctable; in Poland too, sooner rather than later, peasants will give way to a new stratum of family farmers. No doubt they will not be commercial farmers in the Western sense, with powerful unions to defend their interests. However, if they are to be motivated to produce at anything like their potential, they may well have to be assured a standard of living that would disturb some socialist purists. One optimistic scenario would envisage the post-peasants as a pressure group in a kind of pluralist socialism. Polish socialism has not really been like that so far. It has had to accommodate only one other major power centre, the Roman Catholic Church. Some minority groups consider that they are better served by this socialist regime than by an opposition movement too closely identified with the national church. In a sense the peasantry too has, through clinging to its land, also retained a separate power base. Certainly the ethos has survived and peasants are united in their profound suspicion of the authorities. Of course, peasant political opposition has been less effective under socialism than under the populist leaders of the agrarian age. On the other hand peasant religiosity remains at a high level, ensuring that the Catholic Church remains the major solidifying force, in local communities and in the nation. It must be hoped that the power of this church will combine with the idealism of *Solidarity* and the pragmatism of genuine economic reform, and eventually prove conducive to a true pluralist scenario in the socialist industrial state.

Two Immigrants

The texts I translate below describe the experience of two Polish families which have settled in Wisłok in the socialist period. The contrasts between them could hardly be stronger. The first tells the story of Jan Janicki, one of the pioneers in 1948, who was headman of the village for more than thirty years. It is an unabridged translation of a text published in 1953 and circulated in brochure form by the county authorities in Rzeszów. It was intended explicitly to encourage others to follow the footsteps of Janicki. His story is therefore somewhat idealised, but there is no factual misrepresentation.

The second text is a translation of fragments of an article which appeared in a weekly newspaper in April 1980 and won a prize for the journalist Adam Warzocha. It is about the experience of Krzysztof Ołtarzewski, born in a refugee camp in Holland in 1944, brought up in Warsaw, a resident of the Bieszczady region from the early 1970s, and with his own farm in Wisłok between 1978 and 1983. Just as the article about Janicki presents the experience of the early settlers in rather too rosy a light, Ołtarzewski would perhaps admit that this article gives an unduly graphic account of the problems encountered by a recent immigrant whose background, convictions and aspirations are fundamentally different from those of other Wisłok residents. He was not perfectly satisfied with the style of the journalist; but again there is no misrepresentation of the basic facts.

I. Jan Janicki

It was the year 1930. When one of the youngsters from Filipowice in the county of Cracow went courting in the neighbouring village a mischievous whisper would accompany him, which poisoned the life of even the girl who loved him: look, the goatherd is here! This meant that the young man was poor, so poor that no cow's tail lashed the flies in his croft; only goats could survive on the willow twigs and weeds of his estate. Janicki himself wasn't living much better than this. He had just a few acres of land, he had raised a cottage on the common land of the village, paying a rent of 5 złoty. And because he was young and robust he finally found a girl who would marry him; things were supposed to get better that way, two heads being better than one.

But life for them did not work out the way they had promised themselves it would. The yield of a few acres of poor soil couldn't even suffice to meet subsistence requirements. Try as he might, Jan was unable to pick up work in the town, and in the villages it was getting harder to find something all the time, because any openings would get snatched up by workers cast out by the crisis. Meanwhile, around the hearth the hungry mouths were multiplying. Jan went here, there and everywhere to keep his family above the bread line, but Poverty stared them in the face continually. The worst time was before the harvest, for quite apart from the lack of bread the elements wreaked havoc on the unfortunate: the river which flowed nearby was swollen by the spring thaws and flooded the house practically up to waist height. Then he had to carry his sick wife and children up on the kitchen stove.

Years sped by and no help was to be found. To make matters worse his health began to go. After suffering the experience of Nazi occupation he found himself practically devoid of strength in the fatherland now liberated from the yoke of capitalists, both native and foreign; but he was still curious what the rule of the workers and the peasants would bring to him.

At the village meeting he was always present, amongst the poor. Things improved in the countryside, it became easier to sell produce and it wasn't difficult to find work. But he was dreaming of another life altogether. Every night he dreamed about land, having enough land to feed and clothe that swarm of children so that they would not ask for more. Once he went along to a meeting, got there a little bit late and had to prick up his ears to get the drift of what the speaker was saying. Then he started to twitch with impatience — the subject was land, fallow land that was waiting for settlers; and had not been touched by a plough-share for a couple of years. At first he couldn't believe that it was enough to express a desire to take over a farm and without paying any money at all you could obtain land, a house, farm buildings, credits for farm implements and even a free warrant for the railway journey to get there.

Jan put his head down and made some long and careful calculations. So engrossed did he become in them, so captivating was the vision of owning so much land, that he completely lost the track of the meeting. He was brought back to his sense by a sudden clatter as the farmers got up from the benches. Going up to the speaker, he started to ask him all sorts of questions: where was that land? what quality? what sort of houses, and could it all be true?

The speaker burst out laughing — he was saying all this for the umpteenth time — 'in the county of Rzeszów, in the district of Sanok, you'll find land in abundance, houses and barns; and if you think it sounds too good to be true, anyone can check it out with his own eyes and the railway will cost him nothing . . .'.

Janicki went home and he was contemplating and brooding over the next step for such a long time that his wife looked at him anxiously. In the end he did decide. And because he went around the village before setting off on his voyage of inspection, talking about this and that, and the attractions of that land at Sanok, seven others all as poor as himself accompanied him on that first journey. He left without even telling his wife what was really afoot, for it would have been a shame to disappoint her and he was afraid to build up vain hopes of a better life.

What they saw exceeded their wildest expectations. They travelled to Wisłok Wielki in the district of Sanok. There was so much land to be seen that even today, though plenty of families have settled there in the meantime, there are still several hundred acres laying fallow. They walked carefully around the entire village, they had a good look at the houses and the farm buildings; they even scuffed up clods of earth and examined them to see how rich the soil was, to see if it could *produce* . . . It was a beautiful place, a village located on gentle slopes and surrounded by forest. There were flowers everywhere, everything seemed to be in blossom and alive, except that the soil lay covered by a thick layer of green grass, whilst up on the higher slopes the withered hay was almost grey in appearance. 'Land' was all Janicki murmured, neither in sorrow nor in envy, as he strode across the beautiful fields. He selected for himself a house with proper foundations well above the level of the river, remembering the endless flooding they had known in Filipowice. 'It'll never come up this far!' he thought. The farm buildings were not bad at all and there was a garden with a few fruit trees. 'Yes, this one will be the best' Janicki confirmed his choice, and the others who had come with him were also unable to turn down such an opportunity to improve their

179

living standards. Each of them chose a place for himself and informed the presidium of the District Council in Sanok of his decision. There they were assured that everything would be facilitated, that they should fetch their families to Wisłok at once. For Janicki the journey from Sanok to Filipowice had never seemed so long before. In the train he was still deliberating where and what he would have to do, he had his future life already worked out in his thoughts. He had hardly crossed the threshold of the house when he greeted his wife and welcoming children with words that, for him, were now plain and self-evidently joyous: 'We're off to a new life!'.

His wife momentarily did not understand. It was inconceivable to her that they should leave for a region she did not know and leave behind them their bit of land and house. She was absolutely aghast when she heard that Jan had decided to sell everything. 'My God,' she exclaimed, 'what am I going to do with these little ones?' But six little ones, and above all Felek, the oldest of them, supported their father. What was the point in staying on this small plot when, in Wisłok, they would receive enough land so that they all could eat to their hearts' content? There was some other idea lurking in that young head, but Felek was silent.

The migration cost them nothing. The removal operation was a bit reminiscent of a gypsy camp: they had a few bundles of belongings, a pile of children, and a cow on the end of a rope, and this was how they arrived in Wisłok Wielki. Mrs Janicki breathed freely when she saw the house: she liked it. She rejoiced in the knowledge that they now had six hectares of land and could sort out their lives properly at last.

A little later their joy gave way to a certain apprehension. How were they going to plough and sow, and was this really their property? On this score they were satisfied by a representative of the Sanok presidium, who welcomed them warmly and wished them success in their new environment. They talked over what the Janickis would need, and the upshot was that Jan received credits for seed and for essential implements — loans. Altogether he was able to put together about 200,000 złoty of the old currency. He bought a horse and a cow, the agricultural machines they needed, and with the aid of young Felek he started ploughing. The first time they went out the whole family watched them, curious about the soil which the jealous grass and shrivelled weeds had hitherto hidden from them. The sharp blades turned over a dark ridge in the earth, so fertile that it gleamed in the sunshine. That soil would produce fine yields.

Nor did the soil of Wisłok let them down. Barley grew there admirably, each hectare producing about 16–18 quintals. Clover for fodder grew almost up to the waist, while sugar beet, rye and wheat also gave good results. The potatoes grown that year in the Janickis' garden would have graced an exhibition.

Janicki is a wise farmer. 'If the state puts everything into my hands, does all it can to help me, then it's up to me to organise a model farm here. I won't miss a single opportunity,' he resolved.

The Janickis have now been living in Wisłok Wielki for five years. The document conferring full legal ownership of the farm has long been lying in the bottom of a drawer, and all the fears of Mrs Janicki have long vanished. Today in their barn you can see 4 cows, 2 heifers, 16 sheep, a couple of horses and a foal, 4 pigs, and chickens and geese everywhere. In the orchard in front of the house Janicki set up 14 bee hives, collecting 320 kg of honey from them last year. The nearby woods keep the inhabitants of Wisłok well supplied not only with fuel but also with mushrooms, of which there is a superabundance. Last year Janicki got 6,000 złoty for the mushrooms he collected and dried, and though the present year was not a good one he'll still pick up 2,000. The forests also provide extra sources of earnings through the trimming and transporting of trees and logs.

Janicki paid off all his loans a long time ago. Profusion and prosperity have become permanent guests in his house. It is enough to glance at the chubby face of young George, or at the rosy cheeks of the youngest of all, nine-month old Eugene, at their casual clothes, warm sweaters and boots they can put on every day, at all the games and toys in the house — everyone can see for himself how prosperous they have become. Both the Janickis today are happy and contented with their children's prospects in life. They may have nine children, but not one of them is threatened by poverty or destitution; the People's Government has created this life for Janicki.

'I'll tell everyone who comes along here not to hesitate for a moment,' says Janicki, 'but to pack his goods and chattels and join us here. Today the conditions are actually much better than they were six years ago when I settled here. You can get loans for equipment and the seed you need, whilst the loan to buy cows and horses is written off when you have completed three years on the new farm. You don't pay any taxes during those first three years, and for two of them you're free of the compulsory deliveries. This really gives you time to get the farm organised, and the new settlers are given help and protection at every step. Anyway, what's the point in talking so much? Anyone can judge whether it's worth coming or not just by looking at my house, the stables and the yard,' Janicki ended our conversation.

On both sides of the road which leads from Zagórz through Komańcza to Wisłok you can see lands which have to be wrest back from the dead, which the plough-share must bring to life again. They ought to be yielding something. The productive reserves of our agriculture are lying hidden here: thousands of tons of grain, possibilities to breed thousands of head of cattle, sheep and pigs. And for settlers a life of profusion and prosperity is also waiting, a new life . . .

(published in Rzeszów in 1953 by the Agriculture and Forestry section of the presidium of the County Council in a 44 page brochure entitled *Na Nowe Gospodarstwa* (Moving to New Farms), compiled by C. Błońska, E. Jakubowska and J. Ciastoń).

II. Krzysztof Ołtarzewski

How long have we been in Wisłok? Since May of last year, right? — No, we've been here eighteen months. — Nope, it'll be two years in May. — Sure, two years in May, it all began in 1978.

In February the formalities, I gave 140,000 złoty for these putrid buildings and 14 hectares of land. Of course I got credit, I didn't have that much money. I had two horses. We went at it in earnest from the start, set out in grand style — nothing wrong with that in my opinion. I heard there were 10 hectares for sale right next door. The average peasant would spend three years thinking about it: worth buying or not. I wrote at once to the *gmina* offices telling them I'd take it, giving me about 23 hectares altogether. You can appreciate it — I came here at the beginning of May, and by the last day of the month I'd already got forty head of cattle with a cooperation agreement with the State Farm. Do you appreciate it? Here a guy would keep two horses and a cow and couldn't scratch a livelihood, and along comes this madman who takes on forty head of cattle for fattening . . .

Services I got from the SKR, and bloody awful they were at it. In the course of two years they never once managed to execute a job on time and as it should be done. Cutting hay is no problem, but with only a couple of horses and so many fields I obviously have to order the whole range of services. Gierek made this speech on the television, saying that the SKR has to be able to collect the hay, so I went in to them the next day and signed a contract for precisely that. They signed it, they'd have looked foolish if they hadn't.

Losses in 1978 due to badly implemented services I estimated to be in the order of 40,000–50,000 złoty. They did the mowing, then they were supposed to come out to ted and rake it up together, and that was all I wanted from them, even though a trailer and automatic gathering equipment were also listed on paper. I had this absurd way of thinking, I thought that if a firm signs a contract it will stick to it — but here not even 10 per cent. Not to mention the fact that before every job you have to go 12 km to Komańcza several times, which means catching the bus before six in the morning and kicking your heels there until the SKR administrators arrive. There you get these Dantéesque scenes, hollering and brawling, it's such an ugly sight you need to see it to believe it. Eventually your tractor will arrive and it turns out that some screw is missing, so back it fucking goes about 30 or 40 km to Szczawne, which is where they've got their workshop. It's a fine firm.

Nevertheless we made it somehow, got the hay in, the cattle came along well. That first year was a good one, and then I got my photo in the provincial paper, receiving my candidate's membership card in Krosno from the First Secretary of the county.

At the same time there was this stupid situation — I started to have some troubles with the neighbours. In the hamlet where we'd been before it was like this — *your* horses, *your* cart, *you* want to work on Sunday: your own private business! And here the priest damned me from the pulpit for working on Sunday. The people here are unable to understand that there is only the two of us and we can't look to anybody else. Really there's only one and a half, with Jadwiga busy most of the time with the children. There is no Sunday for me, I can't fulfil 200 per cent of the norm on Saturday, all the more so since everything has to be done by hand. I've been shovelling the dung out by hand for two years now because I can't get hold of machines. I've scattered all the fertilizer by hand, imagine, on an area like that! I tell you, you could strain yourself . . .

There's no way you can manage this by physical strength alone, like a yokel or a peasant; you have to devise some sort of strategy . . .

That first year was really a fine one. Come the autumn we sold the cattle, sold hay and sold some grain, we got back what we paid for this farm in the course of a single season.

I spent the winter hammering away in the forest because we

183

needed the money. Jadwiga was at her mother's in Silesia, because you know it was just impossible to live here, things were really a mess. From the spring — more renovation work and tinkering around the house.

As soon as I came here I knew at once that we'd have to get new buildings up. I sent off a request to a firm of architects in Cracow for their current catalogue and possibly something already completely worked out, making it clear to them what I wanted. Five months later they sent me back a scrap of paper, and on this scrap of paper a little wooden outhouse, I just couldn't believe it.

This time I didn't manage to repeat that cooperation agreement with the State Farm and I had no choice but to take on some beef cattle from the Stockbreeding Enterprise. In my opinion there's a big mistake in their assumption, in fact only about 30–40 per cent of their animals are really good enough to be worth fattening up, I'm convinced of that, and I've been through it. Come the autumn, it turned out that from forty head I could only sell fifteen, in other words fifteen head were up to standard in terms of weight and condition, the others were not. Even so I came out the best in the whole *gmina*; there were three of us who tried, the others didn't manage to deliver a single beast, the lot of them were sickly and in lousy condition.

'And what have you been rearing?' they said to me in the State Farm, 'What have you been rearing!' If I'm prepared for a conversation I can talk quietly but I get bloody angry when they talk to me like that. Those cattle consumed eight tons of protein food, 10,000 litres of specially prepared milk, in the spring there weren't any antibiotics to be found, I had to hunt around with vodka and with money, begging, borrowing and stealing in order to wangle some somewhere. I said to those women that maybe they could buy those animals through the regular marketing channels, and they replied that these were full to capacity. Right, let's take them home again! It really stung me, mind, because I am conscious of all the money and all that work, but I just couldn't manage to slobber, kiss the old girl's hand, bribe her with 1,000 złoty or invite her for some vodka, cravenly beseech her; maybe I could have landed some snot somewhere and got something out of her, but that would have been stooping too low, I raised those cattle, that's my work, I'm a productive firm and not a beggar, that's what really hurt me most of all.

The people at the *gmina*'s Agricultural Service and the rest, they ought at least to know their jobs. I don't expect them to be intelligent, but I don't like that director coming out to me here and standing on that little hill to ask about this and that. He's afraid to go and see for himself, he'd get his shoes soaked in the dung, but why doesn't he buy himself a pair of wellingtons for 150 złoty? Then the son of a bitch could go inside the stables and see what it all looks like. He even gets his wellingtons for free because of his job, but maybe he finds he doesn't actually need them. He's a bureaucrat and I'm a farmer, how could we be able to talk like two farmers?

I know that the way that I behave is not going to win me many friends here. When I lose my temper I start to swear, I just can't help it, you know, at times I can't control myself and of course that's not good . . .

The business of building anew from scratch — stable, silos, sties, manure pits, not including a new place for us to live in, that bit was to be our own personal investment — it all worked out to be two million, seven hundred thousand złoty. And people were aghast, people couldn't conceive this, nobody had ever proposed a credit on this scale before. It's a question of the mentality here. People build a stable for ten head, to plan for twenty is pretty awful, and I wanted forty. My neighbour Filozof, that's his family name, has been building his barn for 7 or 8 years and he still hasn't any mechanical equipment in it. What I do by hand in my own eighteenth century barn he has to do by hand in his would-be twentieth century version. It's still not finished, but if he decides to finish it the way it ought to be finished he has another five years' work in front of him. They're surprised at me because I want it all done by outsiders according to their blueprint, for that costs money; but while it's going on I can carry on producing in these old buildings; if I've got to do the building myself I'm not going to have time for agricultural production, and so I prefer to pay half a million more and get the buildings up in two years than to mess around myself for five whilst paying out half a million less.

These are perfectly obvious matters to me, but I don't manage to explain them to the people from the bank or those at the *gmina*; in fact it's difficult to explain anything to those people. Please wait for our letter, we'll contact you, wait for our letter with an answer to your request for credit; and then *silence*, nobody knows what's going on, like a Czech movie. Every one of them is afraid to take a decision, every one just shakes his or her ass when they hear that I want such a large credit: the lady in charge of the local branch of the bank thinks to herself, that's more than I can earn in a hundred years.

My first impulse was to write to the Central Committee, a naive step if you like but that's the way we organise our business, you have to get some piece of paper with an important seal on it supporting you, and then you get things done — this is the established way. Write it down briefly and to the point, it doesn't have to be literary. In fact better if it's specially non-literary, for if one's a bit tense things might spill out too colourfully. Just write down the incontrovertible facts . . .

'That the bank in Komańcza has refused me the credit on the grounds that they don't see any prospect of my repaying it, that after renovating my old stable I had good conditions for production and didn't produce as much as I should have done . . .' I tell you bluntly . . . they don't understand that a barn and cowshed are not like a mass-production conveyor belt. They think that it ought to start producing without a moment's hesitation, but I tell you that it's a cowshed, with living creatures inside it, which might grow but might equally well not grow. In agriculture there is an element of risk, you couldn't possibly run a farm without risk. I've got 450,000 złoty of credits to pay off: 170,000 of this is turnover credit which I'll pay in 1980, 140,000 is for the renovation, that I'll pay the following year though I'm not obliged to for ten years, and 150,000 for the purchase of the farm — that's spread out over thirty years . . .

I can educate my neighbours, you know, on things to do with the land. If I scatter fertiliser in March and collect the first crop of hay in May, with another following in the middle of summer, if I manage to get two crops like this for two or three years in a row, then pretty soon other people will begin to do it, for up to now they've only collected the one crop.

But it's awfully difficult to remodel the habit of doing everything by *asking*. There is this habit — if you as a farmer go to see the administrator and you *demand* from him something he gets paid to do, he'll be shocked. How can a farmer demand anything? A farmer ought to *ask*, he *has to* ask, his grandfather used to ask and his great-grandfather before him; his father asked and so must you.

A gigantic provincial asking process! Well, Ołtarzewski doesn't like this!

Sure, I know it's not going to be easy for me.

(published in the newspaper *Tygodnik Kulturalny*, Vol. 24 no. 17, 27th April, 1980, the words of Krzysztof Ołtarzewski reworked in article form by Adam Warzocha)

NOTES

CHAPTER ONE

1. Paul Stirling, *Turkish Village* (London, 1965), p. 25.
2. Ibid., p. 3.
3. Ibid., p. 25.
4. The importance of agricultural inefficiency in contributing to the general economic collapse has been argued by persons close to the centre of power in Poland (cf. Rakowski, 1981, p. 63) as well as by countless foreign commentators; see, e.g. the articles by Włodzimierz Brus in Alec Nove, Hans-Hermann Höhmann and Gertraud Seidenstecher (eds), *The East European Economies in the 1970s* (London, 1982), and Andrzej Korbonski in Maurice D. Simon and Roger E. Kanet (eds), *Background to Crisis; policy and politics in Gierek's Poland* (Boulder, 1981).
5. This has been persuasively argued in other contexts by Jerry F. Hough, *The Soviet Union and Social Science Theory* (Cambridge, Mass., 1977).
6. See Ian H. Hill, 'The end of the Russian Peasantry', in *Soviet Studies*, Vol. 27, 1975, No. I, pp. 109–27; Roger Whitaker, 'Continuity and Change in Two Bulgarian Communities: A Sociological Profile', *Slavic Review*, Vol. 38, No. 2 (June 1979), pp. 259–71.
7. Influential approaches to peasantry have included, in the American school of cultural anthropology, those of Kroeber (defining peasants as 'part societies' within a wider culture, in his 1948 textbook *Anthropology*) and Redfield (see especially *Peasant Society and Culture*, Chicago, 1956). Eric Wolf's short book (1966), remains a masterly introduction. Some of the theoretical problems with the term and the reasons for persevering with it are discussed by Teodor Shanin in his introduction to Shanin (ed.) (1971), and in Appendix A of Shanin (1972). See also the paper by Thorner in this volume; also further discussion by Shanin in two articles on 'The Nature and Logic of the Peasant Economy', *Journal of Peasant Studies* I, Nos. 1, 2 (1973–4).

   Because of the attention it has received from a number of distinguished social scientists, the Polish peasantry has figured prominently in general discussions of the subject. For example, it is central to the model constructed by Alan Macfarlane in *The Origins of English Individualism* (Oxford, 1978). However, the Polish peasantry has changed radically during the twentieth century, and it seems unwise to conflate studies as far apart as those of Thomas and Znaniecki (1918) and Gałęski (1973).
8. The idea of 'limited good' (as elaborated by G. M. Foster in an article in *American Anthropologist 67*, pp. 293-315) suggests that peasants view progress conservatively: if some are to advance, it can only be at the expense of others, for the economy is like a zero-sum game. Frequently criticised as an explanatory model of peasant behaviour, the idea has nevertheless proved fruitful in later studies of peasantry; it is likely to become, ironically, more apt in Polish conditions, as policies to polarise the peasantry are more vigorously pursued (see Chapter Three).

CHAPTER TWO

1. The most satisfactory scholarly treatment of this period known to me is that of Henryk Paszkiewicz, *The Origin of Russia* (London, 1954) and *The Making of the Russian Nation* (London, 1963). See in particular Appendix II to the second of these volumes, entitled 'The Earliest Rus'ian-Polish Borderlands'.

For more background to these awkward and still controversial questions see articles by R. Smal-Stocki and G. W. Simpson in the Canadian serial publication *Slavistica*, Nos. 8 and 10 (Winnipeg 1949 and 1951). See also what promises to become a definitive study of the issues by O. Pritsak, *The Origin of Rus'* (Vol. I: Cambridge, Mass., 1982).

2. Specialist historians have had difficulty in agreeing on a common terminology to describe the East Slavs, hence authors writing for a non-specialist Western audience face great problems. Against his better judgement, Paskiewicz (*op cit*) uses 'Russian' (written as *Rus'ian* in his later volume) because he judges the plain *Rus'* to be too unfamiliar in the West. He also rejects 'Ruthenian', on the grounds that this is a label applied by Westerners and never acknowledged by any Eastern Slav population. In this book I seek to follow his advice and use the terms employed in self-description by the people themselves. It seems to me that the principal term used in Wisłok and the surrounding region until well into the twentieth century was *Rus* (with *Rusnak* the proper noun denoting an individual — cf. Reinfuss, 1948, p. 177). Latterly, the terms Lemkian and Ukrainian have been more widely employed, as explained later in this chapter.

3. The definitive study of the colonisation of the Sanok lands is Fastnacht (1962). The most influential studies of Vlach impact in these parts are by Kazimierz Dobrowolski, *Migracje Wołoskie na ziemiach polskich* (Lemberg, 1930), and *Dwa studia nad powstaniem kultury ludowej w Karpatach zachodnich* (Cracow, 1938). However, there is no evidence in Fastnacht to suggest that the number of shepherds arriving in this part of the Carpathians from the Balkans was ever very large, and it seems clear that any Vlachs who were induced to settle in places such as Wisłok were rapidly assimilated by the Eastern Slavs and converted to the Orthodox religion. For a more modern assessment of Vlach impact, see Omelian Stavrovsky, *Slovatsko-polsko-ukrainskie prykordonnia do 19 stolitta* (Bratislava, 1967). For an assessment of the complexity of the problems posed by the Vlachs in the Balkans see J. C. Campbell, *Honour, family and patronage; a study of institutions and moral values in a Greek mountain community* (Oxford, 1964), pp. 1–6.

4. This is the interpretation of Przemysław Dąbkowski; *Szkice z Zycia Szlachty Sanockiej w XV stuleciu* (Lemberg, 1923, p. 2).

Most of these details of the early history of the village were provided in a personal communication from Adam Fastnacht. Some of the data can be checked and compared with other areas in the following publications of sources: *Akta Grodskie i Ziemskie*, Vols. 11 and 14 (Lemberg, 1894); *Polska XVI Wieku*, Vol. 8 (Warsaw, 1903); *Regestr Złoczyńców grodu sanockiego 1554-1638*, published by Oswald Balzer (Lemberg, 1891).

5. The phrase derives from Engels and the concept has proved fruitful in a number of recent works by authors seeking to account for the imbalances which generated capitalist development. See Immanuel Wallerstein, *The Modern World System* (New York, 1974), but also criticisms of this approach in the essay by Jerzy Topolski in J. K. Fedorowicz (ed.) (1982). See also the stimulating chapter on the sorry consequences of this development for the Polish state in Perry Anderson, *Lineages of the Absolute State* (London, 1974). The best analysis of the Polish feudal economy of this period is to be found in Witold Kula, *An economic theory of the feudal system* (London, 1976).

6. See Reinfuss (1948, p. 173). It is interesting to compare the fact that the inhabitants of Wisłok today, also identify themselves with a larger entity to the east — now known as the Bieszczady Mountains — to which strictly they do not belong.

7. See Józef Półćwiartek, *Z badań nad rolą gospodarczo-społeczna plebanii na wsi pańszczyźnianej ziemi przemyskiej i sanockiej w XVI–XIX wieku* (Rzeszów, 1974). See also, for more general analyses of peasant resistance in this period, Maurycy Horn, *Walka Chłopów Czerwonoruskich z Wyzyskiem Feudalnym w latach 1600–1648; część 1 — Zbiegostwo i Zbójnictwo Karpackie* (Opole, 1974); Edward Trzyna, 'Stosunki

społeczno-ekonomiczne i walka chłopów starostwa krośnieńskiego z uciskiem starościńskim i militarnym w drugiej połowie XVII w.' in *Rocznik Przemyski* (1962, pp. 9–98); Wojciech Sołtys, 'Pitawal według "Regestru złoczyńców grodu sanockiego" opowiedziany' in *Materiały Muzeum Budownictwa Ludowego w Sanoku*, 26, pp. 63–87.

8. For a detailed history of the birth of this church see the study by O. Halecki, *From Florence to Brest 1439–1596* (Rome, 1958). For background to the delay in the ratification of the Union of Brest by the Przemyśl diocese see the comprehensive church history by the same author, *Tysiąclecie Polski katolickiej* (Rome, 1966).

9. See Roman Rozdolski, *Stosunki gospodarcze w dawniej Galicji*, Vol. 1 (Warsaw, 1962), p. 282(n). The records of the Wisłok parishes and the cadastral maps of 1851 were consulted in Przemyśl (State Archives). For details of the agricultural census of 1787 I am grateful to Iwan Krasovsky (Lemberg).

10. Amongst the many studies of Galician history I have relied upon Styś (1934); also Wacław Tokarz, *Galicya w początkach ery józefińskiej w świetle ankiety urzędowej z roku 1783* (Cracow, 1909), Franciszek Bujak, *Rozwój gospodarczy Galicji 1772–1914* in *Wybór Pism (Collected Writings)*, Vol. 2 (Warsaw, 1976) and, in the same volume, the essay entitled *Wieś zachodno-galicjyijska w schylku XIX w.* Dr Dennis Vnenchak of the University of Massachusetts (Amherst), is presently completing a study of the pressures which caused such extreme fragmentation of peasant lands in Galicia.

11. On the history of the Jewish community in Poland and the early beginnings of its economic role in the countryside see Bernard D. Weinryb, *The Jews of Poland: a social and economic history of the Jewish Community in Poland from 1100 to 1800* (Philadelphia, 1973), pp. 113–4, also the article by R. Mahler in *YIVO Annual of Jewish Social Science*, VII (New York, 1952); cf. F. Bujak, *Galicya*, Vol. 1 (Lemberg, 1908), pp. 101–2 and (for attitudes at a later date) Davies (1981) Vol. 2 p. 412.

12. Interpretations of this period, which develop those offered by Wallerstein (*op cit*) for earlier periods, can be found in Iván T. Berend and Gy. Ránki, *Economic Development in East-Central Europe in the 19th and 20th centuries* (New York, 1974);

and also in a stimulating essay by the anthropologist John W. Cole in Sam Beck and John W. Cole (eds), *Ethnicity and Nationalism in South-Eastern Europe* (University of Amsterdam Papers on European and mediterranean socieities, No. 14, 1981). For a brief account of the migratory process from the *Rus* zone, see Stanisław Fischer, 'Wyjazdy Lemków nadosławskich na roboty zarobkowe do Ameryki' in *Materiały Muzeum Budnownictwa Ludowego w Sanoku* 6 (1967).

13. The standard history of Polish populism is Narkiewicz (1976); see also Peter Brock, *Nationalism and Populism in Partitioned Poland* (London, 1973). It is interesting to note that leaders of the Polish Peasants Party in Galicia had an enlighted approach to nationality problems and did *not* claim that Poles had a right to govern in parts of East Galicia which were not mainly occupied by ethnic Poles. Few other Polish political groupings took such a non-chauvinist position.

14. There is a large literature on political and ethnic problems in the history of Galicia, not to mention closely related studies of nationalism elsewhere. There is a comprehensive study by Józef Chlebowczyk, *Procesy narodotwórcze we wschodniej Europie środkowej w dobie kapitalizmu; od schyłku XVIII do początków XX w* (Warsaw, 1975); a poorly translated version has appeared in English, *On Small and Young Nations in Europe* (Wrocław — Ossolineum, 1980). The best general study devoted to the Ukrainians is that by Ivan L. Rudnytsky, 'The Ukrainians in Galicia under Austrian Rule' (*Austrian History Yearbook*, Vol. III, Pt. 2). A revised version can be found in an excellent collection published in 1982 by the Harvard Ukrainian Research Institute *Nationbuilding and the Politics of Nationalism*, ed. by Andrei S. Markovits and Frank E. Sysyn. The first of three projected volumes on Galicia by Paul R. Magocsi has come too late to be consulted: *Galicia — A Historical Survey and Bibliographic Guide* (Toronto, 1983). The political divisions within the 'Lemkian' zone may be compared with those of Subcarpathian Rus', the subject of a detailed study by Magocsi (1978). On the role of the clergy see John-Paul Himka, 'Priests and Peasants: The Greek Catholic Pastor and the Ukrainian National Movement in Austria, 1867–1900, *Canadian Slavonic*

Papers (1979), Vol. 21. No. 10. Himka argues that in the emergence of the national movement the clergy was soon upstaged by other elements in the intelligentsia, but this could not happen in such an isolated and entirely rural area as the *Rus* zone in the mountains.

15. For a brief account of Shpilka's role see *Nasz Lemko — Kalendarz* for 1939 (Lemberg, 1938), pp. 29–32. For a general account of the revolution in the Western Ukraine see *Ukraine* (1963).

16. See Stephan Horak, *Poland and her national minorities 1919–1939* (New York, 1961), especially pp. 158–70. Cf. Davies (1981), Vol. 2, pp. 404–10.

17. It may be considered erroneous to speak of the invention or fabrication of an identity which is deeply professed even today by 'Lemkians' (or 'Lemkos') in Poland, in the USSR (Western Ukraine) and in North America. Nor would I wish to imply that there are not excellent objective criteria for distinguishing different regional groups within the *Rus* zone. Outstanding ethnographical studies were made by Reinfuss (1948), and these have continued to influence a younger generation of Polish scholars (cf. Jerzy Czajkowski, 'Historiczne i etniczne podstawy kształtowania się, grup etnograficznych w południowej części woj. rzeszowskiego' in *Materiały Muzeum Budownictwa Ludowego w Sanoku* 9, 1969). Definitive dialectological studies were carried out by Zdzisław Stieber and others from the 1930s (one of the distinguishing features of the 'Lemkian' area being a regular stress on the penultimate syllable, as in Polish, and unlike other Ukrainian dialects; but there is also much variety *within* the area). It is significant that Ukrainian scholars also began to contribute to 'Lemkian' studies in the inter-war period, amongst them Ivan Zilynsky in linguistic studies, the ethnographers Jan Fałkowski and Bazyli Pasznycki, and the historian Iuliian Tarnovych: see his *Iliustrovana istoriia Lemkivshchyny* (Lemberg, 1936). See also the article by Mykola Andrusjak, 'Der westukrainische Stamm der Lemken', *Südost-Forschungen*, 6 (1941). Finally, those who have chosen to stick with the 'Lemkian' identity, living mostly in North America, have themselves made useful contributions; see Y. F. Lemkyn, *Ystoryia Lemkovyny* (Yonkers, New York, 1969). Nevertheless the bulk of the literature to

appear on the 'Lemkians' in the inter-war period was produced by Poles to serve political rather than scholarly purposes. Into this category fall some of the contributors to Goetla (1935); also the work by Krystyna Pieradzka, *Na szlakach Lemkowszczyzny* (Cracow, 1939); the brochure by Mgr A. Bartoszuk, 'Lemkowie-zapomniani Polacy' (Warsaw, 1939), and similar publications. The context in which these works should be read is that of government policies towards the Ukrainian minority as a whole, particularly concerning Eastern Galicia. For an alternative account of the inter-war period see the chapter by S. Vytvytsky and S. Baran in *Ukraine* (1963). For later Polish views, protesting the loss of Eastern Galicia after the Second World War see Stanisław Skrzypek, *The Problem of Eastern Galicia* (London, 1948); and Jędrzej Giertych, *O Przyszłość Ziem Wschodnich Rzeczpospolitej* (London, 1946). For an interesting discussion of the lines taken by the communist opposition in the 'Lemkian' region see the article by Stefan Makuch, 'O Początkach Rozwoju idei socjalistycznej w Galicji', *Rocznik Sanocki* (1963). See also Janusz Radziejowski, *Kommunistyczna partia zachodniej Ukrainy, 1919–1929, węzlowe problemy ideologiczne* (Cracow, 1976). In most of this region the Polish Communist Party's attitude to the problem was tantamount to support for the 'Old Ruthenian' line and for the policy of Polonisation; only in eastern sections where a separate communist organisation existed (the Communist Party of the Western Ukraine) was Polonisation more vigorously opposed; Wisłok lay within this eastern section: therefore, communist propaganda encouraged these peasants to see exploitation in ethnic as well as economic terms.

The origins of the term 'Lemko' are obscure. Reinfuss (1948) points out that it was not used at all outside a very small area in the eastern section of the region until after the First World War. This small area was the uncertain borderland between the 'Lemkian' group and the 'Boikians'. *Rusnaks* here were less inclined to accept the name applied to them by others as the basis for a separatist regional identity than the Western *Rusnaks*, more isolated from Ukrainian influence. *Rusnak* was also the term preferred by the people who lived south of the Polish border, in territory that is now part of Slovakia, whose language and culture were very close to those of the *Rusnaks* in Poland. These neighbours have been fortunate enough to survive as a compact territorial group in Eastern Slovakia, with a greater degree of cultural and religious freedom than their kin in either Poland or the USSR; see Paul R. Magocsi, *The Rusyn-Ukrainians of Czechoslovakia* (Vienna, 1983).

18. One can feel this in his published work (e.g. in his descriptions of the 'incredible richness and colour of the folk culture' of that part of the eastern section of the 'Lemkian' region to which Wisłok belonged (1948 p. 173), but I learned more in the course of conversations at the Institute of Folk Art in Cracow, especially when we looked through some of the photographs which he took in the region during his trips in the 1920s and 1930s.

19. The events at Lesko, when incoherent and poorly organised peasant protests at what they feared to be a restitution of feudal obligations by certain large land-owners were drastically repressed by the state, were one of the most notorious episodes in the harsh treatment meted out to the peasantry in the inter-war period. See Inglot (1980), Vol. 3, pp. 312–3, Davies (1981), Vol. 2, p. 412, and Krygowski (1975), p. 95.

20. I have been unable to find any Ukrainian account of the UPA resistance movement, and therefore have had to rely on the Polish military historians Antoni B. Szczęśniak and Wiesław Z. Szota, *Droga do nikąd*, Warsaw, 1973; see also by Szczęśniak, 'Walka przeciw ukrainskiemu nacjonalistycznemu podziemiu w Polsce w latach 1944–47' in Władysław Góra and Ryszard Halaba, (eds.) *O utrwalenie wladzy ludowej w Polsce 1944–1948*, Warsaw, 1982, pp. 385–430. For more background on the movement and its complicated history during the war years see John A. Armstrong, *Ukrainian Nationalism 1939–45*, (2nd edition, New York, 1963). Maria Turlejska has edited two useful collections, *Z walk przeciwko zbrojnemu podziemie 1944–7* (Warsaw, 1966), and *W walce ze zbrojnym podziemiem 1954–57* (Warsaw, 1972); in the second of these the contribution by Mieczysław Redziński describes some minor action in Wisłok. The vast quantity of sensational writing about this period in Polish has served to sow hatred and to prejudice fresh generations of Poles against every-

thing Ukrainian; see the evaluation by J. Lewandowski in Potichnyj (1980). In this same collection there is a good summary of the fate of the 'Lemkos' and of the literature dealing with all aspects of their situation in socialist Poland by J. Basarab. It is worth pointing out that not all Poles approved of the drastic military solution adopted, not even those who believed fervently that Eastern Galicia should be returned to Poland (cf. Jędrzej Giertych, *op cit*). It is now possible to add that hopes raised in 1980–1 have met a fate similar to those raised in 1956; the time is not yet ripe in Poland for an official re-evaluation of 'Operation Vistula'.

21. Cf. Magocsi (1978), pp. 258–9.

CHAPTER THREE

1. Official post-war census data show the population of the village (excluding all convicts and also State Farm workers garrisoned at the upper end of the valley) evolving as follows:

    1950 — 171 persons
    1961 — 304 persons
    1970 — 373 persons
    1978 — 329 persons

    In the census of 1970 it was found that almost half of the Wisłok population (161 persons in all) had arrived from elsewhere in the course of the previous decade. However, during the 1970s there were fewer than forty new immigrants, whilst cases of entire families emigrating from the village also became less frequent. For a general periodisation of the migratory process in the post-war period in the Bieszczady region see Jadam (1976).

2. For criticism of these policies with specific reference to conditions in Bieszczady see Vol. 16 of the periodical *Problemy Zagospodarowania Ziem Górskich* (1976), and especially the contributions by J. Kubica *et al* and by W. Jarosz. The former suggest that the minimum area of a farm in this region should be 10 hectares for each individual employed full time on the farm. Jarosz makes interesting comparisons with the pre-war pattern of land utilisation; he concludes that although the natural balance between the fodder area and numbers of livestock is more healthy today,

there is still much room for improvement in the use that is made of grassland, and also in the types of crops sown. See also the article by Z. Gawlikowski in Vol. 17 of the same journal.

The best general outline of changes brought about by the Land Reform and the agricultural policies of the early socialist period is that of Korbonski (1965).

3. There is a large literature on the Agricultural Circles and their forerunners. See especially the discussion in Jerzy Tepicht, *Marxisme et agriculture: le paysan polonais* (Paris, 1973). For an example of the high hopes placed in them after 1956 see the article by B. Gałęski in the collection edited by Z. T. Wierzbicki, *Aktywizacja i Rozwój Spolecznośći Lokalnych* (Wrocław-Ossolineum, 1973). Although the dangers of specialisation and bureaucratisation were already apparent to Gałęski, he was still at this stage able to conclude that the Circle was an authentic popular institution possessing 'a very elastic organisation, only insignificantly subject to formalism and bureaucracy' (p. 147). On the poor quality of Circle services in the Bieszczady region, even before their forced amalgamation into 'cooperatives', see the article by Halina Kozik in No. 154 of *Zeszyty Naukowe Akademii Rolniczej im. H. Kollątaja w Krakowie* (1979).

4. There is an abundant literature on the agricultural policies pursued in the 1970s, the best short summaries being those of Cook (1984), pp. 407–13 and Pelczynski in R. F. Leslie (ed.) (1982). Useful information may also be found in J. O'Hagan (ed.), 'Growth and Adjustment in National Agricultures' (Rome, 1978) and also in recent English language supplements to the journal *Zagadnienia Ekonomii Rolnej* (e.g. to No. 2, 1976; and to No. 6, 1978). See also Woś and Grochowski (1979) and the two volumes edited by Turowski and Szwengrub (1976, 1977), for much background material on economic and 'sociocultural' conditions in the countryside. A sympathetic outline of the intentions of the Gierek team in this field can be found also in Kolbusz (1978). For more critical assessments see the paper by Gałęski, 'Solving the Agrarian Question in Poland', *Sociologia Ruralis* (1982), Vol. 22, No. 2, pp. 149-66; and also that of Korbonski in Maurice D. Simon and Roger E. Kanet (eds), *Background to crisis; policy and politics*

in *Gierek's Poland* (Boulder, 1981), pp. 271–97. For the no less critical views of farmers who experienced these policies see Raina (1981).

On the agricultural policies of Stolypin see the chapter in G. T. Robinson, *Rural Russia under the Old Règime* (London, 1932).

5. A general inventory of livestock and survey of land utilisation is made each year at the beginning of July. I participated in this work in Wisłok for each of the years 1979, 1980, 1981; unless otherwise indicated all figures quoted in the text refer to the month of July 1981 (including those concerning family size, place of employment, investment credits etc.). Where performance is measured over several preceding years the number of farms included in the tables is smaller, due to the exclusion of one or more newly established farms. On the other hand a few farms which have been transferred to new owners in the same period have been included, despite the modification that may occur under new management. Imperfections are unavoidable. Frequent changes in purchasing prices may not be the only factor which makes these gross production figures a misleading measure of farm performance; however, I believe they give an accurate general impression of aggregate output in this village, where geographical isolation makes the extent of private marketing minimal. I see no reason to suppose that autoconsumption varied significantly over this period, though for most families it may have *decreased* after the full impact of the crisis; for after the introduction of rationing there was *more* food available for rural consumers in the state shop than had previously been the case.

The data concerning family and employment are based on my own household census. Naturally, the age structure of a resettled village will diverge from that of villages with a continuous history of settlement. A high proportion of the present farm owners in Wisłok were born between 1925 and 1935, and the question of a successor will arise before the end of the 1980s. More sophisticated attempts to measure the effects of family labour supply (*pace* Chayanov for the Russian peasantry) have been made for an earlier period by Styś (1934) and recently in relation to farmers' current behaviour by A. Szemberg; see her paper in Turowski and Szwengrub (ed.) (1976), pp. 223–38.

6. See Cook (1984); but note also his caveat concerning the constitutional changes, p. 419.

7. Analyses of the current period must be tentative. However, an indication that a return to Gierek's 'polarisation strategy' may be more actively pursued came with an article by A. Woś (Director of the Institute of Agricultural Economics) in the newspaper *Życie Gospodarcze*, January 22, 1984. Woś called for 'rational pragmatism' to replace emotion and dogma in agricultural policies. In his opinion, rather than enable a large number of medium farmers to accomplish a small expansion of acreage and mechanise, it is essential to favour concentration of land, such that the total number of farms would fall to less than half a million. See also an earlier article by Woś, which deals specifically with the southeastern counties, in which the structural problems of agriculture are most severe, *Życie Gospodarcze*, October 5, 1980.

In the early 1980s favourable climatic conditions, the large price increases and a high level of pressure in the media all helped to maintain production at a reasonable level. However, this was an unusual period; it is difficult to see how any lasting improvement can occur until the structural problems are tackled. Only radical reform of the economy can ensure that farmers will be able to find on the market the inputs they need for production and the consumer goods to make the effort worthwhile in the end. When this happens, official proclamations of the inviolability of private property will perhaps foster genuine feelings of security in the private sector. In 1980–1 many activist groups were calling for 'a public statement that the authorities consider the individual peasant holding to have a status equal in rights and rank as a form of property in the socialist system', (Vale (ed.), 1981, p. 193). The requests were met by an amendment to the constitution passed after the introduction of martial law. However, opinion polls (such as that reported in *Polityka*, March 7 1981) reveal that such declarations have made little impression in the past, since in practice discrimination against the peasantry continued unabated and the goal of gradually extending the socialist sector in agriculture was actively pursued. (For example,

around the time of the Seventh Party Congress in 1975, when it was proudly predicted that the socialist sector would continue to expand its share of cultivated land (Kolbusz, 1977, p. 33). This aggressive ideological stance towards the private sector was one of the main reasons why Gierek's efforts to induce modernisation were resented by the mass of the peasantry.) Signs that this contradiction may have persisted into the 1980s have already been identified by Cook (1982), p. 419.

CHAPTER FOUR

1. Compared with other socialist states, in which they constitute a much smaller part of a socialised sector in which producers' cooperatives are preponderant, State Farms play a more significant role in Poland. However, they remain largely restricted to the areas where previous peasant cultivators were dispossessed at the end of the war, i.e. the 'regained' territories in the west, and Bieszczady. On the social forms generated by this type of farming see Marek Ignar, *Struktura społeczna PGR* (Warsaw, 1978). See also F. Kolbusz and W. Dzun (eds), *Przemiany społeczne w socjalistycznym sektorze rolnictwa polskiego* (Warsaw, 1981). The relative inefficiency of the State Farms in Poland has been well documented. See, for example, Kruszewski (1972), pp. 124–33, on performance in the western territories; and also articles by Szymański in the periodical *Wieś Współczesna*, 1980–1; also the official report on the state of the economy published in July 1981, *Rządowy Raport o Stanie Gospodarki*. The State Farms' role in the diffusion of new technical knowledge to the peasantry is discussed by many official and semi-official commentators on Polish agriculture (see note 4 to Chapter Three for references). However, by the later 1970s more emphasis was being put on the promotion of new forms of cooperation *within* the private sector ('teams' etc.).

2. Forestry also comes in for criticism in the above-mentioned *Rządowy Raport*, the charges including over-exploitation of key reserves and neglect of long term equilibrium. Much of the blame is laid upon the deficiencies in the supply of accommoda-

tion for forestry workers. Jadam (1976), pp. 29–31, claims that out of a total forest area of 200,000 hectares in the Bieszczady region, 70,000 are 'difficult to penetrate' and a further 45,000 hectares cannot be exploited at all.

3. The inefficiency to which the existence of a large worker-peasantry gives rise is noted by (amongst others) S. H. Franklin, *The European Peasantry* (London, 1969), p. 212, and is set in correct economic perspective by Gur Ofer in an article 'Industrial structure, urbanization and the growth strategy of socialist countries' *in Quarterly Journal of Economics* (1976), No. 2. For Poland some of the drawbacks have been pointed out by Maria Dzeiwicka in Turowski and Schwengrub (1976) pp. 75–87 and by George Kolankiewicz, who has defined worker-peasants as a new 'awkward class': see his article in *Sociologia Ruralis* (1980), Vol. 20, No. 1–2. For brief summaries of some of the Polish studies which point up the advantages to households of being able to retain a small holding after taking up industrial employment see Matejko (1974) pp. 74–6.

For the Bieszczady region Jan Mazur has called for a clearer separation of public and private components of this labour process: see his article in *Wieś Współczesna* (1977) Vol. 10, pp. 114–17. Detailed analysis conducted by the Institute of Agricultural Economics in a Bieszczady village (Berezka) with substantial peasant population provided ample confirmation of the problems (detailed statistical data concerning this village served as a useful control during my own survey work in Wisłok).

CHAPTER FIVE

1. An outline of what is meant by 'democratic-centralism', both in general socialist theory and in the Polish practice, is given by Piekałkiewicz (1975: especially Chapter One). For comparative material see Daniel N. Nelson, *Democratic Centralism in Romania*, East European Monographs 69 (Boulder, New York, 1980).

2. For an early assessment of the 'reforms' of the 1970s see the article by Ray Taras, 'Democratic Centralism and Polish Local Government Reforms' in *Public Administration* (1975), Vol. 53, pp. 403–26. For suggestions concerning their effects at higher levels of government see the article by Paul G. Lewis in Woodall (ed.) (1982).

3. For example, Taras, *op cit*, p. 421.

4. Brief accounts of the fate of this 'catacomb church' in the USSR are provided by Wasyl Markus in Bociurkiw and Strong (eds) (1975), and also in Potichnyj (ed.) (1980). See also the article by Ivan Hvat and appendices in *Religion in Communist Lands*, Vol 11, No. 3, pp. 264–94.

5. Sources on the expansion of the bureaucracy in the 1970s and the increase in corruption are numerous; many examples can be read in Vale (ed.) (1981), and in the article by Paul G. Lewis *op cit*. For comparative material from Romania see the articles by Steven L. Sampson in *Sociologia Ruralis* (1984), Vol. 24, No. 3 and in *Folk* (1983), Vol. 25. There is much comparative material from the Soviet Union; see e.g. the feature on 'Clientelism' in *Studies in Comparative Communism* (1979), Vol. 12, No. 2–3.

Although great changes took place during the Gierek period two notes of caution should be sounded. Firstly, despite the later tendency to romanticise the 'puritanical Bolshevism' of Gomułka, in this period there was already a good deal of corruption in local government (e.g. Piekałkiewicz, 1975, pp. 58–9). Secondly, it must not be assumed that the administration was uniformly tainted by the end of the 1970s. On the contrary the Chief Executive in Komańcza could maintain his position in 1981 because his personal integrity had not been questioned in the preceding years. The fact that, unlike most officials, he resided outside his *gmina* and had no personal kin ties with its members, was undoubtedly an advantage in this respect.

6. The best translation of this verb is 'make deals'. I do not know how it entered Polish; but cf. the situation in southern Italy, where peasants are said to be 'with very few exceptions all ... trying to create and maintain successful *combinazioni* of separately inadequate, under-capitalized and peasant-like enterprises'. (J. Davis, *Land and Family in Pisticci* (London, 1973), p. 91; also p. 24).

7. This meant that for the first time 'the directive role of the Party' was formally recognised in electoral regulations, as

Taras *op cit* p. 418, points out.

8. When elections were finally organised in June 1984 this pattern was confirmed. Tremendous interest surrounded the campaign, because the underground opposition was known to be urging a boycott, whilst the church was not taking a position and the authorities were doing their utmost through the media to make participation in these local elections the test of the legitimacy of the central regime. In the event, with turnout at about 75%, they had reason to proclaim themselves well satisfied. The proportion was low in many major urban centres; in the commune of Komańcza it was lowest in the factory settlement of Rzepedź, where the workers' movement had been strong. But in Wisłok the turnout was 85%, a definite indication (in the opinion of the village headman) that the authorities do indeed have a considerable degree of support. This does not mean that he was satisfied with the way in which the candidates were chosen (by the special commission in Komańcza), nor was he entirely sure about the accuracy of the final published figures. He was aware that some individuals voted several times over for absent family members, that many people bothered to vote just because they saw others doing so, and because the polling station could be visited conveniently in the schoolhouse straight after Sunday mass. A few were collected and taken along to vote by special van (this service had to be suspended before the end of polling when the vehicle ran out of fuel). But when all these factors are taken into account, the fact remains that there was no direct pressure upon anyone to vote, and the high proportion which nevertheless did so (though still lower than the usual turnout in communist elections) certainly strengthened the position of Jaruzelski's government.

9. Cf. Narkiewicz (1976), p. 292.

10. Detailed appraisals of the United Peasants Party can be found in Korbonski (1965), Lewis (1973) and Narkiewicz (1975). Of course, one would not expect the party to be particularly strong in a resettled village, where the majority of immigrants had occupied marginal positions in the pre-socialist peasant society. It can also be maintained that the mere fact that a peasant party has survived at all is testimony to the vitality of the populist tradi-

tion and a real element of pluralism in the 'hegemonic' system. Thus, apart from their land, Polish peasants have managed to conserve something else that has disappeared elsewhere in the Soviet bloc, a legal political party to represent rural interests. However, opinion polls conducted before the registration of *Rural Solidarity* showed that most peasants considered this party, like the Agricultural Circles, to be thoroughly discredited. Its leaders had carried their 'agreed policy of compliance' (Narkiewicz, 1975, p. 284) too far, and were seen to be just stooges for the Communist Party. See the poll reported in the newspaper *Polityka*, March 7 1981.

11. Thus, following the long campaign for union recognition which ended with the registration of 'Individual Farmers Solidarity' in May 1981, the authorities went on to award similar recognition to factional groups at loggerheads with the main leadership; only one of these factions kept the title *Rural Solidarity*, which, however, continued as the most popular designation for the whole movement. There is a useful account of these developments by Zbigniew Tadeusz Wierzbicki and Placide Rambaud, 'The emergence of the first agricultural trade-union in socialist Poland' in *Sociologia Ruralis* (1982), Vol. 22, pp. 209–26. However, these authors do not substantiate their claim that the appearance of a trade-union, however vigorous in certain parts of the country, signified the end of the traditional peasantry (p. 224). Nor do they provide a full analysis of the different orientations which emerged within the rural movement. It is clear that the various wings reflected real differences of interest within the peasantry, as well as regional patterns dating back to the partition period that had given rise to different kinds of populist party in the different regions in the past. Overall it would seem that the aspirations of younger, technically qualified farmers, and the more advanced, larger scale farmers of the western territories (ex-Prussian sector) received less prominence in the programmes of the movement than the demands of smallholders in more densely populated parts (ex-Austrian sector) for greater security and assistance to *all* individual farmers, not merely those with the best chances of improving their production.

For the origins of militancy in the countryside in the 1970s see Raina (1981); also the account by Stewart Steven, 'The Poles' (London, 1982), pp. 197–211. A lively report of the crucial events at Rzeszów is provided by Garton Ash (1983, pp. 110–34). An interesting account of developments in two communes in the south-west of the country, one of which showed a high degree of militancy, is Marie-Claude Maurel, 'La commune rurale polonaise entre l'ordre bureaucratique et l'autogestion territoriale', *Revue d'études comparatives est-ouest* (1982), Vol. 13, No. 3, pp. 105–27. However, it seems to me that the extent of peasant militancy has been exaggerated in some commentaries. It is significant in my opinion that strikes and occupations of government buildings tended to be organised only when other specific issues were involved, such as religion (the presence of crucifixes in schools) or the scandal of the government hunting reserve in Bieszczady (where the protesters were scarcely typical of the traditional peasantry in this historically militant south-eastern region). After martial law the emigré press continued to report protests in this region (e.g. the *Voice of Solidarność* (London), 1 February 1984), but I found these to be very misleading. For a more sober assessment of peasant political behaviour see Cywiński (1983, pp. 96–7).

12. Cf. Shanin (1972, Appendix A); Narkiewicz (1975 p. 272) has argued that populism is always 'an ideology of cripples', generating demands (e.g. for abundant land) that cannot possibly be met.

13. For further examples see Tadeusz Zochowski: Konflikt na wsi; reportaże (Warsaw, 1980).

14. Compare the pattern described for a traditionally Polish settlement in the Beskids by Wierzbicki (1963, p. 331).

CHAPTER SIX

1. Janusz Tazbir, *A State without States* (New York, 1972). It is nonetheless true that the climate became progressively less tolerant after the late impact of the Counter-Reformation; see, e.g. the description by Perry Anderson, *Lineages of the Absolute State* (London, 1974), p. 292 and Ciupak (1973, pp. 48–50). A reasoned attempt to show that 'the Polish tradition of tolerance' survived through the centuries, and was not extinguished even in the inter-war period, is that of Francoise Le Moal, 'Tolerance in Poland: political choice and tradition' in W. Stankiewicz (ed.), *The Tradition of Polish Ideals* (London, 1981), pp. 52–84.

The outstanding general history of the Roman Catholic Church in Poland is by Oscar Halecki, *Tysiąclecie Polski katolickiej* (Rome, 1966). See also Georges Castellan, *Dieu garde la Pologne! histoire du catholicisme polonais 1795–1980* (Paris, 1981); and for details of most recent developments see Szajkowski (1983).

2. Kieniewicz (1969), makes very little of the role played by the Church; but see for example the approach of Wierzbicki (1963), and his articles in Turowski and Szwengrub (eds.) (1977), and in Zdaniewicz (ed.) (1981).

3. Orthodox academic analyses of trends in the socialist period are well presented by Pomian-Srednicki (1982, especially Chapter Five), who also brings out well the ambiguous character of the alleged 'secularisation'.

4. Statistical data on the social background of the clergy and many other aspects of Church affairs can be found in W. Zdaniewicz, *The Catholic Church in Poland 1945–78* (Pallottinum, Poznań and Warsaw, 1979).

5. For further examples see Adam Boniecki, *Budowa kościołów w diecezji przemyskiej* (Paris, 1980).

6. See, e.g. Wyszyński's message to the leaders of *Rural Solidarity* on April 2, 1981, 'Nie dać sobie wydrzeć ziemi' in Stefan Kardinał Wyszyński, *Kościół w służbie Narodu* (Rome, 1981). Cf. Szajkowski, 1983, pp. 118–24. These sentiments were echoed by Archbishop Glemp, Wyszyński's successor, at Częstochowa on August 15, 1982.

7. Pomian-Srednicki (1982), p. 71.

8. See the volume *Historia Katolicyzmu spolecznego w Polsce 1832–1939*, especially Part II dealing with the development of 'social Catholicism' in the inter-war period (edited by Czesław Strzeszewski *et al* Warsaw, 1981).

9. Vincent C. Chrypiński in Bociurkiw and Strong (eds.) (1975), p. 241. For more elaborate criticism of these aspects of Pol-

ish Catholicism see S. Czarnowski, 'Kultura religijna wiejskiego ludu polskiego' (in *Dziela*, Vol. 1, pp. 88–107 and Ciupak (1973). The former, writing before socialist transformation was in prospect, identifies several features which were already modifying traditional 'ritualism' and 'sensualism'. Ciupak believes that the church has been deliberately adapting its ideology to socialist conditions, whilst continuing to rely upon affectivity and ritual (see especially Chapter Two, and Chapter Nine, p. 279, pp. 291–94).

10. Amongst those whom the observance of unethical behaviour has caused to suggest the absence of genuinely deep religious convictions, Fiszmann (1972), p. 19, comments that Polish Catholics do not 'internalise principles of piety and . . . practise them in daily life'. However, it may be that such 'immorality' is restricted to a clearly demarcated public domain, identified with the socialist sector, whilst within the family and networks of friends the moral imperatives are highly effective. Of course, this poses grave problems for society, when, e.g. the property of individuals outside the personal circles is treated with the same disrespect as collective or 'socialist' property. Kieniewicz (1969), p. 148 notes a comparable situation in the nineteenth century regarding the peasants' violation of Lordly property rights, especially over forest land. For discussion of the contemporary problem, see: Wierzbicki (1963), pp. 311–13; also Stefan Nowak, 'Value Systems of the Polish Society', *Polish Sociological Bulletin* (1980), Vol. 20, No. 1, pp. 5–20; also Pomian-Szrednicki (1982), pp. 155–5, and the essay by Andrzej Święcicki in the volume edited by Adam Boniecki *et al*, 'Nous chrétiens de Pologne' (Paris, 1979); also the articles by J. Mariański and others in Zdaniewicz (ed.) (1981); also Patrick Michel, 'Morale et société en Pologne: le discours de l'église', *Revue d'études comparatives est-ouest* Vol. 14 (1983), No. 1, pp. 121–32.

11. Dziewanowski (1977, p. 240).

12. Bronislaw Malinowski, *Magic, Science and Religion* (New York, 1954), p. 89.

13. Cf. Stanisław Fischer, 'Obrazki z życia religijnego Lemków nadosławskich na przełomie XIX i XX w' in *Materiały Muzeum Budownictwa Ludowego w Sanoku* (1969), No. 9, pp. 44–8.

14. Cf. Potocki (1974) Part 4.

15. Thomas and Znaniecki (1918-20), p. 275.

16. Cf. Victor Turner and Edith Turner, *Image and Pilgrimage in Christian Culture* (Oxford, 1978), p. 64.

17. Cf. Pomian-Szrednicki (1982), p. 66.

18. In another parish, elsewhere in the Beskids, it was quite clear that the sole obstacle to the holding of Greek Catholic services in 1981 was the attitude of the Roman Catholic bishop of the diocese. Despite the protests of the Catholic population and several appeals to the Pope, it seems likely that many more will transfer to the Orthodox Church if this is the only way that they may participate in eastern rite services. The close identification of *Rural Solidarity* with the Roman Catholic Church inevitably compromised that movement for some members of this minority.

19. See Jadam (1976), pp. 34–5 for a discussion of this settlement; this author is presently engaged on a more detailed comparative study of this sect.

20. It is significant that the successful farmers of this village were no more sympathetic to *Solidarity* as a movement than the Greek Catholic minority described above. They were unimpressed by the talk of moral regeneration, found their own farm management impeded by the dreadful conditions which prevailed in 1981, and identified a regrettable breakdown of law and order; hence, they condoned and even positively supported the eventual recourse to martial law. Certainly, this sect was satisfied with the treatment it had received over many years from the socialist state, and was suspicious of an opposition movement so closely associated with the dominant church.

CHAPTER SEVEN

1. For example, Lucjan Blit wrote of 'the endemic conflict between two churches, one with its Rome vicar, the other with its Moscow chairman': *The Eastern Pretender* (London, 1965), p. 218.

2. Cf. Danuta Jachniak-Ganguly, 'Administration and Spatial Planning as Tools of Land Management in Poland', Centre for Environmental Studies, Occasional Paper (1978), No. 4, pp. 18–19.

3. This does not prevent some employees of

the sawmill from chiding their peasant neighbours, on account of the large areas of uncultivated land; to which the usual riposte is an invitation to the worker to set up his own farm and put some land back into production himself.

4. For example, Cywiński (1983).

5. The extent of this gap is concisely summed up by Tomiak in Woodall (ed.) (1982), pp. 151-2. See also Raina (1981: Part One) for contemporary rural perceptions; and, for interesting discussion of the pre-socialist gap and how it has been closed in different regions of the country, Stefan Nowakowski, 'Town Dwellers versus Village Dwellers', *Journal of Contemporary History* (1969), Vol. 4, No. 3, pp. 111–122.

6. Official statistics show that the incidence of permanent emigration from Poland rose appreciably during the 1970s but then slackened briefly during the *Solidarity* period (the suicide rate also fell sharply at this time). It is impossible to gauge the full extent of short-term migrant labour to Western countries, but this has certainly been very considerable.

7. The disadvantages experienced by rural children are discussed by Fiszmann (1972) pp. 48-9, M. Kozakiewicz in Turowski and Szwengrub (eds.) (1976), pp. 293–304; Tomiak in Woodall (ed.), (1982), pp. 151-2, and by an officially appointed commission of enquiry which published its report in July 1981, *Raport o warunkach startu życiowego i zawodowego mlodzieży*. The report was widely discussed in the press, e.g. in an article by Iwona Derlatka in *Gromada*, a newspaper widely read amongst the peasantry, July 2, 1981.

8. Fiszmann (1972, Chapter 4), reports a much higher degree of 'social activism' earlier in the socialist period; but from his own examples it is not difficult to appreciate the difference between being a 'missionary' in the old gentry tradition and becoming regularly involved in an unlimited number of petty administrative chores.

9. This assertion is based upon my own conversations with young villagers, and attempts to deal with their awkward questions, e.g. 'why did Britain not fight with Poland in 1939 against Fascism, and why did the Allies leave the greatest sacrifices to be made by the Soviet Union?' Cf. Bohdan Cywiński, *Zatruta humanisika: ideologiczne deformacje w nauczaniu szkolnym w PRL* (Warsaw, 1977). For a discussion of Polish writings on subjects with a wartime Ukrainian bearing, including popular works well known in Wisłok, see the article by J. Basarab in Potichnyj (ed.) (1980).

10. See Jan Jerschina, 'Naród w świadomości młodźieży', Prace Habilitacyjne, No. 23 (Cracow, 1978), who also cites as negative features prominent in the consciousness of young persons the lack of respect for public or private property, lack of common interests at the workplace, and the inability on the part of society to organise and cooperate harmoniously. The superficiality of much of the knowledge imparted through the school system is attested by Fiszmann (1972, Chapter 7). On the importance of alcohol in the village see also Wierzbicki (1963), pp. 333-50.

11. The graduation party held every year early in June was cut short in 1979 for the children attending when it was discovered that youngsters had got hold of some wine; having packed the children off home, the teachers and a few parents then carried on with their own vodka party.

12. See the fragmentary evidence collected by Halina Malinowska, Extent and Effects of Alcoholism in People's Poland, *Survey* 25.1, pp. 53–7. For an analysis of the Soviet case see Vladimir G. Treml, 'Alcohol in the USSR: a Fiscal Dilemma', *Soviet Studies* (1975), 27, No. 2, pp. 161–77.

13. With welfare services poorly developed and unlikely to be awarded more funds in the near future, the general health of the population seems to be worsening. Age-specific mortality rates have been rising for several years past for most male groups, but it is impossible to know what part increased alcohol consumption may be playing in this; see the article by Chris Russell Hodgson in Woodall (ed.) (1982), especially pp. 175–8. The most notorious case of alcohol inducing aggression and violence against women in Wisłok involved female affines. Drinking bouts were organised regularly, the men would pass out before the mother-in-law and daughter-in-law came to blows, and everyone would beg each other's forgiveness when they had sobered up!

14. The best that I can offer is the statement by Engels, 'Alcoholism is to a great extent a reaction to frustrations and the lack of prospects in life' quoted in Vale (ed.) (1981), p. 89.

15. Hugh Brody, *Inishkillane* (London,

1973). The greatest contrast with the Irish situation as described by Brody is that in Poland, since drinking behaviour is governed by constantly fluctuating supply conditions, there is no longer any observable seasonal pattern of consumption.

16. There is, of course, nothing novel about such exploitation. Wallerstein has noted that private noblemen were running this sort of business from the seventeenth century onwards (*The Modern World System*, Vol. 2 (New York, 1980), p. 140). The main difference is that when the monopoly is a public one and educational levels are much higher, then the awareness of exploitation is also liable to be greater. The church is well placed to drive the point home, and can justly claim to have played a major part in temperance campaigns in the past (cf. Kieniewicz, 1969; pp. 116–7; Wierzbicki, 1963, p. 333).

CHAPTER EIGHT

1. These figures are from *Rocznik Statystyczny*, 1980, Section 2. As Tomiak (in Woodall ed. (1982), p. 151) points out, this means that the total number of children living in the countryside is about 700,000 greater than the number of urban children. It was not possible to collect exact data for Wisłok for the whole of the socialist period, but the average number of children born by women resident in the village in 1981 and who then had at leadt one child of school age (6-16 years) was 4.6; however several of these women have not yet completed their families. High fertility is discussed by Marek Okólski in an article in *Oeconomica Polona* (1983), Vol. 20, No. 2. The state's responsibility is also made clear in his article, 'Abortion and Contraception in Poland', *Studies in Family Planning* (1983), Vol. 14, No. 11.

2. A short summary of demographic trends in Poland in the socialist period is given by Leszek A. Kosinski in the volume edited by him: *Demographic Developments in Eastern Europe* (New York and London, 1977). For a Polish textbook on the same subject, Part One of which deals with the effect of wartime losses, see Edward Rosset; *Demografia Polski* (Warsaw, 1975). See also Okólski (*op cit*). For a statement of the unchanging pos-

ition of the church see Stefan Kardinał Wyszyński's guidance 'Wieś polska musi być zaludniona' (fragment of a message to *Rural Solidarity* leaders, 2 April, 1981; published in *Kościół w służbie Narodu* (Rome, 1981). Cf. Szajkowski (1983), p. 124. Further analysis of the factors which determine the ideal and actual size of the family in Polish villages will be found in the thesis currently being prepared by Frances Pine (London School of Economics).

3. This is a crude statement of the 'insurance' function of offspring, but it does seem *a priori* plausible that desired family size is higher where welfare systems do not make satisfactory provision for security in old age. For rural dwellers the Polish system has been distinctly less satisfactory in this respect than that of other East European states (where collectivisation required the earlier introduction of pension schemes, even if these compared unfavourably with those of industrial workers).

4. In other words the emancipation of women from what has been termed 'the endless sequence of pregnancy and lactation' (by Michael Mitterauer and Reinhard Sieder in *The European Family* Oxford, Blackwell, 1982) characteristic of peasant society in the past may indeed take place in the peasant sector (or at least part of it) but be adopted afresh in the new socialist sector; this can happen despite the fact that the work-place is now fully separated from the family and the traditional economic rationale for the large family must have changed.

5. Hence, this elderly Ukrainian, having signed his land over to the state in order to obtain a pension, in accordance with the regulations introduced in the Gierek period, found himself obliged to rent land privately in later years in order to maintain a low level of commodity production and supplement his income. The sister-in-law who upset his expectations is nicknamed *Wolna Europa* (Free Europe) after the well-known radio station: a constant gossip and troublemaker!

6. See *Poland* (1977, p. 137 *passim*). Article 81 of the Constitution reads as follows: 1. Citizens of the People's Republic of Poland irrespective of their nationality, race or creed have equal rights in all areas of the life of the state, of political and economic life as well as in social and cultural life.

Contravention of this principle by any discrimination, direct or indirect, or restriction of rights according to national, racial or religious criteria, will be liable to punishment. 2. The spreading of hatred or contempt, the provocation of discord or the humiliation of a human being on the basis of differences in nationality, race or creed, is forbidden.

7. The origins of this attitude towards Ukrainians are discussed in an article by Z. Anthony Kruszewski in *The Politics of Ethnicity in Eastern Europe*, George Klein and Milan J. Reban (eds) (East European Monographs Series, 93, Boulder, 1981). For illustrations of how the hatred has been fanned in the socialist period see the articles by Georges Mond, Roman Szporluk, John Basarab and Józef Lewandowski in Potichnyj ed. (1980). For evidence on the extent of anti-Ukrainian sentiment in a Polish mountain village further west in the Carpathians see the data presented by Z. Chlewiński: 'Dystans społeczny wobec wyznawców innych religii oraz innych narodowości', *Przegląd Socjologiczny*, 32. (1980), No. 1, pp. 157–79. Policies promoting assimilation are given implicit approval by Kwilecki (1974), who also describes many of the difficulties experienced by the 'Lemkos' in the early socialist period. A crude theoretical model of how this assimilation is proceeding has been sketched by Ewa Nowicka, 'Przyczynek do teorii etnicznych mniejszości' in Hieronim Kubiak and Andrzej K. Paluch (eds), *Zalozenia teorii asymilacji* (Wrocław-Ossolineum, 1980). Shortly after this last book was published the emergence of *Solidarity* permitted different voices to make themselves heard. The Solidarity Congress passed a resolution which essentially reiterated the provisions of the Constitution concerning the rights of the minorities (translated in 'Information Centre for Polish Affairs (UK)', No. 16, November 4, 1981); and a long article dealing with the 'Lemkos' appeared in the newspaper *Tygodnik Solidarności*, No. 43 September, 1981; unfortunately it must be pointed out that very similar sentiments were expressed in the media in the liberalised period immediately following 1956, with little practical effect.

8. For example, Jan Szczepański (1970, pp. 133–7) writes of the 'farmerisation' of peasants and the 'reorganisation and decomposition of the peasant class', although he later admits that even the tenuous survival of individual farms does perpetuate pre-socialist class differences 'to some limited extent'; Bogusław Gałęski has argued tentatively (1973, pp. 131–2) that ownership of the means of production and the process of capital concentration are no longer the basic factors which determine the social structure in the Polish countryside. See also the more theoretical discussion of the limited significance of the peasant's legal relationship to the means of production under socialism by Wesołowski (1979, pp. 109–13). See also the article by Turski in Turowski and Szwengrub (eds) (1976, pp. 47–75); also articles by Woś (in Augustyn Woś (ed.), *Społeczno-ekonomiczne problemy rozwoju wsi i rolnictwa w Polsce* (Warsaw, 1978), pp. 16–37) and by W. Dzun and S. Moskal (in F. Kolbusz ed., *Ewolucja społeczno-ekonomiczniej struktury polskiego rolnictwa* (Warsaw, 1979), pp. 97–115).

CHAPTER NINE

1. Cf. Colin Bell and Howard Newby, *Community Studies* (London, 1971). The tradition which goes back at least to Tönnies of postulating community (*Gemeinschaft*) in binary opposition to *Gesellschaft* (society, 'association') is still very much alive (cf. fashionable debates about 'community policing'). Polish authors have contributed much to the ideal type of a peasant village community: see in particular Gałęski (1973, pp. 77–99); but precise definitions have seldom been forthcoming. I do not attempt to put forward one of my own, but follow the simpler procedure of taking the claims made by certain Polish sources and questioning them in the light of empirical data.

2. Jerzy J. Wiatr in his chapter on 'Polish Society' in *Poland* (1977).

3. In addition to the main works cited in the bibliography, both these authors have published many articles, and Jadam is still carrying out fresh research in the region. He has also edited a volume of memoirs under the title *Pionierzy* (Rzeszów, 1975), introduced by a better known sociologist B. Gołębiowski. The general perspective of

integration and stabilisation is shared by a study of a more westerly part of the Beskids, which experienced the same fate after the war: Lucjan Kocik 'Struktura społeczno-zawodowa oraz przeobrażenia wsi regionu muszyńskiego w okresie 1945–75', *Zeszyty Naukowe Uniwersytetu Jagiellonskiego*, DVI Prace Historiczne. There is a much larger literature, similar in content, concerning the resettlement of the 'regained territories'. A good selection can be found in Andrzej Kwilecki (ed.), *Ziemia zachodnie w polskim literaturze socjologicznym* (Poznań, 1970); an early monograph was published by Stefan Nowakowski, *Przeobrażenie społeczne wsi opolskiej* (Poznań, 1960); a good study of a larger area, currently being updated under the supervision of the original author, is Józef Burszta, *Integracja kulturowa wsi koszalińskiej* (Poznán, 1965); for a good overview complementing these Polish studies and doing fuller justice to such factors as the role of the church as a unifying force, see Kruszewski (1972).

4. Jadam (1976), p. 152.
5. Jadam's data are set out in an article Autorytety w bieszczadzkiej społeczności osadniczej, which appeared in *Rocznik Naukowo-Dydaktyczny WSP w Rzeszowie* (1977). The author refers on several occasions to a longer (and in my opinion similarly dubious) study, Stefan Dziabała, *Autorytety wiejskie; studium socjologiczne* (Warsaw, 1973). His data were contradicted for Wisłok by the results of the survey conducted in 1981 by the student whose field research was noted at the end of Chapter Eight.
6. Biernacka (1974), p. 185.
7. Potocki (1974), p. 282.
8. Jadam does pay considerable attention to sects such as the one in Wola Piotrowa described above (1976, pp. 34–5), and Biernacka makes passing reference to folk beliefs and superstitions (1975, pp. 179–82); but neither offers a fair treatment of the role played by the Roman Catholic Church.
9. Cf. Korbonski (1965), p. 163.
10. Cf. Lewis (1973), p. 80.
11. See the front page of *Trybuna Ludu*, January 7, 1981. It is impossible to provide adequate documentation for these summary comments on countries with such diverse histories and natural endowments. For some indication of how diversity has been preserved in the social period see R. Francisco, R. Laird and B. Laird (eds), *The Political Economy of Collectivised Agriculture* (New York, 1979); and for an expert economic analysis, also looking in detail at the individual countries and providing a useful bibliography, see Karl-Eugen Wädekin, *Agrarian Policies in Communist Europe; a critical introduction* (The Hague, 1982). See also G. Lazarcik, 'Comparative Growth, Structure, and Levels of Agricultural Output, Inputs and Productivity in Eastern Europe 1965–1979', United States Congress, Joint Economic Committee, *East European Economic Assessment, Part Two* (Washington, 1981), pp. 587–634; also Ivo Moravcik, 'Une comparaison des résultats de l'agriculture en Pologne et en Tchécoslovaquie', *Revue d'études comparatives est-ouest* 15.2 (1984), pp. 97–110; this author presents interesting comparisons, not limited to Czechoslovakia.

12. Although Poland and Hungary were the two distinctive 'gentry nations' of Eastern Europe and shared a number of features in the pre-socialist period, there were also important differences. For example, the number of manorial workers was much higher in Hungary, whilst in Poland the independent peasantry was proportionately stronger, and this was reflected in the power of its political parties. It seems nonetheless to be true that the failure to collectivise agriculture in Poland has been responsible for some important contrasts to have emerged between the two countries in recent years. This is stressed in connection with the analysis of social mobility in the two countries by Rudolf Andorka and Krzysztof Zagórski, 'Socioeconomic Structure and Socio-Occupational Mobility in Poland and Hungary', Supplement to *Polish Sociological Bulletin* (1978; Warsaw); and in connection with new patterns of stratification by Tamás Kolosi and Edward Wnuk-Lipiński (eds.), 'Equality and Inequality under Socialism; Poland and Hungary compared' *SAGE Studies in International Sociology 29* (London, 1983).
13. For a discussion of developments in Yugoslav agriculture up to 1974 see Branko Horvat, *The Yugoslav Economic System* (New York, 1976), pp. 76–155. It must be noted, however, that even since the 'Green Plan' adopted in 1974, which has given peasants a greater degree of security

as landowners than they have enjoyed in Poland, many serious problems have persisted in Yugoslav agriculture, some of which bear uncanny resemblance to problems in Poland. The crucial difference seems to be that the market has worked more efficiently: the prices for agricultural products have risen, and peasants have been able to command more and more industrial goods, even though drastic inflation has been one of the consequences. For a positive assessment of the progress made in all fields, including inter-sectoral integration, see the article by Vladimir Stipetić in Karl-Eugen Wädekin (ed.), *Current Trends in the Soviet and East European Food Economy* (Berlin, 1982), pp. 309–330. However, it seems that there are definite limits, ideologically imposed and without regard to objective economic potential, to the freedom which even the self-managed socialist economy is prepared to allow its private farmers. See the comments by Robert F. Miller on Stipetić's article (*ibid*), pp. 333–8 and his conclusion that the country faces 'continuing de-agrarisation and disintegration of private agriculture' (p. 338); cf. the prediction by Harry Mydall that 'a critical point' may soon be reached, such that if private sector production is to be maintained it will be essential to do away with the ten hectare limit on farm size, *Yugoslav Socialism in Theory and Practice* (Oxford, 1984), p. 271.

14. Narkiewicz (1976), p. 284.

SELECT BIBLIOGRAPHY

Ascherson, Neal. *The Polish August; the self-limiting revolution*, London, 1981.

Biernacka, Maria. *Kszaltowanie się nowej spoleczności wiejskiej w Bieszczadach*, Warsaw, 1974.

Bociurkiw, Bohdan R. and John W. Strong (eds.), *Religion and Atheism in the USSR and Eastern Europe*, London, 1975.

Ciupak, Edward. *Katolicyzm ludowy w Polsce*, Warsaw, 1973.

Cook, Edward. 'Agricultural Reform in Poland: Background and Prospects' *Soviet Studies* 36, 3, pp.406-26, 1984.

Cywiński, Bohdan. *Potęga jest i basta*, Paris, 1983.

Davies, Norman. *God's Playground; a history of Poland*, (2 vols.), Oxford, 1981.

Dziewanowski, M. K. *Poland in the 20th Century*, New York, 1977.

Fastnacht, Adam. *Osadnictwo ziemi sanockiej w latach 1340–1650*, Wrocław, 1962.

Fedorowicz, J. K (ed.). *A Republic of Nobles; studies in Polish history to 1864*, Cambridge, 1982.

Fiszmann, Joseph R. *Revolution and Tradition in People's Poland*, Princeton, 1972.

Gałęski, Bogusław. *Basic Concepts of Rural Sociology*, Manchester, 1973.

Garton Ash, Timothy. *The Polish Revolution; Solidarity 1980—82*, London, 1983.

Gieysztor, Aleksander *et al. History of Poland* 2nd edn., Warsaw, 1979.

Goetla, Walery (ed.). *O Lemkowszczyźnie (Wierchy 13)*, Cracow, 1935.

Gorzelak, Eugeniusz. *Polityka agrarna PRL*, Warsaw, 1980.

Guizzardi, Gustavo. 'The Rural Civilization — structure of an ideology by consent', *Social Compass* (1976) 23, Nos 2-3, pp. 187-220.

Hann, C. M. *Tázlár: a village in Hungary*, Cambridge, 1980.

Inglot, Stefan (ed.). *Historia chlopow polskich*, 3 vols., Warsaw, 1970–80.

Jadam, Henryk. *Pionierska spoleczność w Bieszczadach*, Rzeszów, 1976.

Kieniewicz, Stefan. *The Emancipation of the Polish Peasantry*, Chicago, 1969.

Kolbusz, Franciszek. *Polityka rolna lat 1971–1980*, Warsaw, 1977.

Korbonski, Andrzej. *The Politics of Socialist Agriculture in Poland 1945–1960*, New York, 1965.

Kruszewski, Z. Anthony. *The Oder-Neisse Boundary and Poland's Modernization*, New York, 1972.

Krygowski, Władysław. *Bieszczady*, 2nd edn., Warsaw, 1975.

Kwilecki, Andrzej. *Lemkowie; zagadnienie migracji i asymilacji*, Warsaw, 1974.

Leslie, R. F (ed.). *The History of Poland since 1863*, Cambridge, 1980.

Lewis, Paul G. 'The Peasantry' in David Lane and George Kolankiewicz (eds), *Social Groups in Polish Society*, pp. 29–87, London, 1973.

Magocsi, Paul Robert. *The Shaping of a National Identity; subcarpathian Rus'* *1848–1948*, Harvard, 1978.

Matejko, Alexander. *Social Change and Stratification in Eastern Europe*, New York, 1974.

Narkiewicz, Olga A. *The Green Flag; Polish Populist Politics 1867–1970*, London, 1976.

Piekalkiewicz, Jaroslaw. *Communist Local Government; a study of Poland*, Ohio, 1975.

Poland — a handbook, Warsaw, 1977.

Pomian-Szrednicki, Maciej. *Religious Change in Contemporary Poland; secularization and politics*, London, 1982.

Potichnyj, Peter J (ed.). *Poland and Ukraine; past and present*, Edmonton, 1980.

Potocki, Andrzej. 'Więź z parafią rzymsko-katolicką a więź z regionem osiedlenia; studium socjologiczne na przykładzie Bieszczadów', Unpublished Doctoral Dissertation, Catholic Theological College, Warsaw, 1974.

Raina, Peter. *Independent Social Movements in Poland*, London, 1981.

Rakowski, Mieczysław F. *Rzeczpospolita na progu lat osiemdzięsiątych*, Warsaw, 1981.

Reinfuss, Roman. *Lemkowie jako grupa etnograficzna*, Lublin, 1948.

Rocznik Statystyczny 1980–4.

Shanin, Teodor. *The Awkward Class*, Oxford, 1972.

Shanin, Teodor (ed.). *Peasants and Peasant Societies*, London, 1971.

Styś, Wincenty. *Rozdrabnianie Gruntów Chlopskich w bylym zaborze austryackim od roku 1787 do 1931*, Lemberg, 1934.

Szajkowski, Bohdan. *Next to God, Poland*, London, 1983.

Szczepanski, Jan. *Polish Society*, New York, 1970.

Thomas, William I. and Florian Znaniecki. *The Polish Peasant in Europe and America* (2 vols.), New York, 1918–20.

Turowski, Jan and Lili Maria Szwengrub (eds). *Rural Social Change in Poland*, Wrocław, 1976.

Turowski, Jan and Lili Maria Szwengrub (eds). *Rural socio-cultural Change in Poland*, Wrocław, 1977.

Udziela, Seweryn. *Ziemia lemkowska przed pólwieczem*, Lemberg, 1934.

Ukraine: a concise encyclopoedia (2 vols.), Toronto, 1963–71.

Vale, Michael (ed.). *Poland; the State of the Republic*, London, 1981.

Wesołowski, W. *Classes, Stata and Power*, London, 1979.

Wierzbicki, Zbigniew Tadeusz. *Zmiąca w pól wieku później*, Wrocław, 1963.

Woodall, Jean (ed.). *Policy and Politics in Contemporary Poland; reform, failure and crisis*, London, 1982.

Woś, Augustyn and Zdzisław Grochowski. *Recent Developments in Polish Agriculture*, Warsaw, 1979.

Zdaniewicz, Witold (ed.). *Religiousness in the Polish Society Life* (sic) (Religious Sociological Studies 3), Warsaw, 1981.

INDEX

administration
  in pre-socialist period, 3, 18-19, 22, 24, 28, 96
  in socialist period, 3, 79-91, 95, 96-9, 161-2
  constraining peasants, 44, 45, 46, 48, 87-91
Agricultural Circle (SKR), 40-2, 44, 45, 50-1, 81, 118, 154, 182-3
agriculture (*see also under* peasants, State Farms)
  structural problems, 5-8, 12-15, 39-40, 42-3, 56-8, 168, 173-5
  sectoral integration, 46;7, 57-8, 63-4, 73-8, 157, 170-1
  socialist sector, 4-5, 7-8, 43, 54, 59-64, 97, 119, 120, 161, 174
alcohol, 67, 68, 86-7, 97, 98, 112, 128-33
  as currency, 88-9

Biernacka, Maria, 157-8, 161, 162, 163, 164, 167
Bieszczady, 4, 5, 15, 33, 39, 43, 68, 94, 114, 116, 157-67, 169, 191 (nn1, 2)
Bishops' letter, 100-1
black market, 21
brigandry, 21
Bukowsko, 25, 36
Bulgaria, 8, 10, 170

capital, 11, 40, 42, 45-6, 50-1, 53
capitalism, capitalist road, 25, 158, 167, 175

churches (*see also under religion*)
  Roman Catholic, 2, 26, 31, 84, 85, 100-12, 114, 115, 132-3, 135, 164-6, 176
  Greek Catholic (Uniate), 2, 21-2, 27-8, 30-1, 83-4, 113-14, 145
  Orthodox, 2, 17, 21, 30, 84, 105
  Protestant sects, 31, 114-16
  Catholic Church as political force, 99, 101-3, 108-9, 176
class (*see also under* capitalist, peasants, status)
  divisions of pre-socialist period, 21, 37
  kulaks, 40
  rural proletariat, 43, 153
  in socialist period, 7, 9, 11, 14, 48, 102, 140, 150-5, 174
Communist Party, 44, 70, 80-1, 84, 92, 93, 94, 118, 165
community
  social integration of, 4-5, 15, 156-67
  absence of in Wisłok, 85-6, 140-3, 157-8, 161
  expressed through parish, 109-12, 164-6
commuters (*see also under* peasants), 12, 39, 71, 72-3, 159, 168
Cooperative, Peasants Self-Help, (*see also under* Agricultural Circle) 81m 87, 88
corruption, 88-91, 184
Council, *gmina*, 82
credit, 41, 42, 44, 45, 51, 55, 88, 115, 181, 182, 185-6
culture, 86, 145, 160, 165-6

205